Timing Space and Spacing Time

Volume 2

Nothing! thou elder brother even to shade:
Thou hadst a being ere the world was made,
And well fixed, art alone of ending not afraid.

Ere Time and Place were, Time and Place were not,
When primitive Nothing Something straight begot;
Then all proceeded from the great united What....

John Wilmot, Earl of Rochester

Human Activity and Time Geography

Edited by
Tommy Carlstein, Don Parkes and
Nigel Thrift

Edward Arnold

First published 1978 by
Edward Arnold (Publishers) Ltd
25 Hill Street, London W1X 8LL

Timing space and spacing time.
  Vol. 2 : Human activity and time geography.
  1. Geography 2. Space and time
  I. Carlstein, Tommy II. Parkes, Don
  III. Thrift, Nigel
  910'.01   G70

ISBN 0–7131–5989–8

Filmset in Great Britain by Northumberland Press Ltd,
Gateshead and printed by Richard Clay, The Chaucer Press Ltd,
Bungay, Suffolk

Contents

Contributors

Tommy Carlstein — Department of Social and Economic Geography, University of Lund (2)*

F. Stuart Chapin Jr — Department of City and Regional Planning, University of North Carolina (2)

Ian G. Cullen — Joint Unit for Planning Research, University College, London (2)

Leslie Curry — Department of Geography, University of Toronto (3)

Leonard W. Doob — Department of Psychology, Yale University (1)

Phillip C. Forer — Department of Geography, University of Canterbury, Christchurch, NZ. (1)

Robin N. Flowerdew — Department of Geography, University of Lancaster (2)

Reginald G. Gollege — Department of Geography, Ohio State University (1)

Derek Gregory — Department of Geography, Cambridge University (1)

Robert W. Grubbström — Linköping Institute of Technology (3)

Peter Haggett — Department of Geography, Bristol University (3)

Torsten Hägerstrand — Department of Social and Economic Geography, University of Lund (2)

Leslie W. Hepple — Department of Geography, Bristol University (3)

Brian P. Holly — Department of Geography, Kent State University (3)

Bo Lenntorp — Department of Social and Economic Geography, University of Lund (2)

William MacMillan — Keynes College, University of Kent (3)

Solveig Mårtensson — Department of Social and Economic Geography, University of Lund (2)

Murray Melbin — Department of Sociology, Boston University (2)

Lars Olof Olander — Department of Social and Economic Geography, University of Lund (2)

John E. Orme — Area Psychology Department, Middlewood Hospital, Sheffield (1)

Donald N. Parkes	Department of Geography, Newcastle University, NSW (1, 2)
Hugh C. Prince	Department of Geography, University College, London University (1)
George L. S. Shackle	Emeritus Professor of Economics, University of Liverpool (1)
Mary Shapcott	The Martin Centre for Architectural and Urban Studies, Cambridge University (2)
Phillip Steadman	Faculty of Technology, Open University, UK (2)
Nigel Thrift	School of Geography, University of Leeds (1, 2)
Yi-Fu Tuan	Department of Geography, University of Minnesota (1)
W. D. Wallis	Department of Mathematics, Newcastle University, NSW Australia (2)
Huw C. L. Williams	Institute for Transport Studies, Leeds University (3)
Alan G. Wilson	Department of Geography, Leeds University (3)

* The numbers in brackets refer to the volume in which articles by the contributors appear.

Preface

This project was initiated in 1974. Since then it has gained a momentum of its own. We hope that it will continue to gather adherents. We have arranged the papers in the three volumes into themes which were unashamedly devised *ex post facto*. In approaching prospective contributors it was the promise of maximum freedom as long as the theme *Timing Space and Spacing Time* was addressed. Which elements of space and time the authors worked with were left entirely to their discretion. We hope that these three volumes unlike a good many collections of papers are performing a much-needed function and that is the mapping out of new areas of human geographic exploration.

Tommy Carlstein
Don Parkes
Nigel Thrift
Saffron Walden, 1976

ACKNOWLEDGEMENTS

We wish to extend our special thanks to Professor Peter Haggett, Professor Torsten Hägerstrand, and the British and the Swedish Social Science Research Councils. Two of the co-editors also want to thank Don Parkes for privately financing a trip from Australia to make the editorial work possible. He in turn wishes to thank Professor K. W. Robinson, University of Newcastle for contributing funds towards living expenses in England.

General Introduction

The object of this three volume collection of essays is to point to the role of both time and space in the structuring of society and environment. The aim of these essays is not to answer the question. 'What is time?'. Rather it is to provide human geographers with a more acute sense of the significance of time(s) in the study of spatio-temporal problems. In this way it is hoped to extend the frontiers of human geography in particular and the social sciences in general. As a matter of policy by no means all the contributors to these volumes are geographers. The contributions from practitioners in other areas of knowledge are intended as further encouragement to human geographers and other social scientists to move outside the traditional confines of space into the realm of time-space. Whether this friendly invasion is part of an attempt to use time and space as structuring agents in a new sociology, or whether it is an attempt to explore spatial pattern from the perspective offered by the multifarious times of other disciplines it is hoped that these volumes will provide the initial wedge whereby others may enter the arena.

The general purpose of these *Timing Space and Spacing Time* volumes (henceforth abbreviated *TSST*) is to present the case for unifying various temporally and spatially structured studies of society and its environment. There are promising prospects for developing a very useful body of social theory employing time and space jointly as primary structuring dimensions. Up until now, however, this has been recognized by only a few, since much of the work done so far has been scattered throughout the literature and has remained unconsolidated. This factor has hampered the emergence of a potentially very fruitful multi-disciplinary approach in social science. Although the *TSST* volumes have a human geographical bias, the contributions represent a variety of disciplines, as do the materials they draw upon. Indeed, a major intention of the *TSST* volumes is to bring together a good many of the relevant ideas, arguments, data, models and theories which are supportive of the development of this general body of theory.

A second main objective is to bring time and the temporal structure of socio-environmental systems to the attention of those who are already familiar with spatial structure and analysis, notably geographers. Unfortunately, time in geography was born outside the traditional form of wedlock and hence remained a bastard-child which received attention only when it cried out too loudly to be neglected. This was especially the case in historical geography or in spatial dynamics. Geographers did not recognize that society and habitat had a temporal structure just as they had a spatial structure. While many human geographers were much distressed by the a-spatial views of social scientists, planners, administrators and economists, their own a-temporal views of human activity systems caused them much less concern. Perhaps this is to state the case too strongly, but time certainly did not evoke the same degree of enthusiasm as the other physical dimensions. As will be argued below and in the other *TSST* volumes, we need a *holochronic* approach to the temporal structure of socio-environmental systems, one which incorporates all the aspects of time, and not merely the macro-chronological features of historical and dynamic models. The contributors to this volume have in common a specific interest in all the various scales and aspects of both time and space in relation to society and habitat at the same time as geographic space is taken into account. Until recently this has been a rare combination in social science.

But this book also aims to introduce spatial concepts to those sociologists, economists or anthropologists who have dealt with time use, time-budgets, time allocation or the temporal organization of society in something of a spatial vacuum. A great deal of work on time and the temporal aspects of society has made little or no use of the spatial dimensions. Perhaps the most notable case is the conventional time-budget survey approach in sociology (cf. Szalai, ed., 1972). This is a great pity since the time-budget tradition has been a useful approach to the analysis of time in social systems. It has explored a wide variety of topics and problems, it has shown how people actually use their time in a host of different places and it has inspired a great deal of enquiry into the temporal structure of social systems.

This book suggests avenues for further enquiry in the light of what has already been done. In assessing existing achievements it is sometimes necessary to take a critical view and to point out things that were missing in the analysis or directions that for various reasons now seem less fruitful. It is of course easy to be critical, but we hope this somewhat negative exercise has produced constructive suggestions and that the reader will be left with the inspiration to pursue some of the topics suggested and to contribute to this exciting field. There seems to be no sector or kind of society which cannot be penetrated by a time-space approach, and often a 'mere' reinterpretation of problems and substance with which the reader is already well familiar will yield new and satisfying insights. It is not in terms of specific kinds of social *substance* that this approach is new and different (cf. Afterword). It is the way of viewing and *integrating* that substance which is at issue.

Many of the time and space structured processes in the minds of people—as related to individual, society and culture—have already been highlighted in *Making Sense of Time*, *TSST* volume 1. The present volume 2 *Human Activity and Time Geography* deals with societal activity systems and 'overt behaviour' as affected by the time-space structure of institutions and the biophysical and organizational environment. The two chapters by Chapin and Cullen below constitute a smooth transition between volumes 1 and 2.

PART I

Approaches to Human Activity

Introduction

F. Stuart Chapin Jr, the author of the first chapter, is a sociologist and urban planner at the University of North Carolina, USA. His work and that of his associates is comprehensive and proceeds from a joint time and space framework. Chapin and his group were among the first actively to adopt a time and space approach in line with other American scholars such as Hawley (1950) and Meier (1959; 1962). His interest seems to stem from a focus on the dynamic aspects of land use and the relation between land use and household time use (e.g. Chapin 1965). At an early stage he also followed up the time-budget tradition in sociology (Chapin 1966a). Since then he and his associates have explored a variety of themes and planning-oriented research topics in the field of time and space use in city and regional systems (Chapin 1968a; 1968b; 1970; 1971; 1974; Chapin and Brail 1969; Brail and Chapin 1973; Chapin and Logan 1969; Chapin and Hightower 1965). His colleagues have carried out research in many directions (Hightower 1965; Hitchcock 1968; Brail 1969; Hammer 1973). Much of this work is reviewed in Ottensman (1972). The range of topics covered is broad and hence the contribution by Chapin to this volume should be seen as one of several lines of enquiry.

In his contribution to this book, Chapin takes a policy-oriented view of time-space concepts and uses a social psychological approach in studying the way people allocate time to different activities in the course of a day, particularly to discretionary activities (cf. chapter 2). Whether a person is likely to consider a particular activity is seen to be a joint function of motivations predisposing him to that activity and of role and personal characteristics pre-conditioning that choice. For propensity to be exercised and a choice of activity made, the person must perceive an opportunity (a place or facility and congenial surroundings) and a favourable situation, the right timing and the right circumstances. The choice process involves a feedback feature in which levels of satisfaction or dissatisfaction from engaging in the activity affect a person's propensity to repeat it or drop it from active consideration in the future. Elements of this framework are then examined using time-allocation data from Washington, DC. The results from exploratory use of key parts of this framework are then presented, although it was not possible to make a full-scale test of the schema.

Cullen is a geographer at the Joint Unit for Planning Research in London, who for several years has applied time to the study of spatial behaviour (Cullen and Godson 1972; 1974; Cullen 1972; 1976; Cullen and Phelps 1975). He has demonstrated in his various studies how useful time is in linking and integrating items of individual behaviour. Other behavioural geographers have done this less successfully due to their a-temporal perspective.

In chapter 2, Ian Cullen discusses the importance of interrelating life choices and behaviour in the life-cycle perspective with daily routine activities and choice. Like Chapin, he incorporates the social psychological dimensions of choice, attitudes and stress with the study of overt behaviour and the settings or time-space contexts where it takes place. Everyday routines are seen as manifestations of long-term life choices such as change of job or residence, thereby establishing a context which has definite time-consuming implications for the way people operate day by day. This is a process of adaptive routinization, and it is against this backcloth of a routine and relatively choiceless daily activity pattern that attitudes develop. Depending on the cumulation of daily positive and, especially perhaps, negative responses such as stress, other long-term responses are produced. Cullen then proceeds to outline a study of stress as generated by daily activities in an urban setting. In this way both the causes and consequences of long-term choice and behaviour are looked into.

Robin Flowerdew's essay (chapter 3) looks into the time and space practicalities of residential choice, which in the perspective of Cullen would be the transition process from routine to long-term decision about changes in routine, e.g. when a decision to alter one's life situation by changing residence has been made, while the practicalities of changing it have to be fitted into the routine of the situation one is about to give up. Decision-making takes time as does the implementation of it and the search for new alternatives. Flowerdew thus wants to show 'The role of time in residential choice models' by looking into the choice and decision process itself as a practical activity that occurs in a context of other temporally and spatially located activities. This essay is in healthy contrast to much of the literature on intra-urban residential mobility, much of which seems to be miraculously effected in a timeless realm. One of the few other scholars who have elaborated on the time elements of residential mobility is the urban sociologist Michelson at Toronto, and he has also worked in the tradition of time-budget analysis in sociology (Michelson 1975a; 1975b, forthcoming).

Philip Steadman and Mary Shapcott at the Martin Centre for Architectural and Urban Studies, Cambridge University, deal with time use as overt behaviour and activity in relation to the use of city space. This is an approach which has been pursued at the Martin Centre for several years, starting with the large study on time use of students and the use of university premises (Bullock 1970; Bullock, Dickens, Steadman *et al.* 1970; Bullock *et al.* 1971; Bullock, Dickens, Shapcott and Steadman 1974). The essay by Steadman and Shapcott (chapter 4) deals with daily time use in the city of Reading, UK in what is essentially a time-budget approach with a spatial dimension (cf. the discussion on time-budgets below). The time uses of individuals are then aggregated statistically to show how the total population behaves and is patterned in its use of time and spatial location. Like previous chapters, that by Steadman and Shapcott combines a temporal with a spatial form of analysis, unlike most of the conventional time-budget or time-use studies which largely ignore the spatial structure of society.

Much of the work in the field of time-budget studies has conventionally employed standard parametric statistical analysis of time-use data both as a means of getting away from individual behaviour to that of aggregate behaviour and as a way of discovering patterns and regularities. This has included processing data so as to arrive at comparisons of numbers of individuals participating in given activities, measures of elasticity or sequential transition probabilities for types of activity, mean durations, similarities in activity profiles over the day, and so on. The range of different forms of statistical processing of time-use data is considerable as evidenced from the *opus magnum* on *The Use of Time* by Szalai and his huge team of research associates (Szalai, ed., 1972). Of course, there have been many other methods worthy of exploration, and Don Parkes, a geographer at Newcastle, Australia, and a co-editor of the *TSST* volumes, has made several pioneering studies on time use in conjunction with the temporal and spatial structure of urban activities on the basis of factor analytic methods.

In a methodological essay Parkes and Wallis (chapter 5) explore the potential of using digraph theory as a means of bringing out activity structure and sequence in diurnal or circadian cycles. In Parkes and Wallis's essay, some of the many problems of quantitative method in time-use analysis are surveyed in relation to graph theory. For a survey of the uses of factor analytical and factorial ecological methods in the analysis of time-space social organization, the reader is referred to other work by Parkes (1974; 1975; Taylor and Parkes 1975).

This is not the place to review the vast number of time-use studies and explanations of activity that are available in the literature. Apart from the seminal study on time-use studies produced by the Multinational Time-Budget Survey team (Szalai, ed., 1972), there are several books and articles which record the history and results of similar time-use studies (e.g. Ottensman 1972; Thrift 1977). This book takes awareness of the classical type of time-use study (or time-budget studies as they are called by most sociologists) for granted. The apex of this tradition is found in *The Use of Time* and the broad range of applications and the general usefulness of the approach are well borne out in that huge study. Hence it should be emphasized that some of the critical assessments of the classical time-budget study made in this book do not derive from a lack of appreciation of all its virtues, but from an ambition to push the frontier forward in new directions. The time-budget as a descriptive record alone reveals a multitude of important features on social interaction, sex roles, ageing, commuting, exposure to mass media, the use of leisure time, the effects of industrialization or innovations, care of children or the aged, and so on which no other kind of method does with the same precision and conviction. Hence the development of this method, which to a great extent occurred within the discipline of sociology, is a very great step forward. But again, this should not lead to complacency but be a challenge to move in new directions. In many respects, therefore, the chapters in Part 1 of this volume start where the conventional time-budget study leaves off.

The range of countries and regions for which time-use records and surveys are available is quite wide. It covers the capitalist-mixed-economy countries of Europe, North America, Australia and Japan; the Eastern European communist countries; and the less developed countries of Africa, Asia, Oceania and Latin America. Most of the studies in this book deal with the rich industrialized nations, with the exception of chapter 8.

The materials from the Third World are, as might be expected, few and far between and anthropologists and sociologists working there have generally given only partial attention to time-use aspects of activities. Some notable exceptions to this rule include the study by Reszöhazy, a sociologist, on Peru (Reszöhazy 1970; 1972) and a village study on Zambia over one year by a geographer (Kay 1964). Even so, once assembled the amount of material for the developing countries dealing more or less explicitly with time use is considerable, as evidenced by the compilation of such studies made by the Institute of Development Studies at Sussex University, UK (Connell and Lipton 1973). The usefulness of this material for the analysis of time allocation and innovations has also been shown by Carlstein (1970; 1973; and his forthcoming study on time allocation, innovation and agrarian change). One of the few studies in social anthropology dealing more explicitly with time allocation also points to the wealth of indicative and partial time-use information (Sahlins 1972). But there is also other important material on time allocation in anthropology, such as that presented by Barth (1967a; 1967b). It goes without saying that most of the material on developing countries has a rural bias, unlike most chapters in this volume which have an urban bias (except for 7 and 8).

Although this has often been the case in the past, studies of time use and time allocation should not be treated as identical, although they are complementary. Time-use studies are invariably accounts of actually observed activities, while the study of time allocation introduces a number of dimensions lacking in time-use studies. For one thing, allocation studies go beyond *ex post* accounting of time use and strives towards an *ex ante* formulation by exploring the mechanisms of time allocation as well as the constraints on possible time uses and the consequences of alternative allocations. In this respect the affinity to economics is clear. But it is not necessary to get entangled in equilibrium formulations and market mechanisms. It is still possible to sort out a demand and a supply side for human time (time resources and time requirements), to examine constraints on alternative allocations and opportunities, and so on. One problem with the conventional time-use study of actual behaviour and activity is that it tends towards behaviourism, empiricism, logical positivism and inductive generalizations in the form of 'patterns". Although these labels are admittedly very fuzzy, they still indicate the notion that it is important to go beyond this towards examining the actual use of time as a sub-set of possible uses within socio-structural and environmental constraints. Since it is hardly possible to observe non-behaviour and alternatives not chosen, analysis cannot be restricted to actual time use. A structuralist framework is necessary to make progress here. Not only must the individual and social mechanisms of choice and constraint be further explored, but also the capacity for action and interaction in given populations, habitats-regions, and sectors of society must be investigated, given certain constraints at the individual level (e.g. indivisibility, limited life span, etc.) and the system level (including both base and superstructure, i.e. technology, production system and economy, political system and ideology).

The time-budget survey as a research tool must be supplemented by more theory building and model construction which in turn will give greater meaning to new generations of time-use surveys. An imperative for further development is the incorporation of the societal and spatial-ecological environment which generates specific forms of time use. In this development, space should be treated as an equal to time rather than a competitor or methodologically obstructing factor. Just as geographers would profit by not treating the world as if it were 'temporally flat' and void of temporal organization and structure, many sociologists and economists who confine themselves to time use or temporal organization should by the same token include the spatial structure of society and habitat.

The sociologist Melbin is a good example of an independent researcher who has explored the structure of urban systems through the use of time and space (chapter 6). These dimensions helped him to grasp the real world. In his contribution to this volume, his main theme is the extension of the active day to around-the-clock activity in the various sectors of modern urban life. This is what he calls the 'colonization of time', as occurring within a spant (a space-time unit or region defined by spatial area and temporal extent). Using this concept among others, he goes on to study certain relationships between time use and energy use and the way energy acts as an 'enabling factor' in the temporal organization of a city.

Two mainstreams of thought which by tradition have incorporated time are historical geography and the geography of spatial dynamics. Common to both is the treatment of time as chronology, as an aid in the ordering of process, while time as a resource or as the temporal organization of activity, society and habitat are largely left unconsidered. But other traditions of study have paid attention to the temporal dimensions of geographic matter, and some of these have made a substantial contribution to time and space geography.

It was typically in the field of rural geography that several inevitable temporal aspects were encountered at an early stage. In hunting and gathering, nomadic and agricultural societies, seasonal and diurnal periodicities were as crucial as they were conspicuous. In the study of urban society, a-seasonality and continuously operating industries gave much less impression of periodicity, apart from the daily cycle of commuting. Looking back through the annals of geographic journals, the rural studies in which seasonal labour profiles and other seasonal variations in habitat and life style are described are too numerous to mention. Perhaps the French *genre-de-vie* school (cf. Vidal de la Blanche and others) deserves special recognition in that time was amply used as a descriptive dimension relating life style to events in the annual and life cycles. The *genre-de-vie* concept has been a source of stimulus to later work by other geographers such as Buttimer (1976) in her more explicit time and space structuring of habitat and life style and in her efforts to grasp the dynamism of the life world. Her work in turn has been strongly influenced by Hägerstrand's time-geographic attempts at regional synthesis (cf. chapter 7) and the tripartite concepts of noosphere, biosphere and socio-technosphere (among other concepts) have in turn proved useful in time-geography (cf. Buttimer and Hägerstrand, forthcoming).

Some of the particularly interesting studies applying an explicit time dimension to rural activities are those by Mead (1956; 1958) on Finland and Kay (1964) on a Zambian village. These were especially focused on how daily time use and land use were related to annual variations, and Kay's study is one of the first explicit time-use studies by a geographer. Another excellent example of an intensive study of annual farming activities and land use is that by Jensch (1957) on Germany. Generally speaking, however, much work on these matters was produced outside human geography and the material available is vast, extending from large studies such as that by Buck (1937) on time and land utilization in pre-revolutionary China to specific agronomic treatises on the farming year (Duckham 1963). Among integrated studies on life style, living conditions and habitat of *local* societies, the best ones seem to be those produced by ethnologists—social anthropologists. At the regional level, synthesis is perhaps more difficult to achieve.

Another area of study in which periodicities over time in rural activity and land use emerge is that of *shifting cultivation* systems. Here both the relations within the daily round and the time spent on travelling to and from fields, as well as the perennial land use, fallow and residence cycles are crucial to an understanding of how these agrarian systems operate. This is again a field of study shared by anthropologists and geographers. Some major contributions by geographers are those by Pelzer (1945), Scudder (1962), Knight (1974) plus many others cited in the systematic comparative study by Spencer (1966). In anthropology the list is longer and includes early pioneers like Linton (1933), Richards (1939), Allan (1949), Izikowitz (1951), Freeman (1955; 1970), de Schlippe (1956) and Conklin (1957; 1961). More recent studies are those by Bohannan and Bohannan (1968), Rappaport (1968) and Stauder (1971), to name a few. (Cf. also the time-geographic approach to shifting cultivation systems below, chapter 8.)

Time has entered rural land- (space) use studies in several other ways. Commuting to fields, fragmentation of holdings and intensity of land use, and distance decay of time inputs (cf. also the prism concept) are some of the topics that have been taken up (cf. the survey by Chisholm 1962.) Other rural land-use studies also dealing with time use are those on *nomadism*. Cattle and livestock tending activities are much timed by the spatio-temporal variations of the habitats used (cf. Barth 1959; 1961; Johnson 1969; Scholz 1974, esp. fig. 54; or Hultblad 1968). Rural space is timed in other ways, for instance in the form of land rotation or periodic redistributions of land according to fixed rules, the latter system found in several places in Africa (e.g. Eritrea) or Asia (e.g. northwest Pakistan). Another interesting example of this is how land use was coordinated in cycles for different adjacent common fields of villages in old Denmark, mainly for reasons of minimizing labour spent on building and maintaining fences (Hastrup 1970; cf. also Parkes and Thrift 1975).

One explicitly time-space oriented field in geography dealing with movements, interaction and spatial flows is that of *periodic markets*. The rationale behind the time-space approach stems from the obvious cyclical-periodic character of the observed phenomena. Some very interesting patterns in the way markets and sellers—buyers—traders shift location have been detected, and the number of studies on periodic market systems is considerable, as evidenced by a recent extensive bibliography by Bromley (1974) covering the whole world. Again geographers and anthropologists have worked hand in hand (cf. for example, Bohannan and Dalton, eds, 1962; Hill and Smith 1972; Stine 1962; Hill 1966; Hodder and Ukwu 1969; Brookfield, ed., 1969b; Skinner 1964-5; Good 1970; Eighmy 1972). The further theoretical development of the field will have bearing on various bodies of theory in human geography such as central place theory, diffusion theory and locational analysis in general, as well as various theories in economic and ecological anthropology. Stine (by organizing a special session at the meeting of the Association of American Geographers in 1975) tried to place periodic markets in a broader theoretical context in comparing them to other 'periodic space-time phenomena', to which also shifting cultivating systems belong.

A rather promising move would be to try to build some bridge between the periodic market field and the time-geographic model of the Lund school. The development of theory concerning these market systems, for instance by geographers such as R. H. T. Smith, seems overfocused on formal space-time structure such as locational spacing and temporal periodicity. This should be greatly applauded by a book on 'timing space and spacing time', and it is. Nevertheless, existing approaches would benefit from the introduction of more substantive aspects of time as a resource for human activity and a more thorough look at the time-allocation aspects of this complex, including the temporal and spatial structure of activities and environments outside the market places proper.

Still much theoretical work remains to be done with regard to rural space and time use, allocation, dynamics, trends and cycles. Although there is a wealth of useful ideas such as that by Brookfield on land-use cycles (1973), one is left with the impression that there is a great need for some more basic and synthetic models for grappling with the joint problems of time and space organization.

It is not surprising that one of the more explicit time-space formulations in human geography grew out of the study of *movement, transport* and *interaction* in space. The very essence of movement is a relation between space and time, especially when the aspect of speed is considered (which it is usually not in migration studies, for instance). But in transport and commuting studies, the time costs of reaching destinations have been an important object of analysis often described by *isochrones* and *velocity fields*. In transportation geography and economics the time costs evaluated in money have also been much looked into (cf. *inter alia* Moses and Williamson 1963; the value of time approach is also discussed in the Afterword). Some of these problems can also be analysed fruitfully with the aid of prism models (cf. the chapters by Lenntorp and Carlstein below).

One explicit time-space approach is that of spatial reorganization and '*time-space convergence*' (Janelle 1966; 1968a; 1968b). Time enters at two scales, first as travel time and friction of distance, and secondly as historical time and transport development. Spatial reorganization becomes a 'process by which places adapt both the locational structure and the characteristics of their social, economic and political activities to changes in time-space connectivity (the time required to travel between desired origins and destinations) ...' (Janelle 1968a). In time-space convergence as a function of *transport innovations*, 'places approach each other in time-space; that is, the travel time required between places decreases and distance declines in significance. ...' Consequently, 'it is possible and practical to adapt the spatial organization of their activities to their evolving time-space framework.' (Janelle 1968a). Forer in volume 1 of *TSST* applies this model to intra-urban changes in Christchurch as a function of transport innovations.

Time-space convergence is, of course, a more technical paradigm for the

more common notion that the world has 'shrunk'. While pedagogically popular, it is sometimes analytically inapt as there seems to be an inverse relationship
between the speed of travel and the proportion of the total population for whom
technical innovations in travel become available. The faster the means of
travel, the more energy per passenger consumed, the more ground personnel
per passenger tied down the more exclusive such travel becomes. Although
motor cars, high-speed trains and super-jet planes are becoming increasingly
available, the use of them is unlikely to be ecologically feasible for the
total world population, and not even for all in the rich countries. The world
has certainly shrunk less in the poor countries struggling with scarcity of fuel
and high energy-import costs. The number of people who can afford to use the
new super-jets is everywhere a small minority.

These aspects aside, the development of transport technology has lead to
overwhelming repacking of human settlement, population and activity in geographic space as well as in daily and annual cycles, and the time-space convergence models have made an important contribution to a time-oriented
geography. The next important step to take is to broaden this specific approach
to make it theoretically and terminologically compatible with other time-space
theories and models.

When looking at human geography from a time-geographic perspective, it is
no longer fruitful to see all human interaction as movement in space. Why
should geography be unduly crippled by not facing up to the fact that much
interaction is in the form of stationary activity which implies *movement through
time* inside stations such as buildings and premises. Whether interaction occurs
with humans, domestic animals, machines or spatially defined areas, it is a
process involving time use and time allocation or even the temporal allocation
of space. Some geographers like Blaut (1961) have noted that the spatial-areal
arrangement of phenomena and processes and their arrangement in time are
part of the same thing. What is seen as spatial structure in a static geographic
perspective is often just a slow process of long duration. But process is not only
an abstract alteration of things in space; much of it is the result of time
consuming human activity—stationary and mobile. To cull out mobile activities from the context of the stationary activities with which they interconnect
is a dangerous form of sectorization which a time-space approach can more
easily avoid. This volume contains many articles illustrating that point.
Taking the materials presented here as a mere starting point, there seems
indeed to be a rich field for further systematic conceptual reorganization of
human geography.

Chapter 1

Human Time Allocation in the City

F. Stuart Chapin Jr

In Western society space has traditionally been bent to social purpose more than time. True, there are a variety of controls society exercises over the timing of activities which serve to narrow the options open to an individual. The most pervasive of these are the institutionalized patterns of hours set for work, shopping and entertainment, which are imposed within the framework of the market system for the economies gained from time synchronization. But time controls are also legislated, for example by shifts in clocks for daylight saving, an occasional imposition of curfews, and the fixing of schedules in the public regulation of transportation and communications. These controls induce patterned forms of activity in the sense of establishing the times when persons may engage in an activity, sometimes regulating how much time is allocated as well. They are used most frequently in urban settlements where, because of dense concentrations of people, it becomes a matter of public safety and convenience to control the timing of activities.

In contrast, public and private actions which fix locations of activities in space are more commonplace. These spatial forms of intervention affect activity choices, often imposing constraints on where people may engage in many kinds of activities and sometimes influencing how much time is allocated as well. Among the most notable are public investment decisions in the location of transportation systems, utilities and public open spaces; these in conjunction with regulatory controls over land use have the effect of shaping the development of a city in density and spread which, in turn, profoundly affects people's activity patterns in time and space. Again, this kind of intervention is more widely used in urban settlements because, where there are concentrations of people, it is more economical and it is considered essential to public health, safety and convenience to provide services and facilities on a communal basis.

Much emphasis has been given in recent years to urban spatial structure, and elaborate models have been devised for simulating market processes. These can be used to show, on the supply side, how the growth of cities responds to policy-oriented interventions in space. However, apart from studies of household moving behaviour and housing choice, little attention has been given to the demand side, particularly to activity patterns of people and the effect that policy interventions in space and time may have in facilitating or constraining human activity choices. This essay focuses on these more neglected aspects of urban structure, concentrating primarily on an approach to describing and explaining activity patterns.

In the course of our work, a number of conceptual frameworks have been explored for interpreting individual behaviour in the choice of activities. Hammer (1973) investigated a utility-maximizing approach in which time and money trade-offs might be taken into account. Brail (1969) used a field theoretic emphasis to explore simulation approaches to patterns of activity. Hitchcock (1968) took a communications view and examined patterns in the utilization of preventive health care services by people from modern as compared with traditional backgrounds, attributing variations in these patterns to differences in 'information states'. And Hightower (1965) used a normative model to explore the conjunction of activity analysis with client analysis in the study of recreation choices.

The present discussion is based on the interpretation of human activity choices following social psychological traditions and extends earlier versions of the framework (Chapin 1968; 1974). The extended framework is spelled out in the initial section below and, using our empirical studies in Washington, an exploratory application of the framework is presented in the last part of the essay.

The context and conceptual framework

In contemplating how people live their lives in time and space and how large numbers of people synchronize their activities in space in the pursuit of a satisfying life, one cannot but marvel that there is not more chaos in human affairs than is actually experienced from day to day. There is a remarkable resilience to human nature, a capacity for man to adapt his living patterns to time, place and circumstance. Yet this accommodation is not without human toll: witness the social externalities steadily accumulating throughout the world. We see these most plainly in large cities—poverty alongside affluence, powerlessness alongside privilege, the nomadic life alongside the settled life, etc.

The structural bases of these contrasts lie deep in industrial and post-industrial societies. Specialization and the division of labour, which have been essential for these societies to evolve, also generate status systems that have a deeply rooted influence on people's values and expectations about the quality of life. In setting out to explore the nature of activity systems, there are thus reasons to conceive of them not only in terms of choice but also in terms of constraints imposed by cultural and social processes.

To understand how patterned forms of human activity evolve, it is essential to begin with the behaviour of individuals at the micro-level of daily routines. Once the regularities in behaviour are understood at this level, the horizon can be expanded to all individuals in the community, with human activity examined in a larger social context. Although not pursued in this essay, eventually patterned forms of human activity thus defined can be interfaced with patterned forms of adapted space, and the effects that policy-related interventions in both time and space have in the fulfilment of policy objectives can be evaluated.[1]

So we begin with the individual. At the most elemental level, human activity can be conceived as consisting of physiological and learned activities. Some

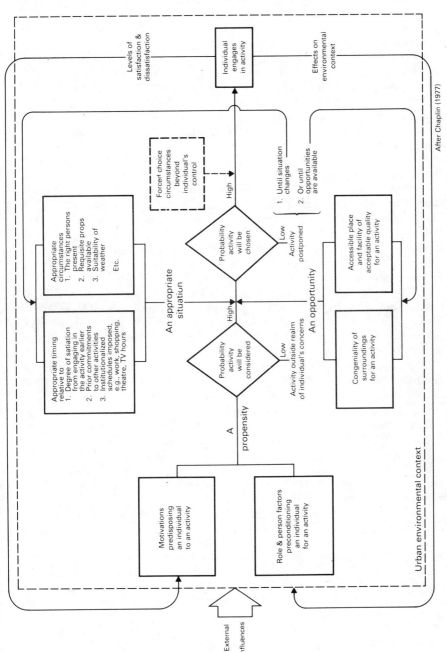

Figure 1 A choice model of time allocation to daily activities in the urban environment.

After Chaplin (1977)

physiological activities such as sleep and other body functions occur in circadian rhythms—rhythms that appear to bear a relation to the earth's motion
relative to the sun (Doob 1971; Palmer 1970). They are involuntary and set
the timing for more voluntary activities. The most involuntary activities can
therefore be thought of as biologically imposed events, and the most voluntary
forms of activity more as experientially conditioned expressions of choice. Most
activities in between are not absolutely classifiable as involuntary or voluntary,
but fall on a continuum extending from the most obligatory to the most discretionary: sleeping—→ ... eating—→ ... receiving medical care—→ ...
working—→ ... buying food (or clothing or shelter)—→ ... attending a
theatre performance—→ ... visiting with relatives—→ ... reading—→ ...
daydreaming—→ ...

The biologically regulated activities are universally attributable to all individuals, but among learned activities, as we move more and more towards the
discretionary end of the continuum, there is a tendency for people to show
increasing variability in their choices. Intuitively, we see that once subsistence
and other needs concerned with survival are satisfied, people have more
latitude for choice. But how are choices made? What factors shape an individual's choices? Are there similarities in the way people make these choices?

Figure 1 approaches these questions in the framework of a conditioned
response model. Learned forms of behaviour are seen to be shaped by four
sources of influence—a propensity, an opportunity, an appropriate situation,
and an environmental context. The propensity is the motivational basis for the
activity but conditioned by person-specific constraints. The propensity element
determines what activities are likely to fall in a person's realm of concerns and
thus defines the scope of choice.

The opportunity element refers to the availability of a physical place or
facility suited to the activity and to the congeniality of surroundings for
engaging in the activity. The situational element refers to appropriateness of
timing and circumstances for the activity. The environmental context is the
milieu within which choices are made; it is everything of a non-physiological
nature influencing a person's behaviour, including his own previous behaviour.

The flow of the diagram is a representation of the choice process. For the
moment, disregarding all elements except the propensity element, we can
conceive of human motivation (upper left-hand box in Figure 1) as the ener-
gizing source for engaging in a particular activity. The type of activity is determined by an urge to satisfy one or more felt needs, with the strength of the urge
determined by levels of satisfaction or dissatisfaction expected or previously
experienced. A first-time choice of an activity, whether by whim or by assessment of the promise of enjoyment, is based on an expectation, articulated or
unarticulated, of satisfying one or more felt needs. Subsequent choices are a
function of levels of satisfaction or dissatisfaction experienced in responding to
these needs previously. After Maslow (1970), the motivation component of the
model can be represented in the form of a hierarchy of needs ranging from those
of a physiological nature to those of a self-actualizing kind which, in an ascend-
ing order, consist of felt needs for safety, affection, esteem and self-fulfilment.

According to this view, motivation comes into play in its most basic form,
beginning at the *security level* in the hierarchy, just beyond the base level of
physiological activity (sleep, food intake, etc.). Security-related motivations are

survival-oriented and, using the institutionalized mechanisms the culture has devised to minister to these needs, they have to do with subsistence (most notably allocating time to 'work' in order to be assured of food, clothing and shelter) and self-preservation (allocating time to medical care and, in times of emergency, to protecting life and limb from natural disasters and human violence incurred in civil disturbances or war).

At the next step up the hierarchy is the *affection level*. This has to do with a need for love and the sense of belonging that goes with it. This need is the basis of the bonds of affection among members of the nuclear and extended family and the friendship ties with others.

At the *esteem level*, there is somewhat more freedom of choice but choices are nevertheless constrained by certain cultural and social imperatives. Self-esteem has two aspects, one concerned with achievement and the other with status. The *achievement component* involves an individual's desire for strength, confidence and independence. Achievement is defined in the context of one's ethnic and social group and the beliefs and values of that group. For example, if the culture or social system places high value on upward mobility, the individual is motivated to engage in activities aimed at 'getting ahead'. The *status component* of self-esteem is concerned with reputation, prestige and recognition; in satisfying this felt need, a person seeks to bolster his sense of identity in relation to others.

Finally, if previous-level needs are substantially satisfied, a person may be motivated to satisfy his own particular inner need for *self-fulfilment*. This is an individual form of self-expression—sometimes creative, often spontaneous, and usually doing things for the sheer enjoyment of doing them.

Thus, as applied here, the Maslow hierarchy implies priorities of choice and it implies an increasing range of choice the higher up the hierarchy a choice is made (two factors which are not unrelated). While consciously or subconsciously lower-order priorities will tend to take precedence, choices are not confined to a serial order of selection. Clearly there are instances in which a person rearranges these priorities, especially when choices fall in the more or less free time periods of the day. For instance, the chance meeting with an old friend on the street and catching up on news of one another; the social interchange in this instance may take precedence over a shopping mission.

Also, people learn that their overall level of satisfaction with everyday life is greater if there is some variety to their activities. This is a basic principle in factory and office management, but it also applies in the more or less free time periods of a day. So people tend to intersperse into the non-work period of the day some diversity of activity to relieve the monotony of routine. Some of these 'filler' activities absorb 'wait time', until the time for a scheduled commitment is reached—for example, talking with the neighbours, browsing through the television channels, or looking at a magazine until it is time to leave for dinner at a friend's house.

Along with motivation predisposing an activity choice, there are constraints which precondition a person's propensity towards making a particular choice. Represented by the lower left-hand box in the propensity element of Figure 1, these consist of certain personal characteristics (e.g., sex, stage in the life cycle, and health status) and roles that society assigns to persons (e.g., the breadwinning role long assumed in Western countries by the male partner of the household and the homemaking role by the female partner). While role definitions are always undergoing change—witness recent changes in the breadwinning and homemaking roles—they obviously precondition choices. Similarly, stage in the life cycle serves as a selection influence in the way motivations are translated into classes of activity. Single persons at a youthful stage of the life cycle respond differently to felt needs and are predisposed to different activities than young couples without children or couples in the child-rearing stage, or spouses in other stages of the life cycle. Obviously, too, one's state of health affects the way in which one exercises choices.

Now let us introduce into the flow diagram the other contingencies. Before an activity can be chosen, the individual must perceive an opportunity to engage in that activity, i.e., there must be one or more places or facilities of acceptable quality in congenial surroundings which make the activity possible and inviting (see lower pair of boxes in Figure 1). As used here, 'an opportunity' has to do with physical and spatial variables affecting the probabilities that a person would choose an activity. Given an unrestrained and responsive housing market, it can be presumed that a household would normally choose a place of residence where opportunities exist for individual members to pursue activities that best fit the activity propensities of all members of the household. However, aberrations in the market, some from social origins (e.g., restriction of housing choice due to prejudice), some from economic origins (e.g., restriction due to shortages of housing within certain segments of the market), and some from inefficiencies in the provision of public goods and services, often circumscribe choice. Consequently opportunities for engaging in particular activities which might otherwise fall in a person's 'choice field' are denied.

But before an activity can be chosen the situation for doing the activity must also be propitious—the appropriate moment and the appropriate circumstances (see upper pair of boxes in Figure 1). The appropriateness of timing depends on a number of factors. First, whether or not a person chooses an activity may depend on how recently he has engaged in that particular activity and how satiated his felt need for that activity is at the moment relative to other choices open to him. Relative satiation becomes increasingly a factor the more towards the discretionary end of the continuum an activity falls. Second, previous commitments to an activity affect choices at a particular moment. Thus, seeing relatives or friends usually involves advance arrangements which effectively limits alternative choices during the times set aside for these visits. Similarly, attending a theatre performance requires a decision to reserve time on a specific date for a specific span of hours, greatly reducing the probability of using that time for other activities.

A third timing contingency relates to the institutionalized schedules society imposes and the necessity for the individual to synchronize with these schedules. While these schedules—work hours, shopping hours, doctor's office hours, theatre showings, television viewing hours, etc.—are phased with biological rhythms, they are set by other considerations as well, and individual activity itineraries must adjust to them. In this respect, the appropriateness of timing not only means that the activity is actively considered during the time of day when there is latitude for that activity to occur but also that the interval of time available is sufficient to complete the activity. Supposing a working member of the household returns home by 6 p.m. on a weekday and the evening meal is ready to serve at 7. After cleaning up, he has a half hour to spare; he might spend this time with the children, working in the garden, helping get the meal ready to serve, reading the newspaper, or possibly watching television. It is unlikely that he would go off to a movie because this requires a commitment of an hour and a half or more. Also, the evening mealtime is an institutionalized occurrence in most families and is scheduled at a particular hour when physiological necessity is ritualized to a social purpose.

Along with timing, the choice of an activity is often dependent upon the right circumstances. Sometimes a choice has to do with the presence of certain people, and sometimes it requires the availability of certain 'props' (remembering to bring a passbook, if one were to do a banking errand; having a swimsuit along, if one were to go swimming, etc.). Suitable weather may be a factor affecting choice. The point here is that in making a choice of activity, an individual consciously or subconsciously reckons with situational contingencies.

But, given all of the foregoing factors impinging on choice—a propensity, a perceived opportunity and a situation—an individual is sometimes forced into an activity by circumstances virtually beyond his control (a neighbour dropping in unexpectedly, a traffic accident with his car on the way home from work, etc.). These chance occurrences may result in activities that short-circuit the choice process described above. In Figure 1, the box outlined in broken lines indicates this contingency.

Finally, we may note that the model has provision for two kinds of change, one from external sources and one from internal sources. The former has to do with change induced into the environmental context from the outside world (see arrowhead on the left in Figure 1 signifying outside influences operating on the environmental context). Thus, in this open system view, the environment is constantly undergoing change from technological, economic, cultural, social and other influences from the outside world. The internal sources of change are reflected in four feedback features in the model. One operates to change the 'environmental context' from within the environment—essentially the pooling effect of each individual's activity added to that of all others and the way this may modify the propensity component (lower long loop). A second operates to change 'opportunities', i.e., the individual takes steps to modify the available space-related options, essentially seeking a change in present surroundings or moving to a place where opportunities exist (lower short loop). Thus, a person may be prompted to press public officials to provide a place, a facility, or surroundings congenial to the activity, or the individual may move to another location where there is an opportunity to engage in the activity. The third internal feedback loop is to make provision for postponement of choice until the 'right' situation for an activity occurs (upper short loop). The fourth loop operates to modify 'the propensity' and is regulated by levels of satisfaction-dissatisfaction experienced from an activity which affect the predisposition of the individual to engage in an activity again (the upper long loop).

Applying the framework to a city

So far we have been discussing individual behaviour. For the purposes of examining the activities of the population of an entire city, it is necessary to work at a more aggregate level. In order to make sense of the otherwise overwhelming factual base of human activity in the city, people are grouped into relatively homogenous segments, and activities are grouped into relatively general activity classes. According to our schema, people aggregated into groups of similar ethnic and socio-economic characteristics will tend to possess similar activity patterns; in short, motivations born of common beliefs, preferences and experiences prompt people to behave in similar ways. In aggregating activities into classes, we group together activities that can be construed to serve a similar function across socio-cultural dimensions and yet provide substitutability in terms of talents and skills utilized, challenge and satisfactions experienced, time involved and surroundings required.

In aggregating, we lose the saliency of matching up precise propensities, opportunities and situations with precise outcomes in activity, but we gain in being able to identify patterns of behaviour arising out of common sources of motivation. Moreover, both forms of aggregation tie in with policy applications of the model. Public expenditure and public regulation are predicated on benefits accruing to entire constituencies rather than to individuals, and so the aggregation of people into ethnic and socio-economic groups, useful in defining constituencies for policy analysis, fortuitously also provides a useful basis for the study of felt needs of a population on an aggregated basis. Indeed, it provides a basis for determining how such public actions affect common felt needs. By the same token, the aggregation of detailed activities into more generic functional categories permits assessment of the fit between activity patterns and community facilities and the spatial structure of the city or the 'opportunity' aspect of the model. In this respect, however, there is work to be done in establishing how aggregation affects the meaningfulness of activity categories to people, particularly sensitivity analysis of the substitutability of choices within activity classes as perceived by different segments of the population.

Table 1 illustrates both forms of aggregation—(a) the grouping of respondents from the 1968 Washington probability sample by segments (by race and income group), and (b) the grouping of the more than 225 possible activities used in the original coding into eleven aggregate activity classes (excluding sleep as a 12th activity).[2] It shows, for respondents in each segment of the population, what proportions engaged in each of the eleven classes of activity on an average spring weekday and the mean hours of time allocated to each such activity class by those involved in the activity. We leave the interpretation of this table to the reader.

Because our 1968 metropolitan-wide study underrepresented the low-income segment of the population (largely attributable to the inner city disturbances which broke out in the period the survey was in the field and the consequent unfavourable interviewing situation that prevailed in the wake of these conditions), we conducted supplemental studies in two low-income sub-metropolitan communities—one in an inner-city black community (summer of 1969), and for comparative purposes, the other in a fairly close-in transitional white community (summer of 1971). Both studies made use of ethnographic and survey techniques in the study of the activities of heads of households and spouses. Participant observation provided a check on the general reliability of infor-

TABLE 1   Activity Patterns of Heads of Households and Spouses During Waking Hours of an Average Spring Weekday by Race and Income^a—Washington, 1968

Activity Measure and Population Segment	Work	Eating	Shopping	Home-making	Family Activities	Church & Orgs.	Recreation & Hobbies	Social Activities	Watching Television	Resting & Relaxing	Misc. Activities	All Forms of Discr. Activity	All Out-of-Home Activities
Per cent of Persons in Each Segment Engaging in Activity													
All Persons (n=1,667)	58	96	36	76	31	6	29	36	67	57	96	99	87
Black (n=358)	59	93	19	71	13	5	13	22	69	41	90	99	78
Nonblack (n=1,309)	54	97	40	78	35	7	34	40	66	62	97	99	90
Low Income (n=592)	44	92	27	73	25	5	21	31	69	50	89	97	75
Middle Income (n=863)	64	97	40	76	33	7	31	37	65	59	97	99	91
High Income (n=212)	64	97	42	76	33	8	40	44	58	69	97	98	94
Mean Hours Allocated Per Participant^b													
All Persons	8.7	1.7	1.6	3.6	1.7	2.2	2.3	2.0	2.5	1.6	2.9	5.9	10.4
Black	9.1	1.5	1.7	3.7	1.6	2.2	2.7	2.2	3.5	2.4	2.9	5.8	10.6
Nonblack	7.6	1.8	1.6	3.6	1.7	2.2	1.8	2.0	2.2	1.5	2.9	5.9	10.3
Low Income	8.8	1.6	1.6	4.3	2.0	2.4	2.2	2.3	3.1	2.1	2.9	6.3	9.9
Middle Income	8.8	1.8	1.5	3.3	1.6	2.2	1.8	1.9	2.1	1.5	2.9	5.7	10.6
High Income	8.7	1.9	1.8	3.1	1.6	1.7	1.7	1.9	1.7	1.4	3.0	5.9	10.8

a Income figured on a per-member-of-household basis. For the derivation of income groups, see Chapin (1974, Figure III–3, p. 64).
b Includes time spent in travel to and from places where activity took place out-of-home.
Note: Table 2 examines the activity patterns enclosed in the boxes using results from supplemental investigations of low income persons.

TABLE 2   Patterns of Discretionary Activity of Heads of Households and Spouses on an Average Summer's Weekday by Sex and Employment Status

	Inner City Black Community Low Income only[a] (1969)				Close-In White Community Low Income Only[a] (1971)			
	(n)	Social Activites	Watching Television	Resting & Relaxing	(n)	Social Activities	Watching Television	Resting & Relaxing
Per cent of Persons in Each Segment Engaging in Activity								
All Persons	(223)	34	71	56	(241)	56	70	48
Women Working FT	(45)	18	67	49	(31)	81	71	39
Women Not WFT	(120)	40	71	56	(110)	59	75	50
Men Working FT	(32)	28	75	47	(50)	32	54	38
Men Not WFT	(26)	42	73	81	(41)	61	73	59
Mean Hours Allocated Per Participant[b]								
All Persons		2·0	4·2	3·2		2·4	2·9	2·3
Women Working FT		1·4	3·6	2·2		1·6	2·0	1·2
Women Not WFT		2·1	4·0	3·2		2·6	3·4	2·0
Men Working FT		1·1	3·9	2·4		2·2	2·4	2·2
Men Not WFT		2·7	6·1	4·9		2·6	2·9	3·5

a Income figured on a per-member-of-household basis. For the derivation of the 'low-income' category, see Chapin (1974, Figure III–3, p. 64).
b Includes time spent in travel to and from places where activity took place.
Note: Table 3 applies the choice model on low-income male heads of households for activity patterns enclosed in the box shown here. WFT means 'working full time.'

mation obtained in home interviews in these community studies and a means of monitoring seasonal variations in activity patterns.

Table 2 presents results from the two community surveys; it shows the proportions of heads of households and spouses of heads in these two low-income communities engaging in selected discretionary activities and the amount of time on the average each segment devotes to the activities. Table 2 may be thought of as supplying special samples for those segments of the metropolitan-wide study enclosed in the boxes in Table 1. The analysis is narrowed to three discretionary pursuits in order to focus on activities where there is some latitude for choice and thus particularly appropriate for analysis using the choice model.[3] By selecting a black community and a white community and narrowing the analysis to low-income subjects only, the analysis controls for such systemic variables as ethno-cultural and economic status, and by selecting out men and employment characteristics it also controls for role factors. Only male subjects are examined here in order to keep the discussion within reasonable bounds.

The results from initial tests of the choice model applied to two segments

TABLE 3 An Exploratory Application of Choice Model to Survey Results from Two Low Income Communities—Washington, DC

	Rank Order Importance of Factors for Male Heads of Households[a]											
	Inner City Black Community (1969)						Close-In White Community (1971)					
Proxies of Motivational Factors	Social Activities		Watching Television		Resting & Relaxing		Social Activities		Watching Television		Resting & Relaxing	
	WFT	Not WFT	WFT	Not WFT	WFT	Not WFT	WFT	Not WFT	WFT	Not WFT	WFT	Not WFT
Predisposing Factors												
Need for security: Concern for violence in neighbourhood	—	1	2	4	4	2	—	1	2	—	—	—
Need for achievement: Evaluation of chances of 'getting ahead'	1	—	3	—	—	3	1	2	1	2	3	3
Need for status: Desire for neighbours of same SES level	—	2	1	2	3	—	3	—	—	—	—	—
General social adjustment: Degree of alienation	4	4	—	—	2	—	2	3	—	1	1	4
Preconditioning Factors												
Stage in life cycle	2	—	4	3	1	1	4	—	3	4	2	2
Health status	3	3	—	1	—	4	—	4	4	3	4	1
R^2	·20	·18	·08	·17	·08	·22	·12	·56	·24	·63	·10	·15

a Rank order established from step-wise regression analysis; beyond the ranks shown, the value of the multiple determination coefficient R^2 changes very little.

Note: WFT means 'working full time.'

of the male population in these study areas (the two segments enclosed in the box in Table 2) is summarized in Table 3. Because our field surveys recorded activities actually engaged in by these segments of the population during a twenty-four hour period, the opportunity and situational contingencies depicted in Figure 1 can be presumed to have been satisfied in order for the activity to have occurred in the first place. Likewise, for purposes of this trial use of the framework, the urban environmental context can be presumed to be constant. So, in this initial experimental use of the framework, we are dealing with predisposing and preconditioning factors as inputs at the extreme left-hand end of the diagram and activity patterns as outputs at the extreme right-hand end of the diagram.

The measures of predisposing factors are crude and extracted from survey items designed for more general descriptive purposes.[4] Some items are not identical in the two studies, and there are no measures of affection or self-fulfilment. However, as an indicator of the extent to which all levels of need were being satisfied, we introduced into the analysis a measure of alienation. We would have preferred to use refined indices for each level of motivation in the Maslow hierarchy. Also, because of the crudeness of the measures used and the variations in the survey items used in the two communities, we did not attempt to identify patterns through factor analysis but chose to make preliminary tests on the basis of step-wise regression analysis. As summarized here, this analysis shows the rank order of importance of factors used and the combined level of explanation these factors supply (the R^2 multiple determination coefficients at the foot of Table 3).

Of the three discretionary activities examined in Table 3, it may be noted that only social activities involve some allocation of time out of the home, with the other two (watching television and resting and relaxing) being passive forms of activity typically taking place in the home. These forms of activity appear to be the most dominant ones in low-income communities. While generalizations from these results must be tentative, it would appear that at the security level of the Maslow hierarchy, among men, the threat of violence on neighbourhood streets has some association with time allocation to all three of these activities in the black community, but little or none in the white community. This would seem to be plausible since, in the black community, there was burning and looting in the area the summer before, and street and alley muggings were common during the period this study was in the field. In contrast, the transitional white community was some three miles farther out from the centre city locations where violence was most prevalent and, according to participant observation, assaults on the streets were relatively uncommon.

At the esteem level in the hierarchy, there were again differences in the two communities. The achievement drive, as measured here in terms of felt need to 'get ahead', did not turn out to be a particularly relevant factor among men in the black community, whereas it did have relevance in the white community. This is not surprising when the much higher rate of unemployment among blacks as compared with whites is considered. According to participant observers, a black person in this inner-city community is so preoccupied with simply holding onto any kind of job that 'getting ahead' seems somewhat irrelevant, but also this kind of achievement orientation is somewhat outside the value system of black ghetto residents. In the blue-collar white community, however, results indicate that 'getting ahead' is a prominent value orientation.

With respect to the status component of esteem (as represented by the importance attached to having neighbours of similar socio-economic background), results in Table 3 indicate that these considerations figure more importantly for men in the black than in the white community in allocating time to the three categories of discretionary activity. Again drawing on results from participant observation, under the deprived circumstances to be found in the inner-city black community, high value is placed on a living environment where children can someday find a better life than their parents. Status has to do with 'escape opportunities' for one's children rather than prestige and recognition that is attributed to, say, middle-class notions of social status. In contrast, participant observation suggests that, in the low-income white community, the blue-collar 'hard living' male ethic attaches little importance to social status (Howell 1973). (This is in marked contrast to the values of women in this community, who do place some importance on the level of attainment of their neighbours.)

With respect to the alienation factor, there is no marked difference between the two communities, and among men in both communities, general social adjustment is a factor associated with the allocation of time to discretionary activities. Similarly, preconditioning factors (both stage in the life cycle and health status) appear to have some importance in the choice of these activities by men in both communities.

Because of the unrefined nature of the measures used in this initial application of the framework, we omit the plus and minus signs of factors ranked in Table 3 and interpretive comments that go with this aspect of the regression analysis. Noting the modest but respectable level of explanation provided by the mix of factors used in this analysis of time allocation, results lend encouragement to making further refined tests of the model, including a fuller representation of predisposing factors.

In a more rigorous application of the model, we would propose tests of the other elements of the model. In addition to refinements in the propensity element, it would be important to establish how variations in the opportunity element and in situational contingencies affect the explanatory power of the total mix of factors postulated as affecting activity choices. Beyond this, through longitudinal studies, perhaps using panels of subjects who are re-interviewed at intervals, an investigation of the feedback features of the model would be fruitful. Finally, it would seem that if these tests prove to be encouraging, the model might then be used in performing experiments to determine how policy-oriented interventions in spatial arrangements of the city affect time allocation and how various controls in the timing of activities affect activity patterns. Indeed, such a model might well have a use for social impact analysis in studying the implications of development proposals—the probabilities that proposals would significantly alter living patterns and generally change the quality of life relative to felt needs of residents.

Footnotes

¹ 'Human activity' is a term used here to refer to the way people live their lives on a day-in-day-out basis. It refers in part to *routines*, i.e., recurrent activities in time and space, say, in a twenty-four-hour time cycle, but it also refers to pursuits of a less regulated nature in the sense that there is less order and regularity in the time chosen and the space used during some recognized span of time. Since the work on which this essay is based carries a bias towards planning and policy applications of human activity, special attention is given to activities, both routine and non-routine, which occur in *patterns*, i.e., activities in which a substantial number of people engage at similar times and/or in the same places in a particular time span.

² The probability sample consisted of 1,720 households drawn from the counties and municipalities making up the 1960 Standard Metropolitan Statistical Area (SMSA). Respondents were selected alternately as the head of the household (following the US Census definition) or the spouse, except where the household turned out to consist of a broken family or an unmarried head, in which case there was only one possible respondent, the head. The usable returns came to be 1,667 households or ·2 of 1 per cent of the households enumerated there in 1970. The area contained a population in 1970 of 2,712,871.

³ In this analysis, we select activities where there is a level of participation amounting to at least one-third of the population. For purposes here, therefore, activities meeting this criterion would constitute an 'activity pattern' as defined in footnote 1.

⁴ For the security level of motivation, we used a graded scale of concern for safety on the streets in the subject's neighbourhood. At the self-esteem level, we used a graded scale of concern for 'getting ahead' as an indicator of need for achievement, and concern about having neighbours of a similar economic level as an indicator of need for status. The alienation measure in the black community was based on an indirect question on the extent of threat felt in relations with others, and in the white community it was based on a scale developed from attitudes concerning the extent people can be trusted, the extent public officials can be trusted, and the subject's outlook towards the future.

Chapter 2

The Treatment of Time in the Explanation of Spatial Behaviour

Ian G. Cullen

In recent years it has become harder to find studies in human geography which have explicitly considered the impact of time upon their explanations and analyses. Time is, of course, fundamentally implicit in the studies of historical geography. Current settlement patterns and spatial forms are interpreted in the light of their development over time. The 'science of places' is seen as a study of chronological sequences just as much as a snapshot of spatial relationships. Yet historical geography certainly does not occupy today the pivotal role it was accorded by writers such as Hartshorne (1946) only a few decades ago.

Today one is more likely to find explicit references to temporal sequence and dynamic process among products of the quantitative revolution of the early sixties than in other branches of the geographical literature. It is not just that statistical and mathematical approaches are becoming far more commonplace overall. It is rather that a significant proportion of the quantitative studies in human geography share in common one ultimate purpose, namely that of achieving a prediction of the future in an accurate numerical form. Their interest in time is thus quite different from that of the historical geographer. They seek not to understand and explain the present in the light of the events of the past, but rather to extrapolate currently observed relationships into the future. Time ceases to be a way of illuminating a situation. It becomes little more than an obstacle which the prediction must overcome. Of course the best of the predictive studies include hard-edged historical data (where available) as well as current observations amongst the raw materials of their analyses. Moreover, they may well be based upon a theory which is essentially historical in character.

However, the predictive purpose of such studies implies the acceptance of a much narrower and more mechanistic view of causation than is implicit in the approach of the historian. Such a mechanistic analysis will often suffice when all that is required is a statistical approximation and extrapolation of the behaviour of an aggregate social phenomenon—the growth of a city or the economic performance of a region. It will not do when the aim is to understand the way the individual uses and responds to the social and physical consequences of that growing city or declining region.

I have argued elsewhere (Cullen 1976) that one of the major reasons why modern behavioural geography so often fails to live up to its promise is precisely because of its insistence upon the appropriation of this mechanistic approach and predictive *raison d'être*. In practice, at the level of individual behaviour, this has all too often meant superficial and inconclusive statistical snapshots of arbitrarily aggregated questionnaire responses about arbitrarily defined aspects of behaviour. The more modest city or region macro-analyses have been able to isolate, describe and extrapolate from broad dynamic processes and trends, but at the level of the individual the various attempts at prediction have always (and I would contend inevitably) failed.

It is not the purpose of this paper to document minutely this failure of behavioural geography to mirror the dynamic and quasi-dynamic prediction achievements of aggregate quantitative studies. It is rather to suggest that the uncritical acceptance of a paradigm which extols the virtues of such achievements beyond all others has possibly blinded its practitioners to more fruitful ways in which *time* might be incorporated within their studies. A penchant for the mechanistic view of time as the biggest hurdle in a predictive obstacle race has meant that its significance both as an integrating medium and a yardstick for the interpretation of spatial behaviour has been missed.

Behavioural geography as comparative statics

The lack of an explicit treatment of time in behavioural studies, apart from the odd desultory venture into the field of predictive analysis alluded to above, has been truly remarkable. This lack has manifested itself in almost all the major research areas. One way of classifying behavioural studies is to ignore the macro-phenomenon (the city, shopping centre or landscape) to which they ultimately relate, and focus upon the link in the behavioural chain which constitutes their primary object of analysis. Thus there is a major group of studies in which ostensibly the chief focus of research attention is the attitudinal or perceptual aspects of spatial behaviour—the way the individual interprets and evaluates the environment. And there is another fairly distinct group which treats overt behaviour more directly—how the environment is used rather than how it is perceived.

In the former of these groups an explicit treatment of time is very rare. There is sometimes a speculative discussion, appended to the major study, of how attitudes change over time, but very rarely do follow-up studies attempt to measure the rate of such changes. Thus we have very little evidence as to the long term stability of the attitude measurements that are taken. Moreover there is hardly ever an attempt made to measure either the relationships between a particular time-specific situation (or event) and the subjective response it engenders, or that between the verbalized attitude and the deliberate action that it fosters. If such attempts were made then time considerations would become more or less unavoidable. As it is attitudes are usually treated as little more than peculiar sorts of verbal behaviour which are the direct products of persistent physical (or social) situations. Viewed in that way the treatment of time becomes irrelevant.

Studies of overt behaviour appear to lend themselves much more readily to an explicit treatment of time. It is relatively easy to monitor when an activity occurs, with what frequency, and for what duration. Empirical transportation studies have been gathering this sort of behavioural information for years.

Shopping and recreation studies normally involve asking respondents at least about the frequency as well as the nature of their activities. And neighbourhood studies in which the concept of action space is employed often establish the frequency of a variety of sorts of local and community participation activity.

Nevertheless, the ways in which this temporal information is used are usually very limited in range. Typically data on frequencies and durations of activities are amassed not to test an hypothesis about the dynamics of spatial behaviour but purely to inform some theoretically peripheral debate. Often this debate is located primarily within a political arena which, whilst overlapping, is certainly not coterminous with that of the academic research which produces these crude time measures.

To take the simple example of shopping behaviour, there have been many studies which have attempted to measure peoples' perceptions of and attitudes towards retailing centres. One of the most meticulous of these was that of Downs (1970) in Bristol. The problems with such studies have been discussed many times—as early as 1968 Harvey (1969) was expressing reservations—but one of the gravest difficulties is that which has already been referred to. Since time is ignored in such studies, we can have no grounds for faith in the long term stability of the attitude descriptions elicited. A typical response to this and other worries is to focus upon action rather than attitude—the traditional economists' approach of revealed preferences. In such studies time enters in the fairly obvious ways noted above. People are asked not only where they go to shop, but with what frequency (see, for example, Rushton 1969). They may, of course, be asked about their attitudes as well, but the point is that these two sorts of question are treated independently. The theoretical interest normally focuses upon the perceptual component of behaviour. Rarely is any attempt made to understand the dynamics of spatial behaviour in terms of these crude frequency measures. In most cases they are there simply to be aggregated and fed directly into some political debate about planning permissions, bus routes or political boundaries.

It is not difficult to understand how the time element comes to enter studies of spatial behaviour more often in the guise of a political rather than theoretical instrument. These studies are primarily about shopping or trip-making or recreation. They are not about the time-ordering of peoples' lives. Time, treated theoretically, links and integrates the items of behaviour, and so studies whose research boundaries compartmentalize activity sequences can have little to say about this temporal structure.

This, however, is no real explanation of why these crude frequency measures are so often found in behavioural studies. It explains only why we should regard them as of limited theoretical interest when they do appear. The more fundamental explanation has, I think, to do with the logical primacy of political motives in behavioural research. This may sound absurd in a discipline in which those who are currently most politically explicit and vociferous are those who have long since discarded behavioural research as counter-revolutionary or worse. However, they would probably be amongst the first to agree that a field of study does not have to be revolutionary to merit the label 'political'. The inevitable primacy of political motivation in such studies derives simply from their expense. The view that social science research should be funded purely and generously for the furtherance of knowledge can last no longer than the medieval concept of the university as a closed institution. (In other words, in this country it is not quite dead, but is going fast.)

The point is that behavioural studies are funded to provide politically use-able information. There need be no *a priori* judgement as to who should benefit and who must lose, just an explicitly political need for information upon which such benefit/loss decisions may be made. (The fact that politicians can be per-suaded that they have such a need when they are not aware of it is neither here nor there from the point of view of this discussion.) When such decisions relate to the distribution of public facilities over space, the need for information becomes particularly acute. These facilities—whether for recreation, transport or health care—are either intrinsically or by virtue of statute, externalities. People do not express their demand for them in the market place and so there is no market price which can be used to guide those charged with their dis-tribution. Time, as Becker (1973) has pointed out, is one of the two major resources which individuals possess as limited assets and which they invest in the consumption of goods and services. From the political point of view, moreover, it has the edge over money in that its expenditure cannot normally be avoided in the consumption of public goods. Thus we observe that most behavioural studies with a practical leaning (i.e. the majority of all such studies) include questions as to the frequency of use of facilities. Such questions rarely illuminate the studies at a theoretical level, but they do aggregate to provide a proxy for the economist's demand curve. They generate indices of intensity of use which can be fed directly into political debates surrounding the facilities in question.

It is worth noting that one class of spatial behaviour study not yet men-tioned is typically used and applied in just the way outlined above even though, as I shall argue below, its potential for a theoretically more respectable treat-ment of time is far greater. This is the time-budget study, in which not only the frequency but also the duration of activity is recorded, normally by means of some sort of continuous diary instrument. Thus all respondents are asked to keep a diary, or recall a sequence, of each of the episodes in which they participated over a period of, say, twenty-four hours.

Such an instrument as this lends itself ideally to a much richer treatment of the dynamics of behaviour than is possible if one focuses separately upon the individual components of daily life. However, in practice the complexity of the analysis procedures and the pressure to provide politically interesting indicators of 'revealed preference' all too often reduces the average diary study to a vast data churning exercise, designed to measure not only the frequency of activity, but also the amount of time allocated to it. We are no longer limited to single categories of behaviour but can present policy relevant indices over the whole range of everyday activity.

I must stress that this is in no sense an inappropriate use of diary tech-niques, nor is it in any way mistaken to include in a study of shopping or social behaviour questions which are designed to reveal frequencies. It is rather that these frequencies and duration measures tell us absolutely nothing about the dynamics of human behaviour. And so even a technique which involves recording uninterrupted sequences of events, if it is processed in this way, is of no use to us in determining how the passage of time really affects human affairs.

The study of behaviour as a dynamically integrated process

How should we study human use of the built environment as a dynamic process? I have already hinted at what may be a useful data gathering technique, but what about the theory? We have discussed above the way in which time enters into the two major classes of behavioural study, if at all, as something of a pragmatic afterthought: many examples in the popular area of environmental perception or attitude research contain no reference to time at all, and the treatment of time in most studies of overt behaviour seems at best purely instrumental to the purpose of answering some immediate practical need. It seems, therefore, that what is required is a quite different way of classifying human spatial behaviour, one in which time is treated explicitly both as an accounting and a linking medium.

An essential first step is a clear differentiation between these two ways of incorporating time. The studies of overt behaviour discussed above treated time purely as a scarce resource and thus a useful unit of value: the amount of time people were prepared to invest in a facility was some index of what it was worth to them. However, time may be incorporated into studies of behaviour in a conceptually quite different way. It may be treated as the path which orders events as a sequence, which separates cause from effect, which synchronizes and integrates. A central argument of this paper is that if we are to understand human spatial behaviour, rather than just monitor it, we must treat time explicitly in this second sense.

A step in this direction is to invoke a typology which classifies actions according to the pattern of their motivation rather than the observable features of their performance. Rather than worry unduly about whether or not an activity counts as shopping for durable goods or for convenience goods, we might approach the event in terms of its level of deliberate premeditation. No one would seriously suggest that a spur of the moment trip to the nearest shop to pick up a toy for a child should be cognitively dissected with the same theoretical device as one would apply to the act of buying a new house in a new district. One obvious feature which distinguishes premeditated action from impulsive or routine behaviour is that in the former case time separates cause from effect. The deliberation and decision come first, the response comes later. In other words, it looks as though there may be a useful parallel to a motivational classification of behaviour which derives directly from its dynamics.

In fact our research of the past few years suggests that these two sorts of classification do overlap in a conceptually productive way. For by and large it is when we view behaviour over the long term, over months and years, that it appears to be most appropriately characterized as a process of premeditation or choice. The infrequent activities such as house purchase, a change of job, or the acquisition of a deep freeze, are the ones which are seriously deliberated. At the day to day level, on the other hand, such activities are swamped by a dominant pattern of repetition and routine. We spend very little time each day either deliberating some future action or executing a previously deliberated one. Most of our time is devoted to living out a fairly sophisticated pattern of well ordered and neatly integrated routine.

The value of an explicitly dynamic classification of behaviour (and behaviour studies) now becomes clear. For if these two sorts of behaviour— infrequent deliberated choices and everyday routines— are contrasted within a theoretical framework which does treat time explicitly they can be seen as related facets of the same overall model of motivated behaviour: the everyday routine becomes a manifestation of the long term choice. Of course this is an over-simplification; just as sometimes we may be faced with no real choice even in the long term, so, on certain days, the things that we do are each separately planned out or arranged in advance. Nevertheless, our research to date suggests that, whatever the balance between choice and necessity in the long term, the average working day of both the members of a university and residents of working-class estate is characterized pre-eminently by a pattern of routine (see Cullen and Godson 1974; Cullen and Phelps 1975). The way in which time may be used explicitly to integrate a humanistic theory of spatial behaviour is summarized in the diagram below:

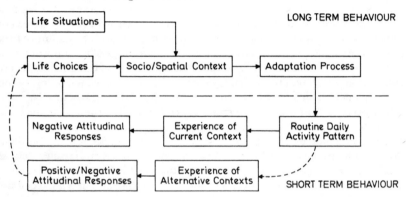

Time 'enters the cycle' in effect to remove a paradox. It seemed clear to us that a deterministic explanation of spatial behaviour was inadequate. The attitudes and motives of individuals are as important as their contexts and backgrounds in explaining key aspects of their behaviour. Yet attitudes are not formed in a vacuum. They are based, at least in part, upon experience. In other words, just as we need information about attitudes before we can fully explain overt behaviour, so we also need information about behaviour and its context before we can understand the meaning of peoples' attitudes. This is the paradoxical circle which the explicit treatment of time helps us to penetrate—by deliberately differentiating the long term attitude-behaviour relationship from that which operates day to day.

The thesis which is crudely represented by the above diagram argues that the context in which we operate every day is the product of a mixture of choice and constraint. In the long term we may seriously deliberate over certain aspects of our situation, and accept that others are beyond our control. Either way, a context is established in the long term which has definite implications—time consuming implications—for the way we operate day to day. The job means one set of activities each day, the home and its equipment (carpets to clean, TV to watch) another, and the relationship between the two, a set of trips. We soon adapt to this complex package of commitments, and fulfil the implications of our 'life choices' and 'life situations' via a highly routinized daily life style (as both the university study at Bedford College and the working-class family study in Hackney adequately demonstrated). This is important because the daily round of routine activities is the mechanism through which we constantly experience, evaluate and revise our responses to our normal situation. Attitudes towards this context develop day by day and week by week, and from time to time we make the sort of long term 'life choice' which will alter our context. A new process of adaptation is initiated, and the circle is set on a new course. A key implication of this thesis is that a person's attitudes normally develop against the backcloth of a routine and relatively choiceless daily activity pattern. We should, therefore, expect to find that the main subjective responses which stand out in the memories of those who have adapted in this way are the annoyances, difficulties and upsets that are occasioned by their contexts. The point is that the process of adaptive routinization may be viewed as an entirely rational response to a highly complex situation. It is a way of negotiating a tortuous path through a difficult environment and a wealth of commitments. Repetitive deliberation and choice are impossible luxuries when it comes to day to day living in a post-industrial city. But just as the spectrum of motivation is narrowed to permit a tractable style of life, so is the spectrum of attitudinal responses. Since we are not continuously choosing what to do, we do not need to be continuously assessing the environment that might have offered us choices. We cannot avoid the annoyances and upsets that are occasioned by circumstances, but the luxurious wealth of positive attitudes we can manage without.

This is, of course, not to say that people only respond negatively to their work-day experiences and situations. However, it appears that the process of adaptation and routinization reduces the necessity for individuals to make themselves consciously aware of the pleasurable events and experiences of the day unless these are also the unexpected or specially deliberated events of their daily lives, and, as we have found, such events are comparatively rare. These occasions are represented by the bottom rather than the middle link in the above diagram, which describes the more varied way in which people may respond to the experience of a context other than that to which they have adjusted. Whereas in these atypical circumstances either positive or negative responses are 'appropriate' in that either may ultimately affect the long term cycle of 'life choices', when experiencing our normal situation it is only a cumulation of negative responses which is likely to affect this long term pattern. Repeated positive responses to everyday situations will only confirm the current set of choices. Thus it seems entirely correct to focus upon the negative end of the spectrum when studying normal daily behaviour, if what is required is understanding which illuminates the dynamics of long term behaviour.[1]

To summarize the above discussion, what we have argued is that an understanding of long term behaviour must be based upon a logically prior understanding of everyday activity patterns for one very simple reason. Whilst the important choices which determine the way people fashion their own environments, and which obviate the need for choice in the short term, are infrequent and oriented to distant time horizons, their implications are experienced day to day as discrete moments of pleasure, indifference or pain.

A fully and dynamically integrated explanation of long term choice behaviour is something which we have yet to achieve. In our most recent studies we have been concentrating upon the day to day experiences which cumulatively help to trigger such choices. However, even at the day to day level we have felt it essential to treat time explicitly by using a diary technique as the core element amongst our survey instruments. This is because if one's purpose is ultimately to explain choices in the long term, the model described above requires one to monitor not only overt behaviour, but also the way attitudes develop against the backcloth of everyday activities. Such a purpose can only be achieved if one ensures that the environment, the activity and the attitude are each recorded with a device which does minimum violence to the way they were experienced. Since they are undoubtedly experienced as a dynamic stream of interrelated events, and since the subtlety of these relationships could never be reproduced in a laboratory simulation, the next best solution must be to use a device which recalls a sequence of such events from the recent past.

The diary device that we have developed over the past few years is certainly far from perfect in that it categorizes, precodes and punctuates everyday behaviour in a variety of more or less arbitrary ways. However, it has already proved itself through some of the time dependent interpretations it has permitted. These are described fully elsewhere (Cullen and Godson 1974; Cullen and Phelps 1975). Two examples drawn from our most recent study should serve to make the point. In that study of fifty married couples living in a Hackney public housing estate, we observed, as we expected, a high level of day to day routinization, and a greater readiness to talk about the stresses of everyday life than its highlights. It should be noted that the only sort of stress we measured was that which the respondent was fully aware of and prepared to discuss with us. The critical index of stress in our study was, however, not so much merely the perception of a stressor but the individual's coping response. We questioned respondents about each of these facets of a problem situation separately, and so we could distinguish in our analyses those situations which were thought to be potentially difficult or unpleasant from those which caused actual distress or annoyance.

The first thing we noticed in performing these analyses was the strong correlation between stress experience and the place of work. Whilst less than 30 per cent of the working day was spent at work, over 70 per cent of all stress was experienced during that time. However, more surprising was the way that stress was distributed throughout the working day. In effect it seemed as if the experience of stress and distress was cumulative— that one's sensitivity increased as morning became afternoon and afternoon became evening. As Figure 1 through 3 indicate, the probability (for men at least[2]) of a work situation being regarded as stressful or upsetting increases as the day progresses. The peak for paid work activity (Figure 1) occurs around 10:00 a.m. in the morning and, in its smoothed form,[3] is some 25 per cent higher than the afternoon peak at about 3:00 p.m. The position is reversed for both the stress and annoyance peaks (Figures 2 and 3). They both occur at around 3:00 p.m.—that for the perception of potentially stressful situations being about 16 per cent higher than its morning equivalent, and that describing the experience of distress being around 21 per cent higher. It would seem that the threshold of tolerance falls as one becomes tired. Difficult conditions, interruptions and inconveniences—the pressure of commitments, the tedium of repetitive tasks or

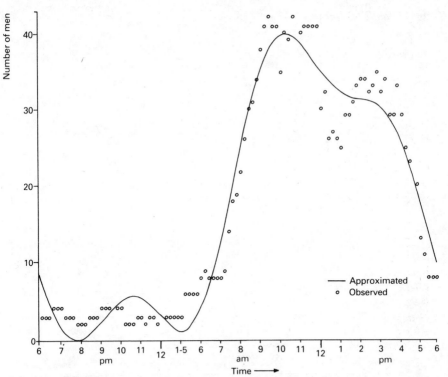

Figure 1 Husbands' work distribution throughout the day.

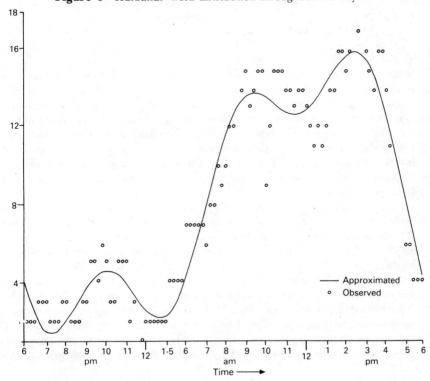

Figure 2 Husbands' stress-time distribution throughout the day.

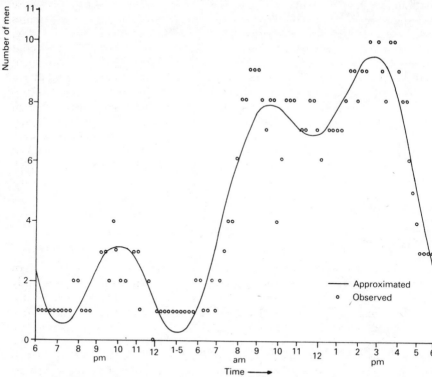

Figure 3   Husbands' annoyance-time distribution throughout the day.

simply an uncomfortable place of work—are more likely both to be noticed as such and to annoy and upset us as the working day nears its end. It is interesting to note in this connection that our earlier study of a university (see Cullen and Godson 1974) indicated that those with the most flexible structure to their working days adopted a typical pattern of oscillation between tightly fixed events and periods of time filling and relaxation. Perhaps this is also a less stressful way of organizing one's life in that it breaks up the process which seems to lead to cumulatively stressful experience. It is, of course, also one not available to the majority.

Apart from the suggestion that the experience of stress was cumulative, our study also hinted that it might be lagged, or displaced in such a way that the annoyance or distress which is 'caused' by one event is in fact ascribed to another. The instance of this sort of effect noted in our study was related to the length and complexity of the journey to work. Travelling on average consumed an hour and a half of the working days of our Hackney respondents. Amazingly, however, only seven of these 90 minutes were regarded as potentially stressful, and only three actually annoying. Moreover, once at work—or wherever else the bulk of the day was spent—the awareness of difficult or potentially upsetting conditions did not seem to vary with the length or complexity of the associated journeys. In other words we have no reason to assume that those with longer or more complex trips to make were in any way objectively worse off when they were not travelling. Yet those with work journeys of 30 minutes and over suffered upsets and distress for an average of 100 minutes per day, as opposed to 77 minutes for those with shorter journeys. And those without access to a car suffered for an average of 110 minutes, whilst those with a car, only 58 minutes.[4] The obvious implication is that whilst people may, after a time, adapt to the rigours of long and complex trip-making routines, that process of adaptation may not be altogether successful. In other words, although the problems of travel may become so familiar that the individual eventually ceases even to notice them as problems, there is a psychic cost. That person's ability to cope with other situations at other times of the day which are noticed as difficulties or problems, is reduced. The probability of distress is much greater. Glass and Singer (1972) focusing upon particular stressors and using simulation techniques, came to similar conclusions.

Conclusions

It would, of course, be very dangerous to generalize on the basis of our own work at this stage. The findings reported above are drawn from a pilot study which has provided us with a firm base upon which to build rather than a definitive answer to any particular question. It has, however, proved indicative in a variety of very interesting ways. It has, for instance, indicated once more the validity of the approach summarized in the diagram presented in the previous section. What this implies is that behavioural research which introduces time as an afterthought is missing a whole dimension of spatial behaviour. Many studies of overt behaviour have realized the fact that time is the unit of spatial experience. If we want a quantitative index of a person's use or valuation of space, time will normally enter that index as an accounting unit. The frequency or duration of an activity will probably be recorded. Nothing else about that study need be disturbed.

What such studies normally fail to realize is that time may be treated in two theoretically quite distinct ways. It is an integrating medium as well as an accounting unit, and its theoretical significance is different when viewed from each of these separate standpoints. Economists have for a long time viewed the intrinsically dynamic processes of accumulation and the lagged response as theoretically very important. Studies of spatial behaviour rarely invoke such concepts. Yet the two examples quoted from our own work indicate their relevance in interpreting the way people use and respond to different environments. Probably of greater theoretical importance than either of these processes, however, is that of adaptation. Also intrinsically dynamic, it is the process whereby long term choices about where to live, what job to take and which clubs to join are translated into a pattern of daily and weekly routines. To ignore the integrating function of time in studies of spatial behaviour is to ignore the way such choices are made; it is to ignore the way those choices are translated via a process of adaptation into a repetitive pattern of spatial behaviour; and it is to ignore the way that that regular pattern provides us with an accumulation of experiences which may eventually trigger a new choice.

Footnotes

[1] From a policy point of view this also appears to be an appropriate strategic decision. To concentrate immediate political effort upon the points where the shoe pinches has a great deal of intuitive appeal, especially in an inflationary situation in which grand designs evoke little more than cynicism, and redistributive philosophies, prevarication and bitter debate.

[2] We have presented here only the diagrams describing work and stress experiences of men. All fifty of the husbands in our sample were employed (most of them full time) and all worked on the day they were interviewed. Though 64 per cent of their wives also had jobs many of these were only part time, and quite a few did not work at all on the day of interview. Thus although there are indications of the same sort of cumulation effect the numbers concerned are very small.

[3] A form of regression model which we used fairly extensively, and which was used to produce Figures 1 to 3, is known as harmonic regression analysis (Bliss 1958). Its great advantage is that it preserves the dynamic aspect of diary information. For many purposes it can be important to discover not how much time people devote to given activities, but when in absolute time they are performed. When do the peaks occur and how do they relate one to another? These questions can be answered by aggregating, not over the full twenty-four hour time span for each individual, but over all individuals for each position of the twenty-four hour clock. The resultant time series thus each describe for every point in time (we actually used twelve-minute intervals for most of our analyses) how many people were engaged in any given activity. Since these are typically rather erratic curves, especially when working with small samples as in our case, we use harmonic regression analysis to smooth them out and highlight the major peaks and troughs throughout the day. The technique fits a sine wave to the major peak in the time series, and then successively decomposes this into a number of harmonics to pick up the smaller peaks and troughs. The continuous lines on each of the diagrams which describe this analysis represent the fitted curves and the 'O' points, the observed time series.

[4] The second set of figures refers to the full sample of 100 individuals, since the question of access to a car was relevant to all; the first set were computed only for those men and women who worked on the day of interview, and thus had a journey to work of a certain length.

Chapter 3

The Role of Time in Residential Choice Models

Robin Flowerdew

In recent years economists have shown increasing interest in the effects of relaxing assumptions about the instantaneous nature of decisions and about the automatic availability of information. This has resulted in the growth of a new sub-field of the subject, the economics of information. Although this sub-field dates back only to Stigler (1961), it has grown rapidly, forming the basis for a collection of readings (Lamberton 1971) and finding important applications in such topics as job search (McCall 1970). At the same time, analytical methods have been developed in which the ordering of information-gathering and decision-making in time has been emphasized; these include dynamic programming (see, for example, Howard 1960), sequential analysis (Wald 1947) and optimal stopping problems (Chow, Robbins and Siegmund 1971). In addition, the Bayesian approach to statistical decision-making, in which probability estimates can be revised as more information is gathered, is well suited to modelling decision processes in time.

Although the remarks above are applicable to economic phenomena in general (and perhaps also to many social phenomena), this discussion will focus on housing choice. In the traditional model of housing choice, the decision-maker compares the cost and desirability of houses of all types in all locations and chooses that house whose qualitites maximize his utility subject to a budget constraint. This neglects, among other things, the continual variation in the sets of vacancies available, the ways in which information is gathered about these vacancies, and the time that the decision may take.

In the main body of the paper, some of the ways in which time may affect the structure of the decision are outlined. They are grouped into twelve categories, each of which is to some degree distinct from the others, and each of which represents a somewhat different context in which time enters into the residential choice process. Some of the terminology used follows the definitions of Parkes and Thrift (1975). At the end of the paper, an attempt is made to compare the different roles played by time in these twelve contexts.

Timing the move

First of all, time may be important in deciding when to move. It is clear in the light of recent British experience, for example, that the nature of the housing market may change greatly over a fairly short period. This is true both in terms of the amount of money, in real terms, that a particular property will fetch, and the ease of obtaining assistance towards house purchase from banks, building societies, or other institutions. There may also be changes in the likelihood that dwellings with certain characteristics will appear on the market, according to social and economic trends in the society at large. For example, the availability and/or the cost of dwellings in one locality may change dramatically once it is known where a new motorway or power station is to be sited.

Thus the timing of his move can greatly affect the ease of finding the accommodation the mover wants; in some cases, these factors may make a move at a particular time impossible. The moving decision cannot then be considered entirely on a time scale of its own; it must take into account temporal variation in the wider society.

In addition, the decision will not be taken without regard to temporal variation in the circumstances of the mover and his household. It seems clear in most studies of residential mobility that most long-distance moves are related to job changes (Johnson, Salt and Wood 1974) and most short-distance moves to progress through the family cycle (Rossi 1955). In both cases, the timing of entry into the housing market will often reflect developments in the employment and family circumstances of the household.

Employment changes may result in home and job being too distant for commuting to be convenient or, often, possible. Sudden changes in household composition, such as increases caused by the birth of a child or the addition of a widowed parent, or decreases, on death or on children leaving the parental home, can cause a change in the perceived suitability of a house. Such changes may be generated also by the gradual processes of growth, as children's space requirements increase and as they come to need or desire rooms of their own. Factors operating for stability are also subject to change in time—these might include the extent of improvements made to house and garden and the ties and responsibilities taken on in the neighbourhood. As the factors influencing the desirability of a move change through time, however, so may the household's ability to finance it: this may be linked to changes in levels of income or expenditure, and to a deliberate policy of 'saving up'.

Again, the basic point is that a move is planned according to the household's time scale, in accordance with changes in its needs and resources. Clearly the relationship between the temporal variations in the housing market and in the household's circumstances is of central importance in determining the feasibility or the nature of any move that is considered.

Synchronization with other events

We have discussed in general terms the timing of a move with respect to other events, including job change by the mover. The point made above was that the occurrence of a job change might greatly affect the probability and desirability of moving. Beyond this, however, there are major problems in co-ordinating the times at which job and home are moved. If the distance of the move exceeds commuting range, then any major discrepancy between the two dates results in considerable inconvenience, either through temporary unemployment or homelessness, or through the expense of temporary accommodation. The problem may be exacerbated if several members of a household are all changing jobs, or if a move is to be coordinated with a change in the school attended by the children. A related difficulty may arise when a dwelling is rented by a group of independent households (such as young single adults), for differences in the timing of arrival and departure may create financial or accommodation problems for those who cannot coordinate their movements with those of the others. Such factors as these may make it highly desirable that a move be accomplished at a precisely specified date, with relatively little leeway in either direction; this need for precise timing and synchronization with other events must influence the pace and strategy of the entire process.

An especially important event with which a move should be coordinated is the abandonment of financial responsibility for the previous residence. It is likely to be unnecessary and expensive for tenants to lease two properties at the same time, but the greatest difficulties are likely to be encountered when one household is unable to sell the house it had previously owned at the time that it buys another. A household may be unable to complete a purchase until its existing house has been sold, regardless of its need to move for other reasons.

Search strategies

To this point, we have been concerned with the time at which a move occurs in relation to other events. Now we consider the process of moving itself, especially in relation to the time it takes, and the factors affecting the temporal arrangement of its components. In general most prospective movers will have little, and incomplete, knowledge of the vacancies available. The two types of activity which must be performed, more or less concurrently, in the mobility decision process, are search—activities leading to the identification of vacancies to which the household could move and of the attributes of these vacancies— and evaluation—activities leading to the assignment of value or utility to the vacancies, on the basis of which a choice may eventually be made. Activities of both types take up time; search often involves time-consuming travel or communication, and evaluation includes the frequently protracted act of 'making up one's mind'. Both of these are discussed below; this section is concerned with the sequence in which the household organizes its search and evaluation activities.

The acquisition of information is of two types—first, the identification of vacancies which the household can consider as potential destinations for its move, and, secondly, discovery of the attributes of these vacancies. Evaluation may take place at any or all stages of search, and may form the grounds not only for opinions about the satisfactoriness of a vacancy, but also for decisions about the most appropriate ways to carry on the search process. There are many different ways in which the process of search can be organized; one important distinction is that between a thorough methodical search for as many vacancies as possible, which are then examined to see if they are satisfactory on each attribute in turn, and a single-minded investigation of each vacancy individually on every attribute until it can be rejected or accepted. Both strategies have limitations, the first because much effort may be wasted on discovering additional vacancies when some of those already available are perfectly adequate, and the second because a wider horizon might enable more promising vacancies to be examined first. In practice, mixed strategies are more likely, with search perhaps being organized on a 'batch' basis, one set of vacancies being identified and information collected on their attributes until a reasonably full evaluation is possible, followed by the identification and investigation of another batch. Information sources are likely to encourage such a strategy, batches being organized according to whatever scheme a newspaper or estate agent may adopt, often based on price range, tenure or location.

Stopping rules

Next we consider the fundamental question of when to stop the search process, and the formulation of this as a stopping-rule model (Flowerdew 1976). The decision-maker is here viewed as making a trade-off between the costs of search and the expectation of finding a better vacancy by continuing to search. Time is considered as being rigidly structured by events, the evaluation of each vacancy occupying one place in a sequence which contains as many items as there are vacancies to be considered. At each point, the decision-maker must decide whether to accept the best vacancy considered so far or to continue the process and inspect another. In general, he should continue if and only if the costs of inspecting another vacancy are less than the expected gain from doing so. This gain will be zero unless the next vacancy is better than the best available of those already inspected, in which case it is equal to the difference between the two. If enough is known about the distribution of the values for the vacancies being considered, it is possible to formulate a rule which lays down the optimal strategy for the decision-maker. Further elaborations can be introduced by allowing him to inspect a vacancy which appears more promising before one which seems less promising (instead of a random order of search).

It is appropriate to consider the nature of the search cost which plays a major role in models of this type. In the search for housing, examining another alternative may occasionally have some direct money cost, in transport costs or perhaps agency fees. More commonly, however, the costs are borne in effort and, especially, in time. Indeed, it will often be the case that time constraints are the major factors leading to a decision to stop search and accept the best alternative so far located. The magnitude of the 'costs', i.e. the importance of the time losses, will vary according to the decision-maker's circumstances and perhaps his impatience also.

Time in bargaining

If a prospective mover reaches the stage of expressing an interest in a particular vacancy, he may be able to affect the terms under which it will be made available to him by negotiation with the seller or landlord (depending on the tenure of the property) or an agent of the latter. This will usually affect the price at which the mover is able to acquire the property, although other features, such as the disposition of furniture and fittings, may also be involved. The outcome of such a bargaining process will depend on several factors, including the alternative dwellings that the mover could choose (he may enter negotiations concerning several dwellings at the same time) and the alternative buyers (or tenants) that the seller or landlord can attract. As Contini (1968) has suggested, however, the pressure of time is of great importance in determining the outcome of bargaining, and the amount of time that each party can hold out may settle the final terms of the transaction.

Chances in housing available

The discussion so far has assumed that any vacancy identified by the prospective mover will be available to him if he chooses it. This is clearly not so in many parts of the housing market, especially where there is great pressure on available vacancies. Although certain would-be movers may be obstructed by discrimination against them on various grounds, the basic problem is one of competition between movers. A policy of delaying a decision on a satisfactory vacancy may be unwise if the vacancy is liable to be snapped up by another mover.

Similarly, in some housing markets, there is no chance of getting some vacancies unless the would-be mover acts immediately. The market for privately-rented flats in some British cities is a case in point. Under such conditions, the time available for search and evaluation, and in particular the time for comparison, is greatly lessened. A greater emphasis is therefore put on search as a means of discovering the state of the market. It may be possible to estimate the chances of a vacancy remaining available over a specified time, and to take this into account in deciding whether to accept the vacancy or to continue looking.

In addition to the loss of opportunities through time, there is also the possibility of new opportunities becoming available. As the search process develops, not only is the mover able to investigate more of the vacancies originally open to him; he may also find new vacancies coming onto the market. The longer he is prepared to search, the higher the probability that something really suitable will come up. This factor makes his search strategy more complicated for it may be worthwhile to recheck sources of information that have been consulted already, in the hope that new vacancies may have appeared.

Time required for search

Implicit in much of the foregoing is the idea that time is required for search, and that the extent of time resources may affect the efficiency and the results of the process. In the first place, the move may need to be made quickly, in which case total time is small, however much is devoted to search. Secondly, it may be difficult for the prospective mover to spend time on search owing to job, family, or other commitments; even if he can find this time, he may be reluctant to do so, preferring to devote it to other activities. Thirdly, those who are intending to move a long distance are handicapped by lack of access to sources of information on vacancies in the destination area, and by the difficulty of acquiring information at a distance. Some search activities can be carried out by mail or telephone, but a large part of the search process for inter-urban migrants must be reserved until a visit can be made to the destination area. This visit restricts the prospective mover effectively to those vacancies which are current while he is there, and its timing may have a major influence on its success. Even though a reasonably long time may be available for search, access to local information will be restricted to the much shorter time which the mover can spend in his destination area.

Short-term temporal constraints

There are several factors which affect planning of search at the detailed level. These include such constraints as the opening days and hours of the various institutions involved in the housing market: such factors affect almost all aspects of everybody's lives. If an estate agent or building society must be consulted, in general this can be done only during business hours. If a newspaper is an important source of housing information, its readers must wait until it hits the streets before they can use this information. If the newspaper is weekly, its day of issue may be particularly significant in organizing the search process. When the mover wants to visit an attractive vacancy, he must plan his visit to accord with the convenience of whoever is to show him around; sometimes these activities must be fitted into a relatively short time in the early evening, after the current resident returns from work and before it gets too late to justify disturbing him. If the mover is reliant on public transport, his movements must fit in with the timetable; unless services are frequent, this can be a major restriction.

As with so many other aspects of life, most of the search process must be concentrated into normal business hours, and into the five working days of the week. This is particularly unfortunate for those whose job makes these times especially difficult to use. The problem is accentuated for those who must make a special trip to search for housing; the times that will be easiest for such people to devote to search are likely to be the times when least can be accomplished. Other minor factors of this nature may affect the decisions that are made; if a landlord or an existing occupant is away for a few days, it will be far harder for the mover to gain information or to take action about the vacancy concerned. Especially if the mover is in a hurry, such an event may effectively remove it from his choice set.

Spatial scheduling

During the course of search, most prospective movers are likely to find themselves in the position of wishing to acquire more information about vacancies than they will have time to gather. If visits are involved, either to vacancies or to information sources, some form of spatial route planning may be desirable. Whatever mode of transport is used, considerable time may be saved by visiting neighbouring destinations on the same trip or by calling in at one place *en route* to somewhere else. If public transport is to be used, route patterns and timetables may make such route planning much less flexible and less effective. Complications are also introduced if appointments must be kept at some prearranged time and place, or if a visit to some destinations is only useful within a particular time range (such as office hours). This type of situation seems ideal for the space-time prism models suggested by Hägerstrand (1970a).

The spatial arrangement of places to be visited, because of this scheduling problem, may materially affect the mover's destination. He is more likely, *ceteris paribus*, to visit somewhere close to other destinations than somewhere isolated. This reasoning has implications, among other things, for the siting policy of housing agencies.

Evaluation time

In addition to time taken up in identification and investigation of vacancies, time may also be taken up in evaluation. It is harder to assess the amount of time taken for evaluation or how flexible this time is. 'Economic man' is able to make up his mind and calculate his best policy instantly, but the real decision-maker wants to think things over, to equivocate, perhaps 'to sleep on it'.

The evaluation process will vary according to the methods used. If the mover has decided what attributes are essential or desirable in his new residence, it may take him some time to check mentally whether a given vacancy possesses them or not. If he has not consciously decided this, he may make a rapid decision on the basis of a perceived match between the vacancy and his image of a 'good place to live'; alternatively, he may mull over possible advantages and drawbacks for a long time before deciding whether it is acceptable. As suggested earlier, decisions may have to be made quickly to avoid the risk of losing the vacancy to a competitor; this may sometimes lead to misjudgements and mistakes. The amount of time needed for evaluation, lastly, may be very much a matter of individual personality.

Evaluation for most moving households is not left to one sole decision-maker. If a household of two or more people is moving, at least two of them are likely to be involved in the decisions. Responsibility for search and evaluation may be shared in many different ways (efficient sharing may greatly increase the person-hours that can be devoted to the tasks and hence diminish the sway of the time constraints), but almost always one decision-maker would wish to consult the other(s) before making a major decision. Consultation will itself take time, the amount of time depending on how soon the decision-makers meet, whether the second decides to repeat the information-gathering activities of the first (for example, by making a visit to the vacancy) and how easily they reach an agreement. Even single-person households may wish to consult family or friends before making a final commitment. The consultation process can cause delay, especially for the inter-urban migrant who must make another trip to show other members of his household the dwellings he is considering.

Time and morale

The amount of time already spent on search may itself affect the behaviour of many people. If a long period has been wasted in fruitless search, morale is likely to sink and behaviour to be altered. One possible repercussion might be a reaction against the stresses of the whole decision process, leading to a temporary abandonment of search, for the day or for a longer period, or even to giving up the idea of moving completely and adjusting to the limitations of the original dwelling. Another possible reaction might be avoidance of those methods of search and those information sources which are most tiring, stressful, or otherwise annoying, regardless of their likely efficiency, in favour of methods which are easier or more pleasant to use. A third possibility might be a desire to settle on some vacancy, even if it is very different from the original aspirations of the mover. In terms of the stopping-rule discussed earlier, such a policy may well be optimal, search costs (measured in effort and frustration) having been raised to very high levels.

Can residential choice be concurrent with other activities?

In much of the preceding, we have talked of search and evaluation as taking up time, and of the problems that may be encountered in setting aside time for these purposes. Here we will consider to what extent time spent on the residential choice process must necessarily involve the loss of time spent on other activities. The answer to this question depends on the extent to which search and related activities can go on at the same time as other activities. Again, an extreme case is provided by the inter-urban migrant who must make a special trip to his destination area in order to conduct his search. Although such a trip may often be coordinated with other activities, such as visiting friends or pursuing personal business, it will effectively prevent him from carrying on most of his normal home-based activities during the period for which he is away.

In contrast, some households moving within the same area may need to set aside very little time expressly for search or evaluation; if there is a vague desire to move, but no urgency about it, households may spend no effort on search beyond listening to occasional news of vacancies from friends and acquaintances and observing notices that appear from time to time in front of potentially suitable dwellings. In such cases, a move may be considered for several years, and eventually accomplished; search of a sort may have been in progress for years, without laying exclusive claims to any significant length of time.

It seems that most movers, other than those who need to go through no significant search procedure, set aside a period of time specifically for this purpose, and that the search procedure takes longer, and is less effective, for those who attempt it while working or engaged full time in something else. This may be explained in part by time-tabling problems, but could suggest that people find it easier to devote their attention to search full time. Some aspects of the decision process, however, such as the setting of aspirations or evaluation of vacancies, require less active involvement and can perhaps be done at the same time as other activities.

The roles of time

An important contrast can be made between ordinal and interval measurement of time. Some of the points discussed depend only on the sequence in which events are arranged in time. This applies, on the whole, to the sections on search strategies and stopping rules; in both cases, the order in which actions are carried out is important, and the time taken to perform them is not considered. In the case of stopping-rule models, one could consider the cost of inspecting another alternative as a direct reflection of the amount of time inspection would take (McCall 1965, develops a model in which the time interval between inspections is a random variable), but the stress is on the ordinal progression of inspections, one at a time, and on the point at which it is stopped.

Other aspects of the process require a quantitative concept of time. The importance of synchronization of the move with other events hinges on the time differences between the occurrence, for example, of job move and home move; the mover's objective would normally be to minimize this difference, with the extent of his loss increasing with the size of this difference. This idea requires time to be measurable on an interval scale.

It is also appropriate to treat time as interval-scaled in considering most of the other points raised. In the discussion of short-term temporal constraints and of spatial scheduling, the sequence of activities is important, but, in selecting a strategy for performing the activities, the amount of time available is also important. In both cases, possible effects of one activity on subsequent activities have to be taken into account; in the first case, the sequence is important because it must be fitted into a set of externally-imposed time constraints which differ between activities. In the second case, it is important because the length of time needed for transition between activities is considered, and these transition times will vary according to the sequence adopted.

A second contrast is between effective time, the time in which the decision-maker is engaged in behaviour directly related to residential choice, and elapsed time, the time recorded by clock and calendar. Again, certain of the topics, including search strategies, stopping rules, evaluation time, and time and morale, are considered largely in relation to effective time, although it would be unwise to disregard elapsed time completely, because of the possibility that the decision-maker may lose the chance of selecting certain vacancies while he is inactive. Other topics, such as timing the move, bargaining time, and changes in the housing available, must be considered in elapsed time. The section on time required for search bears directly on the relation between effective and elapsed time, and the final section is concerned with the extent to which effective time in residential choice can also be effective time in other activities of the decision-maker.

We may also examine differences in point of view in the consideration of time. It is more helpful to think of time in terms of changes in the housing market or in individual circumstances than simply in calendar years. In the first section, the advantages of moving at particular times, as defined first by cycles or trends in the housing market and secondly by progress in family and career life-cycles, were considered, creating two time scales of far greater relevance to the mobility decision than the number of years since the birth of Christ. It is also relevant to point out the different time perspectives which the prospective mover, the landlord or seller, and the housing agency may have. Most of the discussion has been on the demand side of the housing market, but the existence of other perspectives is apparent in the section on changes in housing available, where time might be measured by the addition and deletion of vacancies on a house agent's list and in the section on bargaining, where the time horizons on the supply and demand side come into direct confrontation. A related point is raised by the section on time and morale, in which the mover's time scale is distorted by his feelings about the way in which his time is being used.

Conclusion

This paper has discussed the various ways in which time enters into a series of models of the residential choice process, and has attempted to make some generalizations about the different roles it may perform. The emphasis has been on time rather than on the picture of residential choice that the models present. It is hoped that many similar points might be made concerning the role of time in other models of human spatial behaviour.

There seem to be no simple rules governing how time can best be considered in these or similar models. It seems clear that the most natural treatment of time will differ according to the problem under consideration, but if a coherent, comprehensive model is desired, time, like everything else, should be treated in a consistent and unified manner. In terms of the three specific contrasts drawn in the preceding section, a unitary model should take the more inclusive alternative of the two; thus it should treat time as an interval or ratio-scale measure, should be based on elapsed time rather than effective time, and should co-ordinate the time perspectives most relevant to all the actors involved. The first, however, leads to greatly reduced analytic tractability; the second raises difficulties by making an essential component, the time the mover does not allot to residential choice, exogenous to the model (or else the model must attempt to cover his whole life); and the third raises the problems of complexity normally involved in tracing the behaviour of multi-component systems.

Despite these problems, a clearer focus on the treatment of time in behavioural models must surely lead to a fuller understanding of the processes involved.

Chapter 4

Rhythms of Urban Activity

Mary Shapcott and Phillip Steadman

I.

A team of (Western) social scientists, concerned to study people's use of time in towns, go out to make a series of diary surveys in some chosen city. Each survey lasts one week. The team carries out its first survey, and analyses the results in terms of the time budgets of the various groups in the population, the frequencies of various activities and so on. They make a second survey, and the results—within the limits of statistical error—are broadly in agreement with those from the first. They make a third survey, again covering one week.

When they come to look at the results this time however, very significant changes have taken place in a whole series of the observed patterns of behaviour. The amount of time devoted to shopping has increased considerably. There is an increase in the time-budget for cooking. On two days of the week (not Saturday or Sunday) there is, with some very few exceptions, no formal work recorded by any of the respondents. On the first of these two days it seems that the time of getting up recorded for the younger age groups is much earlier than the norm. There is an unusual amount of religious activity. On both days, the amounts of time devoted to eating, drinking, social activities and watching television are much increased.

What has happened? Is this some statistical freak? Should the team assume that patterns of behaviour are much more variable than they had previously thought? Could there be anything significant or unrepresentative about the particular time they have chosen to make the survey—towards the end of December?

For people who live in the culture—as distinct from our mythical naïve social scientists—the phenomenon of Christmas presents no such puzzle of course. However obvious the explanation, it is still perhaps worth reflecting on the implications of this little fable for the study of human spatial and temporal behaviour from a geographical or social scientific perspective.

It illustrates the fact that variations in patterns of activity at one time scale—that of the day—may occur in a regular and predictable fashion over a cyclic period at some larger scale—that of the year in this instance—and may be attributable to historical causes, or be subject to the influence of particular historical events, over some even longer time scale yet—in this extreme case, over hundreds or thousands of years.

A rhythmic pattern of behaviour is established, and is transmitted culturally in the form of a known 'timetable' of activities—in the late evening of 24th

December there is a church service, on the morning of the 25th the presents are opened, there is another church service at 11:00 and then there is lunch with turkey and plum pudding, at 3:00 the Queen makes a speech on television, and so on. The cultural transmission is carried on through individuals learning the accepted routine, by repeatedly taking part in it, and then by reenacting it for themselves every year. And yet, although this cultural transmission of the activity pattern which is Christmas is *only* effected by the mediation of individuals, and through their individual social and cultural knowledge, it is nevertheless clear that Christmas as a cultural phenomenon quite transcends individuals.

There is no compulsion on *particular* persons to take part (although they will find it very difficult to opt out completely, because of the social activities going on all around them), and the cultural phenomenon will continue whether they celebrate the festival or not—just so long as *sufficient* people maintain the tradition. The individual or the family are to some extent at liberty to alter the accepted routines for themselves—to eat Christmas dinner on the night of the 24th, to open presents in the afternoon—but again, such behaviour will only become part of the normally accepted cultural routine of the Christmas celebration if sufficient individuals or families act in a similar way. This is the explanation for the relative conservatism and cultural 'inertia' of the repeated pattern of the festival; a pattern which changes and evolves only slowly.

The interest of urban geographers and more especially urban planners in patterns of daily activity is clearly in the 'normal' routines of the average working week, rather than in the unusual and anomalous patterns of Christmas. However, similar observations to those which this example has served to illustrate still apply, if sometimes in less extreme and obvious forms.

2.

In our own work we have previously illustrated the various 'normal' constraints on daily behaviour in time and space acting collectively on a group of people, by means of a simple diagram (Bullock, Dickens, Shapcott and Steadman 1974). This diagram (Figure 1) shows a three-dimensional space whose dimensions represent time (the hours of the day), location (represented one-dimensionally as a list of distinct point 'places'), and activity (classified into a series of discrete categories). The daily activity patterns of the population in question (university students in the case of our own work) may then be imagined as a distribution of that population to the cells of this three-dimensional array, each entry in any cell signifying a number of people engaged in an activity at a particular place and at a specific time of day.

The social and spatial constraints on this distribution may be represented in this diagrammatic form by supposing that certain cells in the array are not available. For example locations other than those of shops are not available for the activity 'shopping'; or times of day outside shop opening hours are again not available for that activity. It is clear that this particular example of shopping represents a rather broad global constraint acting more or less equally on all members of the population; and that it does not correspond to any obligation on individuals to engage in an activity, but simply defines the space and time realm in which such activity may go on. Within the same sort of diagrammatic representation it would be possible to show in a similar way

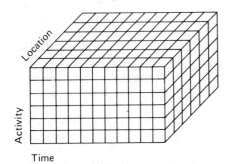

(a) A three-dimensional array of cells representing activity, time and location.

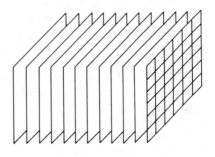

(b) The total population in cells in each activity/location plane must obey the population constraint.

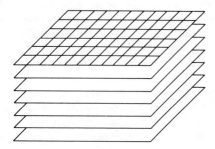

(c) The total population in cells in each location/time plane must obey the time budget constraint for that activity.

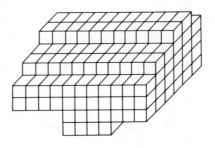

(d) Some activity/location combinations are not available, nor are some activity/time combinations.

Figure 1 The activity system represented in diagrammatic three-dimensional form, from Bullock, Dickens, Shapcott and Steadman (1974).

constraints acting only on individuals (a particular appointment to see the doctor), and constraints which represented definite obligations to engage in activities (the fixed hours of work) rather than simply opportunities for activities of an optional nature.

Our diagram has certain similarities with those of Hägerstrand and his group at Lund, which they have devised in order to illustrate the time-space patterns of systems of urban activities (see for example Hägerstrand 1970a, and the contribution by Carlstein to this present volume). Here again each figure shows a notional three-dimensional space, the principal difference being that two dimensions are used to depict the spatial layout of the city in the plane, and the third (vertical) dimension represents time (so that different types of activity are not explicitly represented).

Various forms of such diagrams have been developed by the Swedish group, to show both individual and group activity patterns. Several different types of constraint are also distinguished; but for example a *coupling constraint*, in Hägerstrand's terms, corresponding, say, to a meeting between individuals localized both in space (at some particular *station*) and in time, would appear in the diagram as a notional vertical 'tube' (Pred's term: Pred 1973) whose position corresponds to its spatial location in the horizontal plane, and to its timing during the day in the vertical dimension. An individual's daily activity pattern or *path* is shown by a line or string which extends vertically so long as he remains in one place, and moves diagonally to correspond to travel, passing on the way through the various 'tubes' which constrain the activities of his day.

Both types of diagram show essentially the same information, although, depending on the specific purpose and detailed form of the representation, emphasis may be placed either on individual life paths and the activities of small groups, or alternatively on the broader social constraints acting across whole groups of the population. It will be apparent however that in both the varying types of Hägerstrand figure and in our own diagram, activity patterns are portrayed in a certain sense from a *subjective* point of view. In neither case is there a particular concern for the psychology of decision-making by which people mentally organize and carry on their daily lives; but all the same the city, and society, are seen and represented only in effect from the viewpoint of the particular or representative individual, who feels their impact as they impinge on him here and there, and restrict the range of action and choices which are open to him.

We may perhaps take some slight liberties with the Hägerstrand diagram format, and adapt it to represent something rather different from individual life paths or the activity patterns of population groups in aggregate. Imagine that the vertical time dimension is very much extended, to show weeks, months and even years, instead of just a single day. Suppose, now, that the diagram is used to show not the particular activity patterns of a single individual, or indeed of any people at all, but instead is used to depict the generally acting *set of constraints* which apply in the society or culture as a whole. (Figure 2)

At the everyday level of ordinary contemporary Western life, such constraints would, for example, include the conventional hours of work ('9:00 to 5:00'—although with many obvious exceptions and differences for particular occupations and trades), the established opening hours of shops (on a daily basis, traditional half-day closing, market day and so on), the opening hours of pubs or cafes, the hours of television broadcasting and the timing of special repetitive programmes (such as the regular news broadcasts), the conventional times for meals, and many other similar phenomena.

Viewed in the larger time scale, these constraints would appear on our modified Hägerstrand diagram as rhythmic structures with generally a twenty-four hour period; for example the fixed hours of work might be imagined as a series of clusters of 'tubes' appearing regularly between the hours of 9:00 and 5:00, the location of the tubes in the horizontal plane corresponding to the relevant spatial positons of the work-places in the city or region in question. School hours, shop opening hours, and the availability of other facilities such as pubs,

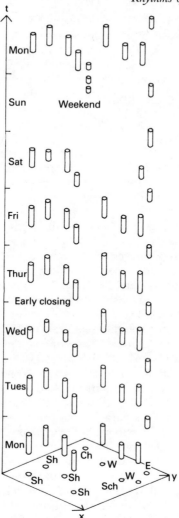

Figure 2 Hypothetical diagram of the rhythmic structure of some generally acting social constraints on daily activities. Sh = shop, Ch = church, W = workplace, Sch = school, E = entertainment, e.g. cinema. *x* and *y* depict the urban space in two dimensions, and *t* represents time in days.

restaurants, cinemas, regular sports fixtures and other entertainments would appear in a very similar way. Weekends would appear as a most significant rhythmic modification of this structure of temporal regularities; as would other regularities in time, of a somewhat less pronounced kind, on a monthly or seasonal basis.

We have been using the term 'constraints' to refer to these socially transmitted temporal regularities; and it is certainly true that many of them do act as such—for instance the hours of work. But 'constraint' suggests limitation, constriction; whereas for example certain phenomena such as the regular hours of entertainments or pubs for example might be better described as 'opportunities' in time and space, or as realms of availability. We might say that the *arrangement* of constraints serves to define the ranges of available opportunity.

Some of these aspects of social timing would be the subject of legislation or of other control by authorities in a centralized and planned manner; as for example the licensing laws for pubs and bars, or the programming of television schedules. In some cases the origin of such legislative control might be found in some particular historical event; since which time the rhythm, once set up, has become established and has persisted (as with the English licensing laws, set up during the First World War). In other cases there is no legal or authoritative force governing the regularities in time, but rather some culturally transmitted convention, such as that relating to meal times, or the timing of festivals and celebrations such as Christmas.

An instantaneous 'time slice' cut horizontally through this picture will reveal the effective map of the spatial area in question, as it is defined in activity terms at the chosen time of day, or day of the week. Thus, while places of residence will appear consistently whatever the chosen instant—because continuously occupied or continuously the potential location for certain activities—other features of the (conventional land use) map will appear or not, depending on the chosen hour or day. Thus most shops and work places would disappear at night time and at the weekends.

In the vertical time dimension these cultural and social rhythms represented by these legal constraints, cultural conventions and temporally organized 'social contracts' could be seen as being overlaid on top of the physiological rhythms of human bodily function, and on the larger underlying biological and astronomical rhythms of the alternation of day and night and the passage of the seasons.

It will be clear that these separate social constraints or rhythmic patterns of availability of facilities or opportunities, are not all independent of each other. On the contrary they must form in effect a highly integrated and co-ordinated structure whose separate rhythms are very subtly interlocked, either in phase or out of phase, all finely timed one in relation to the other. It is, in a certain limited sense indeed, the nature of this coordinated rhythmic structure which defines, in its temporal aspect, the structure of the society.

To go back to the original Hägerstrand type of diagram showing the life *paths* of individuals. One may regard the rhythmic time-space structure of social constraints and opportunities as constituting the *complement* of the diagram of life paths. All individual life paths (except those of hermits or Robinson Crusoes) must take place within the social structure of constraints; and its timing, the phasing of the different constraints by which it is made up, must be such as to allow certain kinds of life paths to be 'threaded' through it. It must facilitate the overall coordination of activities in time and space which allow for the work of society, and social intercourse generally, to go on.

It should be said that Hägerstrand has himself proposed investigations somewhat along these lines. For instance in a recent paper (Hägerstrand 1974) he writes: '... the potential action space is an entity which might be investigated as such quite apart from the observable use people make of the options they have got.' The idea has been further elaborated by the Swedish group, and for example the PESASP model (described by Lenntorp elsewhere in this volume) involves making detailed representations of the 'station structure' of particular cities or regions, through which the movements of the population are then simulated.

The distinction of emphasis which we would like to stress here is that between conceiving of the 'station structure' or action space in Hägerstrand's terms as *something given*, as a complex of phenomena which can be mapped in order then to facilitate the study and simulation of activity patterns, and regarding the action space, as we would propose, as something to be investigated in its own right—quite independent of the specific activities of individuals or groups— as a co-ordinated complex of spatio-temporal rhythms with its own internal organization and structure. This structure is a cultural entity, it consists of conventions, traditions and routines, as much as it describes physical and geographical objects and arrangements; and like other cultural phenomena it undergoes slow changes, as it is transmitted through cultural evolution.

At the very broadest level, in the typical Western and specifically the British case, we have the twenty-four hour cycle split up into three main divisions allocated to sleep, work and leisure, which are roughly in phase for the great majority of the population. These three periods are separated by meals, with breakfast between sleep and work, and the evening meal between work and leisure (or forming part of the leisure; while the third, midday meal serves as a break interrupting the work phase.

The simultaneous timing of many people's hours of work is made necessary by the demands of complex pieces of machinery (both mechanical and organizational) which must be served at the same time by many workers; as well as the need for those in business to communicate with the rest of the world of work. The effects of this broad pattern, of day-time work and evening leisure, are however felt by many others beyond just those in employment. They apply almost as much to housewives and retired people with no formal hours of work, for example, as they do to the worker in the factory or the man in the office. With the housewife, the routine of the day—as we shall see in more detail shortly— is very much governed by the timing of her working husband's activities, as well as by school hours and shop hours (themselves particular examples of hours of work); all of which constrain her own activities, at second-hand so to speak, within the rhythms of the working population as a whole.

Cross-national studies have shown, again, that while there are wide differences in the timing of the general cultural daily routine, as in the timing of work hours and of meals—particularly between Eastern and Western countries, and between climatic regions—nevertheless within any one given country and culture the peaks for the various corresponding activity distributions throughout the day for men and for housewives tend to coincide (Szalai 1972).

A comparable effect may be observed with entertainments; as for example the opening hours of pubs to coincide with the lunch-hour work break and with the period of evening leisure; or the timing of evening television programmes —such as the 6:00 o'clock news, on just at the time when working people return home and are having their tea (television watching being now by far the most important single leisure activity in terms of time consumption). Once again the pattern of leisure activities even of those who are not apparently tied to a rigid work/leisure routine, still often conforms to a general social pattern; as is shown in our own studies of university students for example (Tomlinson, Bullock, Dickens, Taylor and Steadman 1973).

The integration of the structure of rhythmic patterns will be to a great extent self-reinforcing and self-perpetuating. For example any entrepreneur deciding on the routine by which to operate his enterprise—let us say a shopkeeper fixing his hours of opening, or a factory owner deciding on the timing of work hours and shifts (where these are not determined by law)—will do so in relation to an assessment of their convenience to the public or to a potential labour force, as well as their interconnection in time with other enterprises; and hence in relation to many other patterns, of work times, public transport times and so on, which have been already established.

Restaurants are opened at certain hours because these are the times when cultural convention decrees that meals shall be eaten; but to a certain extent the converse is true, and the times at which we choose to eat in restaurants are constrained by the opening hours. The relationship of causality is a circular and self-reinforcing one. People's patterns of activities in the evenings are very substantially affected by the timing of television programmes; and the effects of a single popular programme can be observed even in quite crude time-budget data. But, on the other hand, the broadcasting companies (as for example the BBC: BBC Audience Research Department 1965) devote considerable effort and resources to making time-budget studies for themselves, in order precisely to determine the times of day at which certain audiences will be free from other constraints on their activity, and so free to watch or listen.

It is obviously very important, in the coordination of the whole structure of time patterns, exactly how one particular constraint is phased in relation to others. Thus the extent to which the timing of entertainments is separated in phase from the timing of work hours, will affect how feasible it is, perhaps, to travel from one to the other (depending also on their spatial separation, of course), or to go home and change or eat a meal between the two activities. Again, the degree to which shop opening hours are overlapped with work hours will affect whether or not working women, for instance, will be able conveniently to do the family shopping on weekdays. It is clear that in all these sorts of relationships what is important is the *combination* of the relative phasing of the rhythmic constraints in time with the spatial distribution of the facilities or places involved, in relation to each other. (And the availability of means of transport—including their availability in *time*—between those places. For a discussion, and some quantitative analysis, see Hägerstrand 1973a).

Thus we have the phenomenon, as remarked by Parkes, that 'simultaneity in time encourages propinquity in place' (Parkes 1974), as for example the location of retail shopping or sandwich bars both near to facilities of the same kind, and near to places of office employment. Once again there is a circularity in the situation, as office workers are encouraged to take the opportunity to do their shopping in the lunch hour.

3.

As a consequence of the highly interconnected, coordinated and self-perpetuating nature of the structure of social timing rhythms, aggregate daily patterns of time use would be expected to show a considerable long-term stability. This aspect has received comparatively little research emphasis to date, and there have been few studies comparing activity patterns on a longitudinal basis. The reason is partly that attention has been devoted more to studies of the individual as decision-maker, in relative isolation from the overall structure of social activity patterns already in existence. Although the need to establish linkages with other people is acknowledged, the fact that these other people are likely themselves to be 'tuned in' to the most common allocation of time is not usually regarded as important, and the corresponding reinforcement of the 'normal' pattern is overlooked. Another more practical consideration with long-term studies is the problem of availability and comparability of historical data.

However we have been able to make *some* investigation into changes in daily activity patterns in Britain over the last decade or so, by comparing the results of a survey made by the BBC Audience Research Department in 1961 (BBC 1965) with the results of a survey which we ourselves conducted in 1973. The BBC survey covered a national sample of individuals over the age of fifteen living in households owning a television set or radio. (Fewer than 0·5 per cent of households were excluded by this requirement.) The respondents kept diaries for one week, recording what they were doing in each half-hour interval between 6:00 a.m. and midnight each day.

The 1973 sample consisted of 450 individuals between the ages of sixteen and seventy living in the medium-sized town of Reading. These people were also asked to keep seven-day diaries, but recorded each new activity at the exact time it began so that shorter activities were captured better than by the BBC, and a quarter-hour time interval can be used for the corresponding histograms. These histograms show what percentage of each population group is engaged in each activity during each time period over the day. The reader is referred to the accompanying illustrations for the results of these comparisons (Figures 3, 4), which show separately a selection of men's activities and women's activities on weekdays, with the 1973 patterns shown in heavy line, superimposed on the 1961 in lighter outline. Our 1973 results have been aggregated, so far as activity groupings are concerned, according to the BBC's original classification, in order to effect the comparison. This was possible because our own coded classification is made at a much finer level of detail.

In studying these comparisons one should bear in mind two kinds of consideration. First there are differences which are attributable (although the exact extent is hard to measure) to the different survey and coding techniques used in either case. Most important is the use of the fixed half-hour time interval for recording activities by the BBC. This means that most activities with durations of less than a quarter of an hour or so will have been either lost, or rounded up; and that other longer duration activities will have been altered so as to compensate. This would appear to be the cause of an overestimation of the breakfast peak in 'eating' for 1961, for example; since breakfast is often an activity of short duration, and is being rounded up. Other consequences are the apparent loss from the BBC results of much of such activities as 'personal hygiene', and casual social activities like conversation, which have typically short durations, but which in aggregate add up to substantial components of the time-budget.

A second kind of difference between the 1961 and 1973 figures appears to be

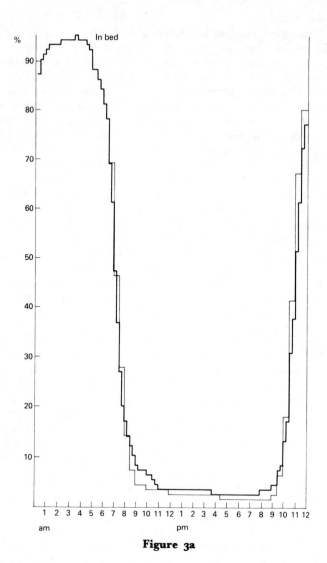

Figure 3a

Figure 3a, b, c and d Selected activities of men on weekdays, in 1961 and in 1973. The graphs show, for each activity classification, what percentage of the sampled population was engaging in that activity at different times of the day, from midnight through to midnight. 1961 data are shown by the thinner line, and are taken from a survey made by the BBC Audience Research Department throughout the country reported in BBC (1965). 1973 data are shown in heavier outline, and relate to a sample of the population of Reading (Berks) made by ourselves. The activity classifications are those adopted by the BBC. For further discussion of the respective survey and analysis methods, see text.

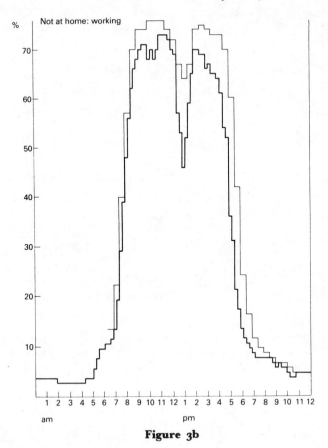

Figure 3b

attributable to the BBC including the journey *from* an activity in with that activity, as well as the journey *to* that activity; while in our own analysis only the journey *to* the activity is included. This would account for the half-hour difference in the ending of work for both men and employed women in the afternoons. There is also the fact of one sample being drawn from a single city, the other from the entire country—albeit a highly urbanized country.

The second sorts of consideration to take into account are the large social changes which have occurred over this period, and which might well be expected to have had a real effect on daily activities: an average increase in real income over the period of something like 30 per cent, a change in the proportion of women in the workforce from 30 per cent in 1961 to 42 per cent in 1971 (Central Statistical Office 1974), and an enormous increase in levels of car ownership.

Despite all these differences however, the correspondences between the results from the two surveys for the major activities—sleep, work, domestic duties, eating and watching television—are remarkably close, and the general impression gained is of a considerable stability in the broad pattern over the period in question.

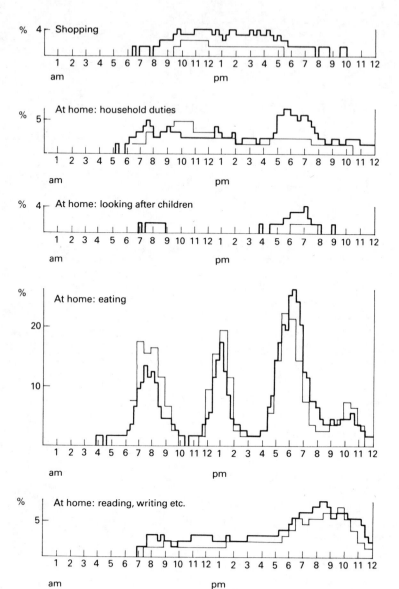

Figure 3c

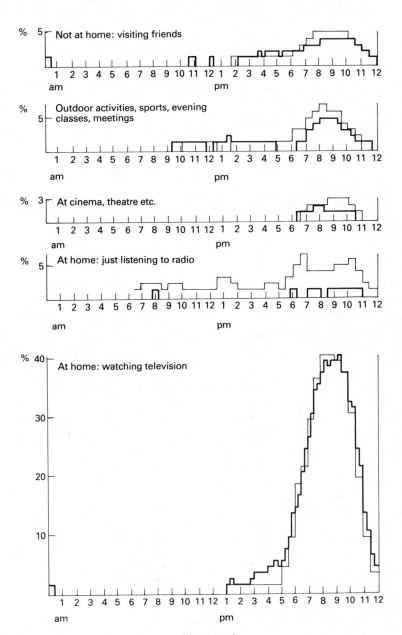

Figure 3d

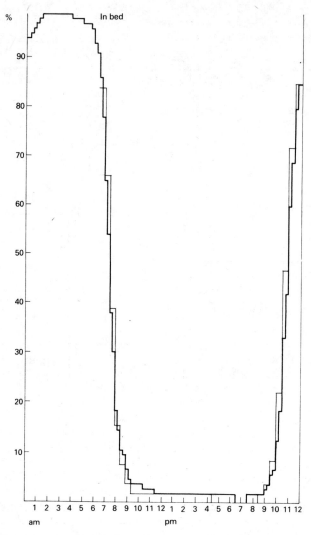

Figure 4a, b, c and d   As for Figure 3, but showing women's activities.

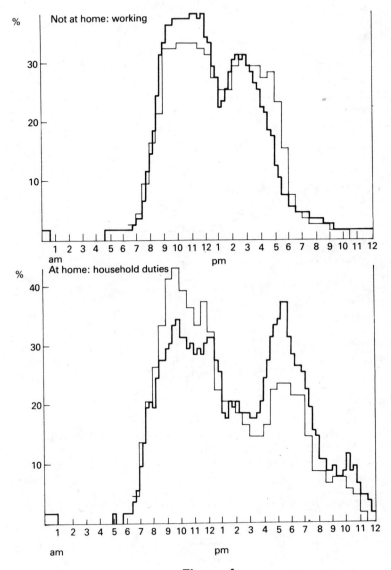

Figure 4b

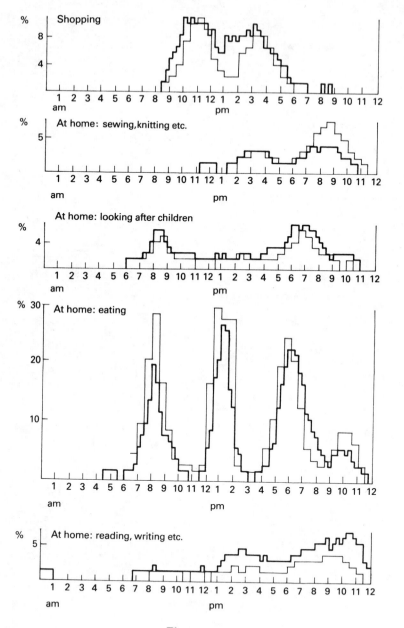

Figure 4c

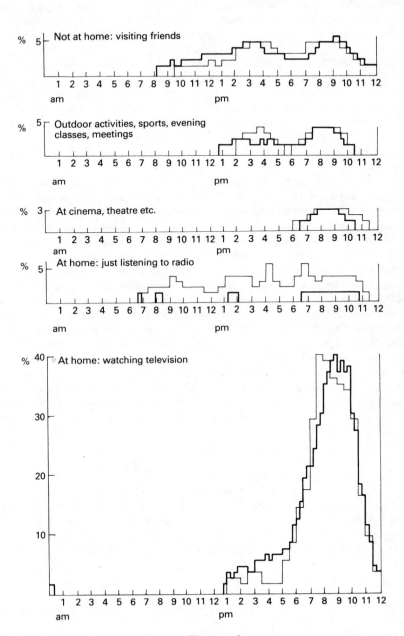

Figure 4d

This is not to say that a finer classification of activities, such as a distinction between modes of travel, would not yield more differences. The increase in car ownership would of course be expected to have brought about a large change in spatial patterns of behaviour, as distinct from the timing of activities. Infrequently occurring activities, too, may have altered in relative terms quite significantly, without this necessarily being apparent; thus changes in participation in sports would be difficult to detect in such samples and with such activity classifications. And such changes might well have important planning implications. (One more minor change in time allocation over the period which is detectable from these comparisons is the well known decline in amounts of time devoted exclusively to listening to the radio.) Nevertheless looked at in broad terms, any overall trends would appear to be slow ones; and there is clearly a great deal of inertia in the system as a whole.

The one factor which does appear to have had an appreciably large effect between the two dates is the greater participation of women in the labour force, and it is some measure of the integration of the whole structure of activity timing that this one change can be seen to have had ramifying effects both on work and on leisure time patterns—and on those of men as well as of women.

The changes are to be observed first, obviously, in the changed pattern of women's work itself, with an increased percentage at work in the morning (many of the new women's jobs will be part-time mornings only), though if anything there is a marginal decrease in the afternoons. Looking at 'household duties', a significant proportion of these activities have been transferred as a consequence from the morning to the afternoon and early evening. There is also evidence to suggest a trend towards the evening meal being regarded as the main meal of the day, rather than lunch (or midday 'dinner'); and the preparation of this meal accounts for much of the domestic work going on around 5:00 to 6:00 p.m. In women's television viewing habits, such small change as can be seen suggests a shift towards a slightly later peak; which could be explained by the greater pressure on the employed woman to fit more domestic work into the early evening.

The graphs for 'household duties' for men show an increase in their total contribution to domestic chores, again occurring mostly in the early evening when they are at home and available; and this too could be related to the increase in women in employment, and a consequent pressure for greater sharing of housework by men. Comparisons for weekends (not shown here) demonstrate further consequences of the changes in women's work; in particular a relative increase in domestic work and shopping on Saturdays, activities which the woman with a job has difficulty in fitting in during the week.

4.

Turning from the question of the long-term stability of the activity system as a whole, on a yearly time scale, to look at the pattern of activities of the individual and of the single household on the daily and weekly scale, we find that here too there is a great deal of regularity in the repetition of weekday behaviour (weekends are more varied)—a great measure of 'routinization' to use Cullen's term. In our own survey in Reading we found that, in terms of the amounts of time spent on activities daily, correlations between successive days of the week are high for any given person. In Cullen and Phelps's study of a sample of husbands and wives on a working-class estate in London, they found that as much as 80 per cent of daily activities were regarded by those engaged in them as 'routine' in nature. Only activities such as shopping and organized leisure—which we find have the lowest day-to-day correlation—tended to be described by Cullen and Phelps's respondents as 'planned' or 'spur of the moment' (Cullen and Phelps 1975).

We can relate this stereotyped character of the individual's daily routine to what has been already said about the stability of the social structure of time rhythms in the longer term. Decisions about the timing of most of the major kinds of activity are not made on a daily basis at all. Instead individuals, and households collectively, commit themselves over a much longer time scale, by a number of 'life decisions'—marriage, taking particular jobs, choosing a particular place to live, sending their children to particular schools—to a series of rhythmic constraints fixed in time and place, which then govern the greater part of their daily routine, and around which and within which those optional and variable activities which do occur at the day-to-day level must be fitted in. 'It is this which enables people', say Cullen and Phelps, 'to cope with the complexity of the urban environment they face by eliminating the necessity of considering anything but a small fraction of its true variety.' (Cullen and Phelps 1975 p. 5)

Even a substantial change in one of the important time constraints on the individual may, it seems, produce relatively little effect. For example, a smaller subsidiary survey which we made in Reading during 1975 has examined the results on activity patterns of the introduction of flexible working hours into a particular Government office in the city. Workers participating in the scheme filled in seven-day diaries, covering out-of-work as well as work activities, before the introduction of flexible hours; and then again six months later, after the scheme had been put into effect. Despite several months having elapsed during which individuals might have experimented with changes in their routine, and despite generally expressed enthusiasm for the freedom which flexibility of hours confers, there were many participants who had not altered their previous times of arrival and departure at all. (Only one third had altered their habitual time of arrival in the morning.)

This could partly be attributed perhaps to psychological inertia and long-ingrained habit. But just as important, these people were still constrained by a whole series of other established commitments set up around their previous fixed hours—to coordinating with their wives or husbands, to taking lifts in other people's cars and so on—which the change to flexible work hours in itself did nothing to alter.

The process of making this kind of series of 'life decisions' might be imagined in relation to the picture provided by the modified Hägerstrand diagram already described. On the longer, month by month and yearly time scale which the diagram is taken to illustrate, an individual may be thought of as engaging in a progressive and interrelated series of commitments which in effect 'lock him in' or constrain him to daily and weekly cycles of activity, as determined by the overall rhythmic pattern of the social time structure (Figure 5). These will be combinations of commitments in space and in time, as for example purchasing a house in a particular location, or taking a job at a specific place of work and

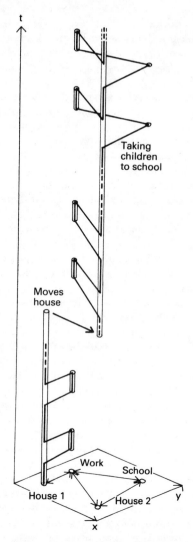

Figure 5 Hypothetical daily routine of an individual, and changes in that routine resulting from long-term 'life decisions', in this case moving house, and sending children to a particular school. The children are dropped off at school by the individual on his way to work in the morning. *x* and *y* depict the urban space in two dimensions, and *t* represents time.

with given fixed hours, and once again it will be evident that such decisions will not be made independently of each other, but that the commitment to a job will condition the spatial choice of place of residence, that both decisions may be made in relation to other aspects of the local social space-time structure, such as public transport facilities and times, where friends and relations already live, the availability of shops and other services, and suchlike.

5.

For the great majority of people, the factors affecting their commitments in this respect to long-term spatial and temporal constraints on their daily activity patterns will be those which occur at the level of the household unit, and which arise from their relationship to other members of their family.

Of these linkages, probably the most important commonly agreed timings within the household are those associated with meals. We have already seen the correspondence in timing of meals for different groups in the Reading population. For working men and housewives this has a great deal to do with the effect on family meal times of the men's hours of work (as well as of children's school hours).

As fewer men and fewer working women return home for the midday meal, its significance as a household tie is probably diminishing. A survey of London housewives made in 1947 found that two thirds of the women interviewed then cooked the main meal at midday (reported in Hole and Attenburrow 1966). But by 1973 only about 15 per cent of working men in our Reading sample were going home for lunch. Nevertheless the timing of breakfast and of the early evening meal are still very much conditioned by work and school hours. A survey by the Building Research Station showed that meals were the most common form of shared activity in the household, and that in families of between four and seven people it was the later afternoon meal which typically had the largest number of people at it (Hole and Attenburrow 1966). The later evening meal more often had only two people. Breakfast had three or four people and lunch also three or four people.

The study of housewives, previously mentioned, demonstrated how cooking and food preparation controlled and dominated a great part of their day; and in our own 1973 survey we find that the same is still true, and that over half the time allocated to housework as a whole is associated with meals. (Despite the fact that men are in general undertaking more of the household work than previously, this does not appear to include a much greater share of the cooking.)

With roughly 7:00 a.m. to 9:00 a.m., 11:00 a.m. to 2:00 p.m. and 4:00 p.m. to 7:00 p.m. taken up with these activities, the housewife tends to slot her remaining household duties into the remaining daytime—so shopping by housewives shows strong morning and afternoon peaks around 10:30 a.m. and 3:00 p.m. Housewives generally spend less time working in the afternoon than in the morning, often reserving some time for visits to friends and relations, watching television and generally relaxing, before preparing the evening meal. At about 3:00 p.m. we find roughly 20 per cent of housewives out of the home either visiting friends or involved in other leisure activities. Those women who go out to work usually finish earlier in the afternoon than men, so that they too can get home and cook the evening meal.

Apart from cooking for the family the housewife may be occupied with the care of young children, a major determinant of time use. In our Reading survey we found that the presence of young babies in the household was associated with three or four hours of child care per day on the part of the mother, and men too helped, averaging one or two hours of baby care daily. Most mothers had a routine for waking, washing, dressing, feeding and putting their babies to bed which was highly regularized.

Older children require less direct attention, but, because of their greater contact with the world outside the home, may have almost as constraining an effect on the household timetable. They may require to be taken to and picked up from school, and ferried to and from other leisure and sports activities, visits to friends and so on. Unfortunately we have little such information about older children's activities from our Reading survey because of their exclusion from the sample. Household time-budgets currently being analysed by the BBC Audience Research Department, from a new survey made in 1975 which included children from the age of five upwards, may however shed some light on these effects.

A further important type of linkage within the household concerns the use of the family car; and such linkages have no doubt assumed greater importance as car ownership has increased. The convenience of car travel over public transport allows all sorts of out-of-home leisure activities which before would have been inaccessible (both in space and in time). But the penalty, when the household has only one car, is that a great deal of coordinating behaviour must go on between wives, husbands and children, with typically rather complicated travel patterns resulting for car drivers.

In our sample 60 percent of all respondents recorded 'having the use of' a car; although this in fact included quite a few people who mainly got lifts. Generally it is the man of the family who has effective control of the car. (Thus all men in our flexible working hours survey in car-owning households had unrestricted use of the car, but less than half of the women had free use of it. All of the men drove themselves to work, but half of the women who travelled by car got lifts.) Overall in the Reading diaries there were recorded 1,387 car passenger trips and 3,870 car driver trips, most of the car passengers being driven by other members of their own household. The complication of car journeys which results from this pattern of coordination within the family—giving lifts, picking up and setting down—means that more stops and more separate legs are involved in car journeys than in journeys by public transport or walking (cf. Jones 1975).

The use of the family car has undoubtedly had its effect on patterns of shopping. Where the car is monopolized by the man of the family on weekdays, such effects however will be confined to Saturdays; and the fact that the time-budget for men shopping on Saturdays has risen from 0·43 hours in 1961 to 0·66 hours in 1973 has probably a lot to do with this. (Another factor is that the peak number of men at work on Saturdays has dropped, from 43 per cent to about 30 per cent. The greater proportion of *women* in the workforce would also tend to have the effect of increasing the total amount of shopping by both themselves and men at the weekends.)

We have presented our general argument here in a sequence which perhaps might suggest that the larger structure of social time rhythms is to be regarded as primary; and that the activity patterns of the individual household must be fitted into this greater system. Such an idea would however, we believe, be an incomplete one and it is our argument that at the same time the larger structure is, for the most part, the cumulative product of the aggregate of many separate households and their organization. There is once again a circular relationship involved.

There is in society, of course, a significant minority of people who are not members of households. And the coordination of hours of work is certainly governed crucially by considerations of industrial organization and commercial communication. Nevertheless the household is the most important, most universal and one of the most highly structured of social units; and it is arguably the patterns of interlinkage and coordination in time that it sets up among its members which are collectively responsible for establishing many of the larger rhythms of society as a whole.

If this idea is accepted, then we can interpret the effects of the various longer term social changes going on in activity patterns, which we described earlier, in this light. The large structure of social time rhythms, we can say—speaking very broadly—is set up by, and for, behaviour patterns and interrelationships at the household level which cater to the traditional male/female roles and to the 'man at work/housewife at home' stereotype of the division of domestic labour. The much discussed difficulties which are faced by the working woman in organizing her daily life can thus be seen in terms of a kind of dissonance between the demands of her job and family commitments, and the larger organization of society in time according to the needs of the established working husband/non-working wife arrangement. The societal rhythms—of shop hours, official hours of work, even school hours—have changed much more slowly than have women's availability and willingness to do paid work, thus making it less likely that a feasible solution can be found to the woman's problem of running a house while holding a job.

Largely as a result of women's ties to home, their jobs are often part-time ones; women are more frequently absent from work than men for domestic reasons (Department of Employment 1974); and the most frequent explanations for their leaving jobs are changes in domestic circumstances (14 per cent in 1966) and having babies (13 per cent), followed only then by the sorts of reasons which apply more commonly to men (poor pay, a better job elsewhere, redundancy, ill health and so on) (Harris 1966). Despite the general increase in women working, the numbers at work in the 25 to 29 age bracket have remained fairly constant over the last twenty years at around 30 per cent—a fact which, for this group, is no doubt attributable to the very important ties to home represented by young children. Fewer than 20 per cent of married women in households with children under five were at work in 1966.

As a result of the combination of the demands of their job and their domestic work, women in employment are subject to considerable pressure on their time (cf. Young and Willmott 1973). Most studies, and ours is no exception, show that housewives have more time for sleep and for leisure activities than do working women. (Where housewives miss out, is on out-of-home leisure. They spend comparatively little time outside the house, especially if shopping is discounted.) Women with jobs get much less domestic work done than housewives —only about two-thirds as much. However this, in combination with their hours of paid employment, naturally adds up to a much greater work load in toto. Weekday household duties tend to get squeezed into the hours between 4:00 and 7:00 p.m., and evening leisure activities are reduced by comparison with both men and housewives (33 per cent of working women are watching television at the peak hour of 9:00 p.m., by comparison with 50 per cent of housewives). The leisure activities such as visiting friends which housewives do in the afternoons are, for the working woman, also forced into the evenings.

Working women's activity patterns during the day show greater complexity than do those of housewives. This is particularly apparent when one examines trip-making behaviour, where, in the Reading survey, housewives recorded 3·3 trips per day, and working women recorded 4·7 trips.[1] Working women also, though they make about the same number of trips overall as men, tend to be obliged to use modes of travel which are less convenient and physically more tiring (0·8 bus journeys per day compared with 0·4, 2·0 walking trips against 1·2, and only 1·8 car trips as compared with 2·7 for men).

We have already remarked on the difficulty which working women experience in getting the family shopping done. In many cases shopping is done on the way to and from work, on weekdays, or during the lunch hour (20 per cent of women in our flexible hours survey were shopping between 12:30 and 1:30), the net effect for all working women being to produce a more or less even distribution of shopping during the whole day, compared with the distinct mid-morning and mid-afternoon peaks for housewives. A great amount of shopping is done by working women on Saturdays—as would be expected— compensating for the constraints during the week.

Some changes in shopping hours have been mooted, and to some extent instituted, in response to this situation, specifically the practice by a few supermarkets and big stores of opening late—up to 8:00 p.m.—on one or two evenings a week. If the law in relation to Sunday opening were to be relaxed (the Shops Act of 1950 forbids shops to open on Sundays in England except for the sale of perishables and newspapers) it is to be expected that this would prove popular amongst shoppers— witness the present popularity of Sunday markets.

Neither of these two kinds of change in shop hours is without its drawbacks however. In the case of weekday evening opening, many of those working women who might especially benefit are at home cooking, eating with the family and looking after children at just this time; and so it is largely single people or those without children who can take advantage. And with both late evening opening and possible Sunday shopping, there is the problem that shop workers will have *their* leisure time linkages with family and friends cut as a result of such changes.

And so once again we are brought back to our theme of the self-perpetuating nature of the social time structure, of its general resistance to change, and of the high degree of coordination between the established rhythms of work, leisure, and the domestic life, such that those slow changes which economic and social movements do bring about affect the system not just in one part only, but in multiplying and ramifying effects throughout.

6.

Much recent work in social science and geography on human spatio-temporal behaviour has stated the problem to be investigated, in its essentials, as that of a direct interaction between two terms: the material (urban or geographical) environment, and the subjective world of individuals and individual minds.

The alternative view which we have tried to present here, of a culturally transmitted structure of temporal regularities and routines, in effect introduces into the picture a third term which mediates between the subjective decision-making of the individual (or household), and his physical surroundings in time and space. This cultural structure is part of Popper's 'world three' of 'objective knowledge' (Popper 1972). Like natural language, it is a cultural product which arises originally *only* out of individual actions and behaviour; but once produced, it acquires a certain autonomy and a degree of relative independence from the thoughts and actions of individuals. It is a question of the subjective 'world two' of minds—in Popper's terms—interacting with this quasi-autonomous 'world three' structure of inherited and historically accumulated cultural products, and of the interaction of 'world two' with the 'world one' of material objects and physical environment going on for the most part *via* the cultural structures of 'world three'.

Our purpose in introducing the fable about Christmas at the beginning of this paper, was precisely to demonstrate that in the terms of a 'two world' paradigm, of a simple interaction of individual behaviour with the physical environment, such culturally determined patterns of activity are quite inexplicable. Only an approach which recognizes the existence of mediating structures of a cultural evolutionary character could be capable of accounting not just for the temporal organization of such special occasions as Chistmas, but for the whole range of more everyday routines of which the same is equally true. To study daily activities without reference to these cultural structures would be like studying speech without any reference to language.

As Popper himself points out in relation to investigation of psychological and cultural problems in general, such a 'three worlds' view in effect reconciles the long-standing and vexing opposition in social science—an opposition which has found its particular expression in contrasting attitudes to the study of daily patterns of urban activity—between a wholly subjective, free-will 'psychological' point of view on the one hand, and a rigid cultural and environmental determinism on the other (cf. Hillier and Leaman 1973). There *is* a social structure of temporal regularities, routines, conventions, which has its own autonomy and dynamic, and which evolves in relative independence of the actions and thoughts of individuals; and yet the structure only owes its existence historically to the sum of these individual behaviours. At any specific point in time it is a 'given' so far as the individual is concerned; he must take it as he finds it. But the social space-time framework which it constitutes nevertheless offers the opportunity for wholly novel, creative and subjectively motivated activities at the individual level.

Again, the broad analogy with natural language is an illuminating one. Language is a socially evolving cultural product which, as a whole, is relatively independent of any single person's speech behaviour. And yet it is language which provides the structure whereby individual speech is made possible; and the possibilities allowed for particular written or spoken utterances have an enormously rich and varied—in effect infinitely varied—range. Paradoxically then, it is the structure of constraints making up the language—of vocabulary, grammar, established forms—which precisely confers freedom of expression on the individual speaker. A similar observation applies to our cultural structure of time rhythms. It is the pattern of constraints which, although they certainly restrict and limit social and spatial behaviour, do so in fact in just such a way as to confer freedom and possibilities for a variable choice of patterns of personal activity on the individual.

ACKNOWLEDGEMENT

The work described in this paper has been supported on a grant from the Social Science Research Council.

Footnotes

[1] A trip being defined as a movement from one distinct location to another by one transport mode with the exception of bus travel, where walking and waiting for buses, and change of bus, are included all in the same trip.

Chapter 5

Graph Theory and the Study of Activity Structure

Don Parkes and W. D. Wallis

In this essay we consider the utility of certain graph theoretic principles for the study of activity structure, with some emphasis on sequence.

To date the main thrust in the analysis of human social activities has centred around classical parametric statistical analysis of time-budget data, based on samples of urban, rural or national populations. Techniques used include calculation of the mean duration of activities, measures of elasticity based on the variance about mean activity durations, comparison of proportions of participants in activity sets discriminated on various socio-economic factors, measures of similarity in activity profiles based on correlational methods and identification of 'simple structure' among activities using factor analytic methods. The citations which follow are by no means comprehensive of all such studies, but each adopts one or a number of these analytical methods in order to analyse activity structure and process (Sorokin and Merton 1937; Chapin 1974; Hammer and Chapin 1972; Parkes 1974; Cullen and Godson 1972; 1975). The most ambitious study has been that undertaken through the European Co-ordination Centre for Research and Documentation in the Social Sciences (Szalai, Converse, Feldheim, Sceuch, Stone *et al.* 1972).

Three approaches to the study of time, space and activity have been of particular interest to us. The first of these is by Hägerstrand *et al.* and may be called the time-geographic approach. The particular value of this approach has been its emphasis on the essential indivisibility of the individual, of flows or paths through space-time and the conceptualization of a set of constraints which confine activity profiles within a so-called space-time prism (Hägerstrand 1970; 1974; Carlstein 1975). Development of simulation models of an individual's activity path within a daily prism has also been a major contribution to the understanding of space timing and time spacing (Lenntorp 1974; Carlstein 1975a). One such computer based simulation is known as PESASP and is referred to elsewhere in this book (Lenntorp, chapter 9).

The second approach is that taken by Chapin and his research associates. Unlike the Lund scheme referred to briefly above, Chapin's work has been essentially inductive in its approach. Time budgets have formed a framework for his data collection and analyses. His classification of activities (treated as a partially ordered set in our study) ranging from obligatory activities which are essential to the maintenance of life through to discretionary activities for which there is a high level of participation choice, as well as timing and spacing choice perhaps, has been particularly useful (Chapin 1974). Relatively little attention is paid to sequence analysis however (Chapin and Hightower 1965;

1966). This is so in spite of Chapin's statement that sequence is an important part of activity analysis (Chapin 1974).

Finally the work of Cullen, Godson and associates has been concerned with the identification of structure within activity systems. The 'critical question of sequencing of activities' has been given explicit consideration (Cullen and Godson 1975, p. 10). They have used conventional statistical measures to isolate structural elements in the activity profiles of their sampled populations. The techniques which they adopt include calculation of transition probabilities of change from one activity to another as well as harmonic analyses of one form or another. These may indeed be the best way to tackle the study of sequence; but having adopted these approaches they comment on the need for further development of methodologies.

We investigate methods for the study of activity *structures*, including sequence, rather than the study of activity *process*. Emphasis is on identification of certain uniformities, similarities or differences in the structure of individual and group activities over a period of time, such as a day. Although the data which we use were generated from a small survey of twenty subjects, there is no sense in which that data is being treated as representative of a population. The data might just as well have been generated 'artificially' but this would have made the task of evaluating the application of graph theoretic methods that much more difficult and we wished to avoid the somewhat annoying tendency of some writers to use entirely unsympathetic 'examples' to illustrate a methodology. A further aim was to adopt as simple an approach as possible, in the firm belief that many more complex methodologies possibly do not contribute much, if any, more to an understanding of social science problems. The sort of answers we are interested in are inherent or otherwise in some of the methodology available to us in finite combinatorics and graph theory and especially in that branch of graph theory relating to digraphs. For the purpose of this paper we are not concerned with the real characteristics of the particular sets of ten females and ten males who provided an activity diary for us, or with their 'representation' of behaviour in a population. The same conditional comment is relevant to the coarseness of the time intervals used for recording activities.

> Much of social behaviour depends for its orderly qualities on common definitions, assumptions, and actions with regard to the location of events in time. Certain activities, for example, require simultaneous actions by a number of persons, or at least their presence at a particular time.... Thus one element of temporal ordering is *synchronization*. Other activities require that actions follow one another in a prescribed order; thus *sequence* is a part of temporal order ... frequency of events during a period of time is critical; thus *rate* is also one of the ways that time impinges on social behaviour. For all of these elements of social coordination the term *timing* is useful ... timing is an intrinsic quality of personal and collective behaviour. If activities have no temporal order they have no order at all.
> (Moore 1963, pp. 8–9).

Although, for any single individual, life itself is a *path* rather than a *cycle* (as it is somewhat euphemistically described) any single life-path is made up of many cyclic periods. There are familiar daily, weekly or monthly cycles, described elsewhere as *small time* cycles and the annular cycle described as *big time* (Parkes 1974). It is the fact that the cycles are of such apparently rigid and fixed length that 'constrains activity and makes allocation and priorities essential' (Moore 1963, p. 6). Indeed, time itself has been described as a device to give order to events by identifying them as coexisting or successive (Lynch 1972, p. 120).

Within the period of a single particular cycle, for instance the *circadian* cycle, certain structural attributes of activity sequence have been identified. For example, 'the working day begins to break up into something more gregarious after midday and the variety, speed and complexity of behaviour must be at its highest from mid-morning to mid-afternoon' (Cullen and Godson 1975) and the 'sequential distribution of activities may be interpreted as [a] manifestation of values, habits and life styles' (Chapin and Hightower 1966, p. 63). However, despite Chapin's

> use of time-budget diary techniques to collect information, which suggests an interest in the sequencing of an individual's activities, there has been very little development of either ideas or data relating explicitly to the inter-dependence between activity choice decisions over time. The task of pattern recognition has not yet taken the form of identifying sequences of activities which can be viewed as activity modules ... (Cullen and Godson 1975, p. 6).

Activity sequence study in effect, puts social events into a system which is ideally timed by the succession of events relevant to that system, that is by *social time*. In other words, reference to universal or clock time becomes secondary to the internalized timing which is defined by the nature of activity sequence structure. We have yet to develop a timing system which is internalized to the relationship between events in a socially relevant cycle. Clock time still dominates.

Characteristics of activity structure and sequence

In order to relate our proposals and those of the existing approaches to activity analysis and *time-space* study it is worth considering some of the characteristics of activity structure that have been identified and some of the models that have been used in order to do this.

As used in this study the term activity refers quite specifically to the act which a person was engaged in at predefined points in time, *instances* over a twenty-four hour period. These reported acts are then classified according to the scheme proposed by Chapin (1974):

> An *activity* is a classificatory term for a variety of acts grouped together under a more generic category.... Furthermore an activity has a number of properties. It has duration, a position in time, usually designated by the start time, *a place in a sequence of events*, and a fixed location or a path in space (Chapin 1974, pp. 36–7).

The need to develop a taxonomy of activity types remains as an important objective for time-space research, in spite of the valuable contribution that the classification schemes devised by Chapin (1966 *et seq.*), Szalai (1972), Stone (1970) and Cullen and Godson (1972; 1975) have made to date. Perhaps the most useful developments are going to occur in the analysis of activity descriptions on semantic data, see for instance Kranz (1970), who identifies one of the critical limitations of past time-budget research as the difficulty of 'activity classification'. In this exploratory study we have indeed used what Kranz describes as 'large and inclusive categories' fully appreciative of the fact that this 'necessarily obscures differences' between groups and between activities (Kranz 1970, p. 287). To overcome these and other problems in activity classification, Kranz (1970) and Stone (1970; 1972) have considered ways and means of using the semantics adopted by individuals to describe an activity profile, as a basis for activity classification. Kranz uses a semantic dictionary for time budgets which is able to deal in very fine detail with activity descriptions.

For a number of years Stone has been developing a method for analysis of activity descriptions of co-occurrences of events based on a search for matching symbols among 'lists and lists of lists' (Stone 1970, p. 7). 'Complicated patterns of symbols could be searched' using his so-called general sequence analyser. Sequences could thus be picked out of the stream of events and connected (Stone 1970, p. 7).

He has proposed three levels of time-budget data analysis in relation to the international time-budgets study of twelve countries (Szalai *et al.* 1972). Level 1 is of simple durations or frequencies, level 2 average duration or frequencies for combinations of duration, and level 3, in which 'each activity is considered by itself apart from its place in the stream of events ... search procedures were needed to search the stream of activities for certain sequence patterns' ... (Stone 1972, pp. 96–7). However, he adds, 'few sequence studies appear in the volume (Szalai *et al.* 1972) [and] we would expect future time-budget studies to not avoid sequence issues, but to develop more sophisticated ways of handling them' (Stone 1972, p. 107).

As for any classification or taxonomic scheme the problem of scale selection becomes critical not only for the interpretation of empirical studies in conjunction with some theoretical viewpoint but also in terms of the analytical methods that can be applied to the data after classification. For instance, it is not unreasonable to argue that the very fact that we conceptualize human activity as forming a stream flowing through time (and space) suggests that a classification into activity types, sets or modules is either not possible or that it produces a severe and unacceptable abstraction of reality. In other words we are confronted with the very difficult problem of infinite divisibility or *density*:

> Not only can we always consider any interval as made up of smaller ones, but we are entitled to apply even irrational numbers to the measurement of time.... Quite apart from Zeno's difficulties with infinity, and Hume's empiricist objections, the notion of denseness and continuity is incompatible with the notion of *nextness*, and hence, on one of its interpretations, of *succession*. If time is dense there cannot be a next instant after this one; because for any instant after this one there is, by the definition of denseness, *another* instant between it and this one (Lucas 1973, p. 29).

We do not consider the philosophical issues associated with instants and intervals here, these and many other matters are discussed by Lucas (Lucas 1972). In the particular study of activity structure and sequence which we address ourselves to, it is the *instant* rather than the *interval* that we are concerned with. Our instants in other words are a particular classification of time, appearing as regular intervals on a clock-time scale. It is the activity occurrent at time (instant) t_o which we *relate* graph theoretically to activities located at $t_o - t_n$ and at $t_o + t_n$. The time-space separating t_o and t_n is always an interval of thirty minutes length. This is obviously no more than an operational expedience at the moment.

It may be the case that the approach we are suggesting is less sensitive to variation in scales of space, time and substance classification than are the 'parametric' methods which have been applied to date. However, such methods rely heavily on the variance of the data or impose conditions of independence between observations or attributes which may prove to be severely limiting model demands.

Other methods impose certain constraints such as the dependence of any state on the immediately prior state. Stone (1972, p. 180) and Cullen and Godson (1972, p. 16) refer to the disadvantages in the use of Markov models for instance *at this stage in the development of studies in human activity sequence*. However, Markov models and the graph theoretic approach we are suggesting are not entirely independent of each other, to the extent that graph theoretic methods may simplify mathematical treatment of Markov chains.

Markov approaches may be used with only limited confidence in time-budget data analysis, in fact they have been rejected for the time being by some workers (Stone 1972, p. 180; Cullen and Godson 1975, p. 16).

When an activity A is followed by an activity B which is followed by an activity C, then A is followed by B and C. Such a sequence may be considered in terms of A, B and C or in terms of A and B or A and C or B and C. The fact that A and C are in sequence can only be accepted if the two activities have some functional connection; lunch (C) follows breakfast (A) or tea (C) follows lunch (A) for instance, but there have been a number of activities (B) in between. The functional connection which satisfies the notion of sequence in such a case is obvious; they are more or less obligatory activities demanded for survival or at least they are activities that have become so socially institutionalized into the structure of the day that they appear to be necessary for survival! Thus even the nature of 'sequence' in social terms is not easily determined. Mere adjacency in clock-time is an oversimplification. But *adjacency* and *connectedness* are important concepts in graph theory and may be found to be useful in the solution of some aspects of activity structure, for instance sequence.

As we have pointed out earlier, Cullen and Godson were particularly 'concerned' to examine the sequencing of activities. They were looking for highly organized episodes which gave pattern and structure to the 'whole stream of behaviour' (Cullen and Godson 1974, p. 8). Such highly organized episodes are not easy to identify. Graph theoretic methods may reveal them, if darkly, through the isolation of subgraphs, and the concept of connectedness. Using a range of statistical methods, the most important of which were factor analysis, lagged covariance methods, harmonic analyses and transition matrices they were able to consider a number of fascinating hypotheses relating to activity structure. Of particular interest to us are their comments about sequence and degree of commitment, level of arrangement, fixity in time (they also considered place fixity) and the extent to which the activity was planned or unplanned.

Some aspects of graph theory

Basically a graph is a mathematical entity which makes explicit a relationship between objects. A graph consists of a collection of objects (called *vertices*) and a collection of relations between the objects (called *edges*). For example if we want to model the relationship between people in a gathering which is induced by conversations, we could take the people in the gathering as vertices and include an edge from X to Y whenever X speaks to Y: if A spoke to B twice, A spoke to C once and C spoke to A and B once each, then the graph would have two edges from A to B, one from A to C, one from C to A and one from C to B. (Figure 1).

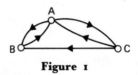

Figure 1

We represent a graph by a diagram in which each vertex is a distinguished point and each edge is a line joining two vertices. In some cases the relationship is symmetrical and the graph is *undirected*, at other times it is not, and the *direction* of the relation is shown by an arrow on the edge. Our example was one of these *directed* graphs. In this essay we assume that graphs are directed unless otherwise stated and may be referred to as *digraphs*.

As a matter of terminology we say that the two vertices joined by an edge are the *endpoints* of that edge, and we say that the vertices are *adjacent*. The number of edges which touch a vertex X is called the *valency* of X; in the directed case one may also speak of the *in-valency* and *out-valency*, the number of edges directed *into* and *out of* X.

A graph or digraph can be represented by an *incidence matrix*. Given a graph on p vertices, label its vertices as 1, 2, ... p in some order. Then form a matrix whose (i, j) entry is the number of edges from vertex i to vertex j. The matrix will be symmetric in the undirected case, but not usually symmetric in the digraph case; for example, labelling A as 1, B as 2 and C as 3, we obtain

$$\begin{bmatrix} 0 & 2 & 1 \\ 0 & 0 & 0 \\ 1 & 1 & 0 \end{bmatrix}$$

as the incidence matrix of the graph in Figure 1. Various matrices are possible —different labellings of the vertices lead to different matrices—but the matrices for one graph are equivalent in an obvious way. The sum of row i and the sum of column i will be the out-valency and in-valency respectively of vertex i.[1]

The basic reason for using graph theory is that it is a general modelling system for relations. The vertices are undefined objects and may be used to represent anything whatsoever. The use of the graph underlying a situation enables us to strip off *initially* unessential details. Even when some information is lost in looking only at the graph, this method of modelling may bring new insights by directing one's attention to the structural aspects of the relation being studied. Where theory exists about the nature of structural relations a graph or diagraph theoretic approach provides a means for testing theory, where no theory exists or in the more likely situation of ill-defined theories in the social sciences, graphs and digraphs may generate well-defined schemes. Sometimes it is useful to concentrate on part only of the relation being studied; instead of the whole graph, one looks at a *sub-graph* formed by deleting some verices and /or edges from the original.

A graph very often represents *sequential* events (say, activities):[2] the existence of an edge from X to Y represents the fact that the state X immediately precedes state Y in some sequence, and the edge in fact represents the transition from X to Y. It is then often reasonable to say that there is a 'second stage' connection between X and Z if there are edges from X to some Y and from Y to some Z, so that X and Y are only two steps apart. More generally we define a *walk* from X to Y to be a sequence of vertices and edges starting with X, then an edge from X to (say) Y_1, then vertex Y_1, then an edge out of Y_1, and so on, ending at Y. We say 'X is connected to Y' if there exists a walk from X to Y. In the figure (2) below, there is a walk from A to E which goes A, (A,B), B, (B,D) (either edge), D, (D,E), E (or more concisely we could say $ABDE$; this may lack precision as it is sometimes necessary to know which (B, D) edge is used, but more usually it is not).

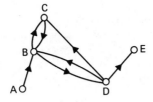

Figure 2

Another such walk is $ABDCBDE$ (the repetition of vertices of edges is of no consequence). There is no walk $ABCDE$, since the edge (D,C) is directed the wrong way, although such a walk would exist in an undirected graph. There are walks joining twelve ordered pairs of vertices in the graph, but not the pairs starting with E or ending with A.

We say that a graph[3] is *strongly connected* if there is a connection from every vertex to every other, and (weakly) *connected* if all vertices are connected in the undirected sense. There is an undirected walk from any vertex to any other vertex. To say a graph is connected means intuitively that it 'consists of one piece'. Even though two graphs are both connected, we may think that one is 'more connected' than another, in order to describe this we may define the *connectivity* of a graph to be that number n such that deletion of n vertices will leave the graph connected but deletion of $n+1$ will result in a *disconnected* graph. The *edge connectivity* is a similar number defined in terms of deleting edges. In the analagous way we define *strong connectivity* and *strong edge-connectivity*.[4]

If a graph is disconnected it will consist of two or more connected pieces. Each of these maximal connected subgraphs are called a *component*. Figure 3, below, shows a disconnected graph with precisely two components.

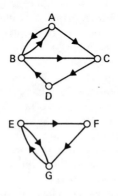

Figure 3

Two graphs are called *isomorphic* if there is a map, or way of associating vertices of one with vertices of the other, which preserves adjacency. Precisely, an *isomorphism* between graphs G_1 and G_2 is a map Φ from the vertex-set of G_1 to the vertex-set of G_2 which sends vertex X to vertex $X\phi$, such that X and Y are adjacent in G_1, if only if (iff) $X\Phi$ and $Y\Phi$ are adjacent in G_2: G_1 and G_2 are isomorphic if and only if there is an isomorphism between them. We consider that the relationship of isomorphism between graphs is one which needs generalization. For example, the two graphs in Figure 4 are not isomorphic, but they are very similar; it is for such cases that we need a generalized measure of 'relative isomorphism'. One such measure is suggested below in section (c).

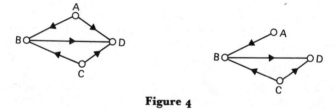

Figure 4

A graph theoretic description of an experiment

(a) The data base

In order to generate data related to activity structure, twenty subjects, ten female and ten male, were asked to keep a diary of their activities over a twenty-four hour cycle, from midnight on a specific Saturday through to midnight on Sunday. In free format description the activity being undertaken at each of forty-eight *instants* was self-recorded. The instants were thirty minutes apart—on the hour and half-past the hour. Additional information to be recorded included (a) the level of choice attached to the activity, based on a five-point scheme where 1 meant choice to engage in the activity was at a maximum (highly discretionary) and 5 meant that there was no choice (obligatory), and (b) whether the activity was planned (or expected) to occur at that time, at least twenty-four hours ahead. A simple yes/no dichotomy was used. For the choice level category, the five-point scheme was also dichotomized during analysis.[5]

The free format activity description was then transposed into a Chapin activity classification with up to 233 categories. These 233 categories were then reduced to nine major categories following the Chapin scheme (Chapin 1974). This reduction was no more than a matter of expedience in the analysis of the 'experimental' data. The Chapin scheme was considered most practicable because it allowed us to follow a further useful theme in Chapin's work, the consideration of his quasi-scale of obligatory-discretionary activity types. Once again, however, this partial ordering must be considered merely as a device, in this instance, in the full realization that a finer taxonomic scheme will be necessary when representative sample data are being used for predictive and normative studies.

Owing to the recurrence of 'sleep' activity as the 'norm' between say midnight Saturday and 08:00 Sunday, our analysis began only with the final sleep instant unless the Saturday midnight instant was not sleep. Furthermore, in the representation of activities as the *vertices* of a graph G_f for females or a graph G_m for males, Figures 5 and 6, the *edges* representing the transition or link between time instants were only recorded if there was a *change* in activity. Loops therefore mean that there was in fact a change of activity, in terms of the 233 category classification, but not in terms of the nine-category (nine vertex) scheme adopted for digraph representation.

Figures 5 and 6 represent the activity profiles of twenty subjects as *digraphs*. The vertices representing activities have been ordered 0, 1, 6, 2, 8, 4, 3, 5, 7 to represent the quasi-scale of high order obligatory to most discretionary activities. As a matter of almost diversionary interest, remember that the day in question is a Sunday, discretionary activities 'should' be well represented, i.e. 4, 3, 5, 7, say, except that the obligatory activities related to biological functions 0, 1 and movement 6 must remain dominant.

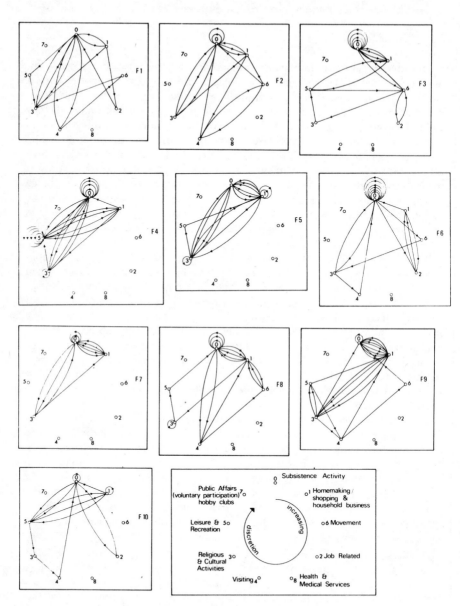

Figure 5 Examples of activity digraphs for ten females (Sunday). Activities are ordered clockwise obligatory to discretionary.

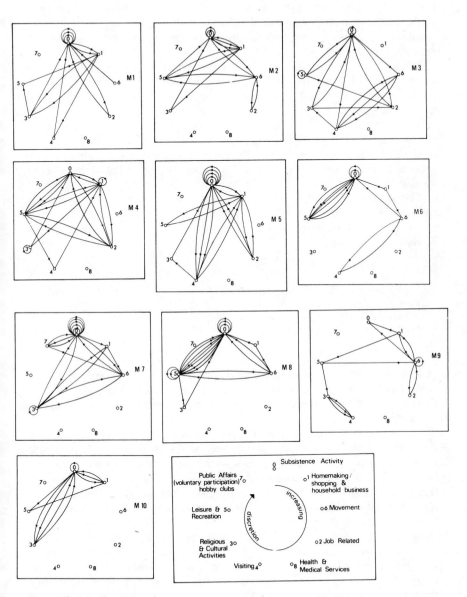

Figure 6 Examples of activity digraphs for ten males (Sunday). Activities are ordered clockwise obligatory to discretionary.

Using a basis which will be explained when we discuss the measures of generalized *relative isomorphism*, four of the set of twenty graphs will be used to explain and evaluate our approach. The twenty graphs in Figures 5 and 6, are in fact sub-graphs of the graph G, which would represent all the subjects in the experiment, but they will be referred to as graphs from here on. Large graphs with a high valency on a number of vertices are more conveniently represented as matrices.

For instance, the graphs of the set of all males, the set of all females and the set of all subjects each have large valencies and large multiplicities on the edges. Matrices representing them are to be found at the end of Table 2 (see p. 89 below).

The four graphs we have selected are of two pairs. A pair G_s^1 and G_s^2 being the most similar or relatively isomorphic, and a pair G_d^1 and G_d^2 being the most dissimilar or least isomorphic. In Figure 7 they are shown with the activity sequence represented by integer numbers on the edge between (activity) vertices.

The graphs G_s^1, G_s^2, G_d^1, G_d^2 are the graphs G_j^7, G_m^{10}, G_m^9, G_m^4 respectively, shown in Figures 5 and 6.

For each of these graphs the activity sequence may be shown as a string of vertices as follows:

G_s^1 : 0 0 1 0 3 1 0 1 0 3 0 0

G_s^2 : 0 0 5 1 0 1 0 1 0 3 0 3 0

G_d^1 : 5 6 0 1 6 6 2 6 1 5 3 4 3 4

G_d^2 : 0 2 1 0 5 2 5 1 2 0 5 4 1 5 0 1 1 3 3 0

The difference in the length of the strings results from the incidence of the same activity occurring in two or more sequential instants. A narrative description of the activity sequence in terms of common instants can be readily developed.

It is particularly interesting to be able to look at the *triples* of activities. For our four graphs shown above these appear as shown in Table 1. The *triples* consist of a sequence of three activities, so the triple indicates a sequential link between the *links between* activities. As soon as we discuss *triples* we have moved from graph theory to the related theory of *generalized* graphs or *hypergraphs*, but the structural considerations are similar to graph theoretic considerations. The data we collected were not sufficient to enable us to look at the structure of triples (or of longer sequences), but some interesting results occurred. For example, consider the triples which occur in the sequences for the four subjects and their relative frequencies, as shown in Table 1. The similarity of G_s^1 and G_s^2 and their dissimilarity from G_d^1 and G_d^2 is striking. Such considerations throw further light on the possible structure of activity sequence and furthermore permit the use of other measures of structural similarity from non-parametric statistic theory and practice. A complete list of all possible triples was produced from the data generated by this small study but cannot be presented here, nor would the results have any definitive value. The use of triples or larger sub-sequences does suggest itself as a possible alternative to the use of Markov

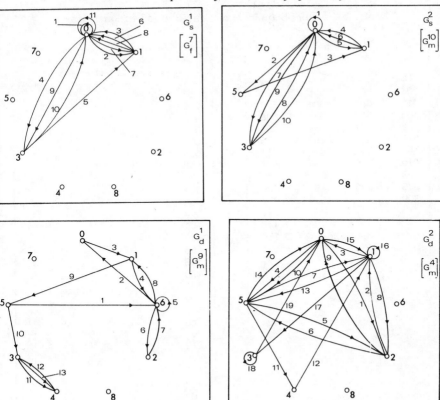

Figure 7 Most similar and most dissimilar pairs of digraphs. Based on measures of relative isomorphism.

models. Those sub-sequences which occur with high frequency would be 'activity modules' in the Cullen and Godson sense. However, in order to discuss such analyses, we would need data in which the triples occurred with higher frequency.

(b) The related matrices

The incidence matrix for each of the twenty graphs showing the sequential associations between activities was calculated. For the set of all subjects (female and male) and for each sex sub-set, similar matrices of incidence were produced. By way of illustration examples are shown below (Table 2) for the same four graphs that we have used above.

In Table 2 the principle diagonal shows the number of times that an activity was followed by an activity in its own class (but not the same activity for reasons which we have already explained). For the female sub-set this accumulates to a value of thirty-three and for the males to a value of twenty-nine. This

TABLE I   Triples/Sequences of Length 3 and Frequencies

G_s^1	G_s^2	G_d^1	G_d^2
001	005	560	021
010	051	601	210
103	510	016	105
031	101	166	052
310	010	662	525
101	103	626	251
010	030	261	512
103	303	615	120
030	030	153	205
300		534	054
		343	541
		434	415
			150
			501
			011
			113
			133
			330

Triple	G_s^1	G_s^2	G_d^1	G_d^2
		Frequencies		
001	1			
005		1		
010	2	1		
011				1
016			1	
021				1
030	1	2		
031	1			
051		1		
052				1
054				1
101	1	1		
103	2	1		
105				1
113				1
120				1
133				1
150				1
153			1	
166			1	
205				1
210				1
251				1
261			1	
300	1			
303		1		
310	1			
330				1
343			1	
415				1
434			1	
501				1
510		1		
512				1
525				1
534			1	
541				1
560			1	
601			1	
615			1	
626			1	
662			1	

measure would indicate that females tended to have a less varied activity structure than did males. Though our data are not designed to be representative, the result is in the expected direction. For each of the row sums, interpretation would follow the same reasoning, for example while subsistence activity Ao was followed by a greater variety of activities in total for females, there is no consistency to this result in terms of pairs of activities. Housework A1, for instance, accounts for much of this difference in conjunction with religious and

TABLE 2 Incidence Matrices for G_s^1 G_s^2 G_d^1 G_d^2

$G_s^1: (G_l^7)$

PREDECESSORS \ SUCCESSORS (ACTIVITY)	A0	A1	A2	A3	A4	A5	A6	A7	A8	σ
A0		2	2							4
A1	3									3
A2										
A3	1	1								2
A4										
A5										
A6										
A7										
A8										
σ	4	3	2							

$G_s^2: (G_m^{10})$

PREDECESSORS \ SUCCESSORS (ACTIVITY)	A0	A1	A2	A3	A4	A5	A6	A7	A8	σ
A0		1		2		1				4
A1	2									2
A2										
A3	2									2
A4										
A5		1								1
A6										
A7										
A8										
σ	4	2		2		1				

$G_d^1: (G_m^9)$

PREDECESSORS \ SUCCESSORS (ACTIVITY)	A0	A1	A2	A3	A4	A5	A6	A7	A8	σ
A0		1								1
A1				1					1	2
A2						1				1
A3					2					2
A4									1	1
A5		1		1						2
A6										
A7										
A8	1	1	1							3
σ	1	2	1	2	2	1			3	

$G_d^2: (G_m^4)$

PREDECESSORS \ SUCCESSORS (ACTIVITY)	A0	A1	A2	A3	A4	A5	A6	A7	A8	σ
A0		1	1			2				4
A1	1		1	1		1				4
A2		1								1
A3			1							1
A4						1				1
A5	2	1	1		1					4
A6										
A7										
A8										
σ	3	3	3	1	1	4				

TABLE 2 —cont.

SUBSET MALE TOTAL

ACTIVITY	A0	A1	A2	A3	A4	A5	A6	A7	A8	σ
A0	22	11	3	4	4	10	3		1	36
A1	5	1	3	5	1	4	4			22
A2	5	1				2	2			10
A3	9	1	2	2	2		1			15
A4	1	3		2	1					9
A5	10	5	1	2	3	3	2	3	1	22
A6	7	1	2	1		3	1			17
A7	2									2
A8										
σ	39	22	10	15	11	20	15		4	

SUBSET FEMALE TOTAL

ACTIVITY	A0	A1	A2	A3	A4	A5	A6	A7	A8	σ
A0	23	17	2	11	3	5	2			40
A1	21	3	2	8	1	3	2			37
A2	2	2					1			5
A3	9	5		3	3	7				24
A4	4	2					4			10
A5	3	9		2			4	1		16
A6	3	2	1	3	1		1			10
A7										
A8										
σ	42	37	5	24	9	15	10			

(SET) GRAND TOTAL

ACTIVITY	A0	A1	A2	A3	A4	A5	A6	A7	A8	σ
A0	45	28	5	15	7	15	5		1	76
A1	26	4	5	13	2	7	6			59
A2	7	3				2	3			15
A3	18	6	1	5	5	8	1			39
A4	5	5		5			6			19
A5	13	14	1	4	2	7	4			38
A6	10	3	3	4	4	2	2	1		27
A7	2									2
A8										
σ	81	59	15	39	20	34	25		2	

(σ is the row-sum or colum-sum minus the value in the principal diagonal) cultural activities $A3$. For all of these activities males have higher scores. Ao, which is an obligatory activity category has a greater number of activities preceding and following it than any other activity category. For females, domestic work $A1$ is a close second, and while Ao for females and males shows very little difference, as ought to be the case for physiological-need related activities, the same cannot be said for category $A1$. Thus activity discrimination on an obligatory-discretionary scale is quite obviously sex specific to a considerable degree. Although the particular results that we have referred to may be no more than artifacts of the data classification scheme that we have used, we do not think that this overrides the significance of such a simple device as the incidence matrix in the study of activity structure.

Finally, the 2×2 tables which follow, while in no way graph theoretic, provide a promising point for the investigation of particular attributes of activity structure and sequencing. These tables describe in a simple way the level of choice and degree of expectancy associated with a set of activities undertaken for a period such as a day. For our now familiar graphs $G_s^1\ G_s^2\ G_d^1\ G_d^2$ we have the following situation as described in Table 3.

TABLE 3

G_s^1 CHOICE			G_s^2 CHOICE			G_d^1 CHOICE			G_d^2 CHOICE		
1	0		1	0		1	0		1	0	
1	0	3	1	1	4	1	4	3	1	11	3
0	3	(11)	0	4	1 (10)	0	3	3 (13)	0	3	2 (19)

G_s^1 EXPECTANCY			G_s^2 EXPECTANCY			G_d^1 EXPECTANCY			G_d^2 EXPECTANCY		
1	0		1	0		1	0		1	0	
1	4	1	1	4	1	1	4	3	1	5	6
0	1	5 (11)	0	1	4 (10)	0	3	3 (13)	0	6	2 (19)

(The values in brackets represent the sum of different activities undertaken)

The *bits* 1, 0 represent (1) for maximum choice thought to be associated with a particular activity (discretionary) and (0) minimum choice (obligatory). For G_s^1 in Table 4 on no occasion was a discretionary activity followed by a different type of discretionary activity, but on three occasions a discretionary activity was followed by an obligatory one. On three occasions an obligatory activity was followed by a discretionary one, and on five occasions was followed by another and different obligatory activity. For the expectancy level, unexpected (unplanned in terms of the particular time instant) activities followed unexpected activities four times. Once, an unexpected activity was followed by an expected one, which may be an indicator of activity elasticity.

TABLE 4   Relative isomorphism Non-Squared Values—Digraph with Loops Included

	F1	F2	F3	F4	F5	F6	F7	F8	F9	F10	M1	M2	M3	M4	M5	M6	M7	M8	M9	M10
F1	0·0																			
F2	12·5	0·0																		
F3	20·7	17·5	0·0																	
F4	17·7	13·8	13·8	0·0																
F5	15·1	13·0	15·3	9·6	0·0															
F6	12·3	14·1	16·5	15·9	16·1	0·0														
F7	10·5	6·4	13·5	11·1	6·7	10·3	0·0													
F8	14·3	17·7	17·2	13·8	16·2	12·7	13·8	0·0												
F9	18·2	14·6	15·3	12·6	12·1	19·8	12·2	20·0	0·0											
F10	18·5	12·8	15·0	14·8	12·0	16·2	10·8	15·5	12·1	0·0										
M1	16·7	11·4	14·1	14·3	11·3	14·3	11·2	12·8	15·3	11·2	0·0									
M2	21·7	16·5	5·7	13·2	14·6	17·5	12·5	17·7	16·7	14·3	13·5	0·0								
M3	17·3	17·0	21·9	18·2	20·5	15·7	14·7	19·0	19·2	20·0	17·5	20·7	0·0							
M4	19·7	24·8	21·7	14·8	15·3	19·3	18·8	15·3	18·8	18·2	17·7	18·3	22·3	0·0						
M5	13·5	16·2	14·7	13·8	13·9	14·5	10·1	13·2	14·5	13·4	12·8	13·7	16·4	14·0	0·0					
M6	15·5	8·5	14·1	15·0	16·3	17·5	10·3	15·5	11·0	13·0	13·5	14·8	14·9	20·7	15·3	0·0				
M7	18·3	14·3	18·5	17·9	14·1	16·0	12·1	24·7	17·7	19·0	17·0	17·8	21·7	25·0	20·2	15·5	0·0			
M8	16·9	14·0	15·3	14·6	17·3	18·3	11·5	16·8	15·8	16·5	14·7	12·4	18·0	21·8	16·1	7·7	16·7	0·0		
M9	21·0	18·5	13·3	22·0	20·3	21·3	16·3	17·3	18·7	19·0	19·3	14·3	24·0	26·0	17·0	14·0	21·0	13·3	0·0	
M10	10·7	10·2	12·9	8·7	8·2	11·7	4·2	11·0	14·0	10·5	11·2	12·3	15·7	16·0	9·3	9·8	15·4	11·4	17·0	0·0

That is to say, in spite of being preceded by an unanticipated event at $t-1$, a planned activity at t still occurred.

(c) *On relative isomorphism*

The four graphs G^1_s G^2_s G^1_d G^2_d were selected on the basis of the coefficients derived from a simple measure of relative isomorphism developed in this study. In Table 4 these coefficients are shown as the lower triangle of a symmetric matrix. Values approaching 0·0 mean that a high relative isomorphism exists between a pair of graphs. The 0·0 shown in the diagonal is equivalent to actual isomorphism (in fact automorphism). In Table 5 we have shown the averages of the measures for female and male sub-sets and for the total. The smallest values obtained were 4·2 for G^{10}_m and G^7_f, 5·7 for G^2_m and G^3_f. 6·4 for G^7_f and G^2_f, and 6·7 for G^7_f and G^5_f. The largest coefficients were 26·0 for G^9_m and G^4_m, 25·0 for G^7_f and G^4_m and G^2_f, and 24·7 tor G^7_m and G^8_f. Accordingly we chose G^7_f and G^{10}_m and G^1_s and G^2_s and chose G^4_m and G^9_m as G^1_d and G^2_d.

TABLE 5   Averages for Non-Square Values of Relative Isomorphism

Digraph no.	Sex Average	Total Average
F1	15·53	16·37
F2	13·97	14·59
F3	16·12	15·66
F4	14·05	14·69
F5	12·93	14·13
F6	14·90	15·81
F7	10·60	11·44
F8	15·70	16·05
F9	15·22	15·73
F10	14·20	14·89
M1	15·25	14·21
M2	15·32	15·17
M3	19·02	18·67
M4	20·21	19·40
M5	14·98	14·36
M6	14·03	13·85
M7	18·92	18·06
M8	14·68	15·23
M9	18·44	18·62
M10	13·12	11·59

$$\overline{F} = 14\cdot32 \qquad \overline{FT} = 14\cdot94$$
$$\overline{M} = 16\cdot40 \qquad \overline{MT} = 15\cdot92$$
$$\overline{F+M} = 15\cdot36 \qquad \overline{FT+MT} = 15\cdot43$$

$\overline{F}$ is female average
$\overline{M}$ is male average

The isomorphism measure was computed as follows. Suppose G^1 and G^2 are two graphs with the same vertex-sets, and suppose G^k and d^k_{ij} edges from vertex i to vertex j. Then

$$D_{ij} = \frac{\left| d^1_{ij} - d^2_{ij} \right|}{d^1_{ij} + d^2_{ij}}$$

(where $|X|$ denotes the absolute value of X and d^x is a descriptive superscript and not an exponent) is a measure of the difference between the two graphs in the (ij) connection. If they are identical, D_{ij} will be zero for all i and j. The factor $(d^1_{ij} + d^2_{ij}) - 1$ seems to be a reasonable way of weighting the relative importance of differences. The fact that one graph has two more edges (i, j) than another is relatively unimportant when the graphs have a lot of vertices joining one to another, but quite important when they do not—and this is precisely the case when $d^1_{ij} + d^2_{ij}$ is smallest. Our isomorphism measure is just

$$\Sigma \Sigma D_{ij},$$

where the sums are taken over all pairs (ij) and where $D_{ij} = 0$ when there are edges (ij) in either graph. This means the formula we used is

$$\Delta 12 = \sum_{i=0}^{8} \sum_{j=0}^{8} \frac{\left| d^1_{ij} - d^2_{ij} \right|}{d^1_{ij} + d^2_{ij}}$$

$$d^1_{ij} + d^2_{ij} \neq 0$$

Applied to undirected graphs, the measure would be summed over all i and over j equal to or greater than i, to avoid double counting.

This choice of a measure has been quite arbitrary. Two other measures were considered—one being

$$\frac{\Sigma \Sigma (d^1_{ij} - d^2_{ij})^2}{d^1_{ij} + d^2_{ij}}$$

$$\frac{\Sigma \Sigma \left| d_{ij} - d_{ij} \right|}{\max d^1_{ij}, d^2_{ij}}$$

The final choice of measure was made on purely subjective grounds, after examining the figures resulting.

There are other problems associated with measures of similarity or relative isomorphism. For example, suppose G^1, G^2, G^3, G^4 are graphs which are to be tested for isomorphism: G^1 and G^2 have n vertices each, while G^3 and G^4 have m vertices each. How should $\Delta 12$ and $\Delta 34$ be compared? This problem does not, of course, arise in our present study, as all graphs have nine vertices, but if m and n are unequal, there is a serious problem. Our intuition is that in order to achieve a standardized measure, Δij should be divided by the sum of the number of vertices in G^i (and G^j). We shall investigate the problem further at a later date.

In any event, the graphs which are 'closer to isomorphic' or 'less dissimilar' under our measure appear to be so in fact, according to judgements based on visual scrutiny of the graphs.

Other measures of similarity of sequence might involve the triples or higher order sub-sequences. We have not attempted any calculations of this sort as yet, but clearly our formula can be generalized to cover these cases. The most similar pair by our measure of relative isomorphism also appear to have very similar triple structure (Table 1).

(d) Connectivity

The concepts of *connectivity* and *edge connectivity* were defined earlier.[6] We shall be concerned essentially with the edge connectivity, because it seems to us at present to fit better with our intuitive ideas of connectivity in the case of multiple edges. For example, Figure 8 shows four graphs; under each is shown its connectivity κ and its edge-connectivity ϵ.

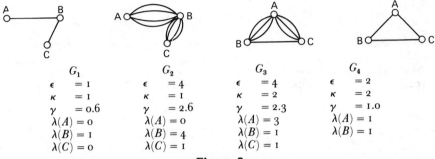

	G_1	G_2	G_3	G_4
ϵ	= 1	= 4	= 4	= 2
κ	= 1	= 1	= 2	= 2
γ	= 0.6	= 2.6	= 2.3	= 1.0
$\lambda(A)$	= 0	= 0	= 3	= 1
$\lambda(B)$	= 1	= 4	= 1	= 1
$\lambda(C)$	= 0	= 1	= 1	

Figure 8

For our sort of purposes we wish to think of G_2 and G_3 as being noticeably more connected than G_1 and G_4, and there is no way we want to consider G_4 as being more connected than G_2, or G_1 and G_2 as having the same connectivity. Of course, different types of data—especially data in which multiple edges were rare—might require different measures, and the ordinary connectivity might be more appropriate then.

In order to measure how *critical* a particular activity is, i.e. its relative importance as a link between different types of activity, we are trying to develop a measure which might be called a *linkage coefficient* of a vertex. One possible candidate for the linkage coefficient of a vertex v is $\lambda(v)$ defined by the formula

$$\lambda(v) = \epsilon(G) - \epsilon(G - v)$$

where G is the original graph (with any isolated vertices deleted), $G - v$ is the graph derived from G by deleting precisely the vertex v and all edges which touch it, and ϵ denotes strong edge-connectivity in the case of digraphs, and edge-connectivity in the case of undirected graphs. However there are some obvious difficulties involved in the interpretation of λ; for example the existence of vertices of very low valency may lead to anomalous results. A higher linkage coefficient will suggest a more critical role.

One would expect the linkage coefficient to have little meaning in small graphs, where the edge-connectivity was small. Another anomaly can occur when *one* vertex has very low valency. For example, consider the graph of Figure 9. This has $\lambda(v) = 5$ simply because of the one vertex w which has small valency. To avoid such anomalies we would only suggest using it on dense graphs and digraphs, such as the graph of all subjects (see Table 2)—and that

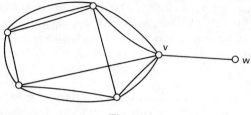

Figure 9

even in these cases, vertices of small valency (such as $A7$ and $A8$) should be deleted.

To clarify the calculation of λ, we now give an example. Consider the digraph G of Figure 10. (Numbers next to edges denote the multiplicity of edges in the direction shown.) $\epsilon(G) = 5$. We find that $\epsilon(G-a) = 5$, $\epsilon(G-b) = 0$, $\epsilon(G-c) = 7$ and $\epsilon(G-d) = 0$, so $\lambda(a) = 0$, $\lambda(b) = 5$, $\lambda(c) = -2$ and $\lambda(d) = 5$. As a further example, the linkage coefficients have been added to Figure 8.

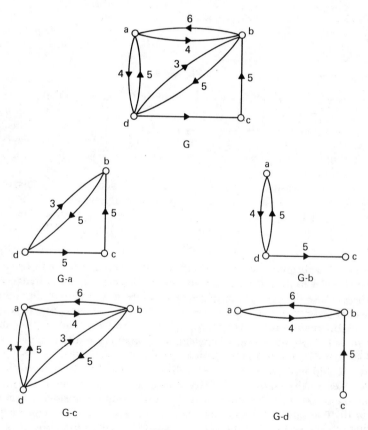

Figure 10

Suppose the data are such that our $\lambda(v)$ is an acceptable measure of linkage. Consider the case where the deletion of vertex v causes a 'large' drop in the edge connectivity of G, where $\lambda(v)$ is relatively large compared with $\epsilon(G)$ and that $\epsilon(G-v)$ is only a small part of $\epsilon(G)$. One interpretation is that v acts as a pivot between two sets of activities which are not closely related to each other. Our activity category 6 would normally be such a pivot. This leads us to consider the connectedness of parts of a large graph.

Consider again the 'sequence of activities which can be viewed as activity modules' (Cullen and Godson 1975, p. 6). Such sequences can be studied by hypergraphs if data are sufficiently large, as we have suggested above; but they may also appear as parts of subsets which are highly connected.

We suggest as an additional idea to the activity module concept a set of activities which are frequently *directly linked*, in which it is often true that one of the set directly follows another. This is a different idea, but one which may well lead to new structural information about activity patterns.

We need to examine the connectivity of sub-graphs in relation to the connectivity of the whole graph. By the *induced* sub-graph on a set of vertices we mean the sub-graph whose vertex set is the set of vertices and whose edges are all the edges of the original graph which joins two vertices in the set. We shall define the *strong connectivity* of a set of vertices to be the strong edge —connectivity of the induced sub-graph on the set. A *set of high connectivity* is a set whose connectivity is greater than the strong edge connectivity of the original graph. A *compact* set is one in which the addition of any vertex decreases the connectivity of the set.

If a large graph is obtained (say the union of X days diaries of the sort we have used for only a single day) for each subject, one can investigate the compact sets of high connectivity for individuals. (Our data are—intentionally —too small for such a study to be carried out). Various possible interpretations will arise. For example, at our scale of enquiry, traditional views would suggest that activity $A6$ and activity $A2$ should form a compact set for male subjects but not for female subjects. But questions as to which are the most prevalent compact sets, and why, in different geographical or social spaces, form an area which we consider to be worthy of further study.

The possibilities for effective manipulation of human behaviour are improved if critical activities can be identified. Just what 'effective manipulation' might mean of course is dependent on the nature of the normative objectives of the agency with power of authority to initiate change (for instance statutory government planning bodies or industrial and commercial management in shift rostering schemes). However, while a vertex (v) with a high linkage coefficient $\lambda(v)$ might indicate the most probable critical or pivotal activities in some set, it is clearly not the case that a vertex with a low linkage coefficient may not be critical, or pivotal in certain circumstances. Levels of stress may result from the need to develop complex coping strategies if a particular activity is no longer possible or is possible only after a considerable rescheduling of a given activity profile, within a finite time period such as a day.

These and other ideas expressed in this essay seem to fit quite comfortably within the conceptual frame of this book, in that the timing of space and the spacing of time seem to be the very essence of human activity dynamics.

Concluding remarks

This paper has considered certain aspects of activity structure analysis through the use of simple graph theoretic methods. The study of human activity may be approached in a number of ways. In this paper and in other essays included in this book some of these approaches have been outlined. Specifically, our perspective has been towards methods of activity structure identification. In other words it has been with the descriptive modelling of human behaviours, set in some socially familiar cycle such as the day. The individual has been the object of our analysis. Activity classes have been the manifest basis for examining behaviour.

Although our data set has been small and our activity classification scheme coarse, there is no reason why the principles of activity structure analysis which we have tried to present should not be applicable to much larger numbers and much finer classificatory schemes. In fact, as we have suggested, certain graph theoretic methods become more powerful as the vertex set (activity set) increases, through use of hypergraphs for instance. Certain other advantages of using combinatorial methods have been suggested above. This does not discount the fact that multivariate parametric methods such as those used by Cullen (chapter 2) have an important role to play.

With further study of activity and graph theoretic methods it will be possible to develop measures of relative isomorphism and linkage for instance, which are more stable than those we have proposed. Hopefully some interested readers will take up this challenge.

ACKNOWLEDGEMENT

This study was partially supported by the Australian Research Grant Committee (ARGC) through its support of work being undertaken by Professor Wallis into the construction and investigation of block designs.

Footnotes

[1] Although not considered in this essay there are certain operations which can be performed on the incidence matrix which do provide valuable additional information about structure. The most familiar operations relate to the powering of the matrix. For instance the second power of the incidence matrix for Figure 1 will isolate all two-step linkages between the vertices (activities). If the rows of the incidence matrix represent *predecessor* activities and the columns represent *successor* activities, then row and column sums may be thought of as summarizing the 'status' of the activity in terms of predecessor and successor characteristics. An activity with a zero row sum after raising to the pth power may be thought of as a *terminus*, no activities ever follow it. In terms of the study of activity structure, a *detour* matrix of a digraph may be particularly useful; it simply represents the length of the longest path from i to j and is ∞ if there is no path (Harary 1969, p. 199).

[2] The planning and scheduling of commercial, industrial and engineering *projects* is often approached by graph theoretic methods known as CPM and PERT. The Critical Path Method (CPM) and the Programme Evaluation and Review Technique (PERT) differ from the approach taken here in that EDGES represent activities with weights

related to durations, hence weighted digraphs are developed, and VERTICES represent (what are confusingly called *events* in some texts) the beginning and end of activities. Numerous interrelated activities may be analysed and programmed by these methods. Such activity graphs are by their nature acyclic and this condition is not always going to be acceptable in human activity analyses of the sort we are likely to be interested in social sciences. There is certainly considerable scope for the direct application of these established methods of project or activity analysis to social activity studies and accepting that certain activity studies have used the vertex to represent the activity (Deo 1974, p. 408) as we have done; so far as we are aware there have been no attempts to compare and describe *activity structures* using graph theory in the way we are proposing.

[3] Observe that terminology varies from text to text in some parts of Graph Theory; in particular Harary (1969) uses 'unilaterally connected' for what we define as 'connected' digraphs.

[4] For technical reasons it is necessary to define separately the connectivity of a 'complete' graph, one in which every vertex is joined to every other by at least one edge. Such a graph has connectivity equal to its number of vertices. A similar remark applies to the strong connectivity of a 'complete' directed graph.

[5] Only brief attention will be given to these aspects of the 'diary' later in this section. We hope to develop our ideas relating to choice level and 'expectancy' in future work.

[6] In transport and settlement-linkage studies in geography the gamma index is a familiar measure of connectivity. For planar graphs it is simply

$$\gamma = \frac{e}{3(v-2)}$$

and for non-planar graphs

$$\gamma = \frac{e}{v(v-1)}$$

The index will vary between 0 and 1. (With multigraphs as in Figure 8 this range does not hold.) This measure is not very useful for our purposes.

Chapter 6
The Colonization of Time
Murray Melbin

The last great frontier of human migration is occurring in time—a spreading of wakeful activity throughout the twenty-four hours of the day. There is more multiple-shift factory work, more police coverage, more use of the telephone at all hours. There are more hospitals, pharmacies, aeroplane flights, hotels, always-open restaurants, car rental and petrol and auto repair stations, bowling alleys, and radio stations always active. There are more emergency services such as auto towing, locksmiths, bail bondsmen, drug and poison and suicide and gambling 'hot lines' available incessantly. Although different individuals participate in these events in shifts, the organizations involved are continually active.

It is useful to speak of this growth as *colonization*. It parallels the human occupation of space, and attention to the similarities will help us better understand the four-dimensional space-time context of social life. First, time is part of the container. It is occupied along with space, if we think of filling it with people and activities rather than with people and structures. Secondly, expansion by using more hours of the day leads from well-used hours into adjacent ones. As with geographic migration, this is initially the venture of a few bold pioneers. What is first a tenuous foothold later becomes an established colony. Some industrial plants, transportation systems, and newspapers have operated incessantly for more than a century. We know that St Augustine was the first European settlement within the boundaries of the United States, but it will be harder to learn the name of its first twenty-four-hour restaurant. And although they are relative newcomers, the gambling casinos of Las Vegas are among the densest and most vigorous permanent settlements on the twenty-four-hour scene. Just as great land areas on Earth are still not occupied by humans, so activities continue to be sparse during the early hours of the morning. Yet even in cities about which it is said 'they roll up the sidewalks at ten in the evening', there is still likely to be all-night police and telephone coverage, a late-hours dining place, and perhaps some truckers delivering foodstuffs to the local stores during the dark. Luther College (Decorah, Iowa, USA) decided to keep its student union open until midnight because nothing else for young people was open in the town. We can speak of *density in time*. We can perhaps measure it according to the number of different activities and the number of people involved in them hour by hour. The *temporal ecology* becomes an issue—the relative proportions and different types of people who are up and about outside their residences around the clock.

The spant

The expansion in time is taking place largely in urban areas. In this respect the growth of cities is outracing our concepts and our research. We have not studied systematically the circadian cycle of human *social* life. There is not even a single word to refer to the four-dimensional space-time unit that is actively occupied. There is no comprehensive knowledge about the scope of activities showing this trend. Government bureaux do not assemble adequate data of this type. (An estimate for the state of Massachusetts set the labour-force figure at 4 per cent of the industrial work force, but the recreation, entertainment, and service industries deserve to be counted too.) There is no clearly economical, advantageous way to start gathering this information.

Of course growth of activity in time never happens without the use of space as well. I point to the temporal aspect because it has been neglected. We have the discipline of geography but where are the volumes on *tempography*? Where, outside of philosophy and relativity physics, are the writings about the four-dimensional existence of which we all partake? It is no trivial item that the word geography is familiar to grade-schoolers while tempography is a word I coined in order to make this point.

The words and the lack of a word are telling. A single word matters because objects of thought that are familiar are often phrased in abbreviated form for easy utterance. Brown proposes that the shortness of a name for a category is directly related to the ease of perceiving and thinking about that category, and to the readiness with which a community will agree about what is being referred to. There is a tendency—in a variety of languages—for word brevity (whether measured in phonemes or syllables) to be associated with greater frequency of usage (Brown 1958, pp. 235-41).

Though Locke asserted that 'expansion and duration mutually embrace and comprehend each other' (Bk. II, Ch. xv), he did not bestow a name on this union. Minkowski declared that space by itself and time by itself were doomed to fade from scholarly thought, but he neglected to suggest a phrase for their combined reality. Einstein did not use the same phrase consistently (cf. Einstein 1922). One of his shortest references was to a 'Minkowski space', and one of his favourites was the lengthy 'four-dimensional space-time continuum'. Alexander termed a space-time point a 'pure event', but the name did not catch on (Alexander 1920, p. 48). Some present-day physicists use the word 'interval' in this sense. It is not so apt because it may be confused with the interval of pitch in music, or with confidence intervals in statistics.

I suggest the term *spant*, an acronym for *SP*ace *AN*d *T*ime unit. The size of a spant could be noted as appropriately needed, by subscripts referring precisely to longitudes, latitudes, dates and hours of the day,. Several diverse understandings suggest themselves for this label. History is the study of spants. A treatise on Elizabethan England refers to a certain place during a certain era. When a parent tells a youngster 'this is not the time or the place to behave like that', the child-rearing effort has been focused on a spant. The idea of human density is improved by thinking of *people-per-spant*. For if urban crowding has a significant psychological impact, then four-dimensional density is conceptually and methodologically superior to three-dimensional density in dealing with the experience. Measuring people-per spant may help explain why some recent studies have found no link between mere spatial crowding and social pathology, while earlier studies and some hypotheses say that these are linked.

The ebb and flow of people in cities occurs in the four-dimensional sphere. To chart a city in spants, one would have to set the sizes of the space and time boundaries per unit. It could be one hundred metres square times one storey high (if there are buildings on the site) times one hour, or the unit spants may be one cubic kilometre times six hours. To be sure, far fewer of the latter sized units would be needed to encompass a city. In either case the amount of wakeful activity varies among the units. The spants for day-time in the central business district will be very dense. Those for night-time in the same place will be extremely sparse. It will be conspicuously more manageable and precise to use spants than having to say 'traffic on the South Circular Road is most congested during the evening rush hour on weekdays'.

We can trace movements of individuals along series of spants. Two people may not encounter one another merely by having been in the same place. Nor are there good odds that they will meet just because they are up and outside their dwellings at the same time. They will probably meet if they are in the same spant. Making appointments is just that—agreeing to join one another in a given small spant.

To interpret this trend of growth in the number of active hours, I assume that there is a predominant daily cycle of human activity, concentrated in the day-light period from sun-up to sunset. Colonization, then, begins with migration into pre-dawn and post-nightfall times. Active use of the maximum twenty-four hours I will call *incessance*. I now turn to a prime question about this trend: What are its causes?

Causes of extending the active day

This expansion is like the geographical spreading that took place in earlier times across the face of the Earth. Certain resources and technologies have to be at hand to accomplish the moves. There are various pressures to disperse. There are lures as well, to move in certain directions. For example, Hawley (1950) writes that the cause of spatial migration is twofold, consisting of an excess of numbers in the area of origin and underpopulation in the area of destination. And the ability to live permanently in a new realm is resolved by mutual influences among a number of factors—such as ability to endure hardships, and being able to ensure adequate steady supplies of needed resources. I will discuss these causes, which ordinarily work in combination, as *enabling factors*, *demand push*, *supply pull*, and *stabilizing feedback*.

Enabling Factors

A number of important achievements over the centuries lie behind the enlargement of the active day. These include improvements in street and house lighting and the development of long-distance transportation and communication technologies. Bellan notes that the introduction of coal-gas illumination along throughfares enabled people to come and go as never before. It not only made night work feasible, but permitted the emergence of the modern night-time entertainment industry (1971, pp. 67–8).

The developments of the telephone, the wireless, and more recently the communications satellite have brought all time zones around the globe into a single instant-access network. For the multiple embassies of more than one hundred nations that are in constant contact with their capitals, the news networks, the field offices of international corporations that keep in touch with their firms' headquarters, worldwide brokerage offices, military organizations and commercial airlines that maintain contact among their widespread bases, the communications system makes it possible for people to be in touch with one another even if they are out of phase in time. Someone in Manilla in the early afternoon who telephones New York will rouse his party at 1 a.m. Thus people do not have to be physically close in order to be drawn into activity at all hours. The ports, train and bus terminals, and airports provide similar opportunities around the clock. Passengers can arrive and disembark and cargo can be unloaded at any time.

Two other factors deserve acknowledgement. One is the availability of a labour pool, since much late-day or early-day activity depends upon employed persons. The other factor, in the city, is heat. Lowry explains how cities tend to be warmer than the surrounding countryside. The city's masses of buildings and pavements accept, store, and conduct heat faster than does wet, sandy soil. The activities of its inhabitants are a considerable source of heat in addition to that coming from the sun. At night the concrete sidewalks and brick buildings still give off heat stored up during the day (Lowry 1967, p. 15). Ehrlich and his colleagues estimate that the heat released by human activities in large urban regions is equivalent to 5 per cent or more of the incident solar energy falling on those regions (Ehrlich *et al.* 1973, p. 15). Since more people go out into the streets under warmer conditions, the city uniquely provides extra aid to being up and about long after dark.

Demand Push

Demand is a most impelling force to extend the active day. As suggested in the preceding section, some stimulation comes from outside the city. Outputs from one location are inputs to another. Workers are mobilized to unload the planes, trains, trucks and ships that arrive. Taxis are marshalled to transfer people from arrival points. Inasmuch as a portion of the travellers go to hotels, the staffs of those organizations are roused to accommodate them. Similarly, governmental and commercial telephone lines carry newsworthy messages that prompt people in faraway places to go into action. A more stable form of this demand is the time-zone relationship between a dominant institution and its liaisons elsewhere. A securities dealer in Beirut stays open late to maintain contact with the Paris Bourse and the London Stock Exchange. A federal office in San Francisco begins earlier than usual because its operations are tied to its headquarters in Washington DC.

By *chained activity phases* I mean a series of procedures, each of which depends on an event preceding it and in turn prompts another that follows. The chain reaction set off by disembarking passengers mentioned above is an example. Such sequences have been extended also into the early hours to meet the daily nutritional demands of an urban region. Deliveries of fresh foods must be made between 7 and 9 a.m. to be in the shops at opening time, necessitating purchase and loading at the wholesale markets to go on from 5 to 7 a.m. Since truckers will bring in the foodstuffs from outlying districts, and need travel time before then, farmers must rise at 2 a.m. to gather eggs, fresh produce, and dairy products in time for the trucks' departure.

The complexities of today's civilization foster evening and night activity. There are more scientific laboratories about. Those that house plants and animals sometimes require surveillance at all hours. Rising crime rates call for more police surveillance at all hours. The need for faster customer service and more management information has dictated late hours at banks and offices (*Wall Street Journal* 1967). Elecricity, gas, telephone, hospital, police and fire protection have become incessant utilities. The demand for service as a proportion of total activity has been increasing. Services, especially emergency forms, have to be available whenever people need them. So skeleton staffs are usually on duty, and always on call, at ambulance fleets, locksmiths, plate glass installers, bail bondsmen, insect exterminators, auto towing stations, and car hire agencies.

By *density push* I refer to crowded conditions in one time period driving people and their activities out of that period into earlier or later time spans. In the first century A.D., Rome was obliged to relieve its congestion by restricting chariot traffic to the night hours (Tomlinson 1969, p. 243). Today, because there is often no room to build another airport in a metropolitan area, the terminals restrict their cargo operations until night-time when passenger traffic declines. Individual commuters choose to travel to work earlier to avoid the 'crush hour'. In 1974 this tactic was adopted by the Mid-Town Task Force, which appealed to 1,000 New York companies to change their scheduled hours in order to help alleviate commuter congestion. Meier, citing a similar case of work-staggering for a section of Moscow, proposes that this timing plan and the strategy of wholesale multiple shifting is a way of creating space (1967, pp. 575–6).

Economic motives count heavily in organization-based expansion into early and late hours. Night work is resorted to when the demand for a product cannot be met by normal day operation of a plant and when it is impossible or inadvisable to expand plant and equipment (National Industrial Conference Board, pp. 1–2).

Yet while economic reasons help explain much of the movement, this growth has a non-economic base as well. For example, when a tornado wrecked a high school on the southeast coast of the United States, a full second shift was introduced in the evening at another high school nearby to house the displaced students.

A subtler, individualistic movement resembling emigration to escape persecution also takes place. The city harbours a myriad of life styles, some more deviant than others. There dwell individuals who are treated publicly as deviants, such as homosexuals, people with a physical stigma (deformed, obese, ugly), and social stigma (pimps, former mental patients, petty criminals). Contacts between the majority and deviant individuals are often strained and tinged with intolerance and harassment. So the deviants escape into emptier spants where fewer confrontations occur, and live more at ease in their newly established territory.

Finally there is *secondary demand* generated by the initial moves. CBS Radio estimated that 25 per cent of the industrial workers in the United States were employed on non-daytime shifts. (*Newsweek* 1973a). Such a pattern requires structures of support. The lonely guards and watchmen scattered throughout the region seek radio programmes and television broadcasts to keep them company. Regular arrangements must be made for protecting, feeding and transporting workers. They also need shopping centres open at hours convenient to them, and auto service stations. These enterprises then invade those hours too. Again, though economic forces predominate, secondary demand is spurred in other ways as well. At the Polaroid Corporation in Massachusetts, an in-house educational programme was started, through which employees could receive instruction during periods on the job. At first this was offered only to workers on the day shift, but the courses were so popular that night-shift personnel demanded the same educational privileges. The corporation in 1973 established a night-shift schedule of courses, which in turn called for hiring teachers to work at those hours too.

Supply Pull

Richardson notes that with few exceptions theories of urban growth are demand oriented (1971, p. 193). That would not do to account for the growth in time. Certain resources, available during the vacant hours, attract people and activities to them. In this way the pressures of demand are augmented by the lures of supply. And those who own or control such resources try to maximize and smooth their usage.

A *maximizing* strategy is one in which deliberate additional use is made of facilities at hand, in order to reduce the overall cost of owning them, by drawing the greatest possible yield from them. A form of this was recognized by Marx a century ago. He pointed out that multiple shifting in factories was often introduced without concern for workers' lives in order to utilize idle plant capacity (Marx 1867, III, x, p. 4). This scheme is understandably more common in capital-intensive undertakings. In the past this was limited mainly to the manufacturing industry, but expensive equipment is now more widely used. For example, the high cost, rapid obsolescence, and liberal depreciation allowances for tax purposes have become incentives for keeping electronic computers busy around the clock in banking, insurance, and brokerage firms and in universities. Also, where shutdown and startup costs are prohibitive, as in metal smelting because of the lengthy cooling and heating periods for the furnaces, incessant operation is inherent in the decision to build the plant in the first place. The aluminium smelters at Alcan's Arvida works in Quebec have been in continuous operation since 1957.

The quest for full exploitation of facilities has spread beyond industry and commerce. Citizens concerned over the high cost of building schools argue that the same educational facility should be used on a two- or three-shift basis instead of constructing more class-rooms that will remain empty twelve to sixteen hours a day. A Boston lawyer suggested using vacant courthouses at night for job training, family counselling, and public meetings. He maintained that the huge public capital investment in courthouses was largely wasted by the failure to utilize the buildings after regular court business (Doherty 1973).

A *smoothing* strategy aims to even the load on facilities by making off-hour usage more attractive, thereby redistributing the demand. This is tried where building a facility to cope with peak demand entails huge capital costs, but the daily cycle of demand fluctuates widely. Electricity, transportation and telephone usage are familiar examples. Their activity levels keep rising, straining equipment that was installed to deal with peak loads of former eras. When further plant and equipment investment is hard to justify on economic grounds, the organizations turn to pricing tactics. Pricing smoothes the 'load curve' by luring more activity into slack periods through combining bargain rates for usage then with high charges during peak demand periods. In the United States the cost of a long-distance telephone call fluctuates with the load curve for the trunk lines. It is highest during weekday daytimes and far lower after nine p.m. and on Sundays. Eastern Air Lines, to cite another instance, advertised 'The cost of living goes up every day, but the cost of leaving goes down every night,' and offered 20 per cent fare reductions on its flights leaving after nine in the evening (*New York Times* 1973a).

Another reason for increased activity in the off-hours can be labelled *inducement*. The sheer availability of an opportunity induces some people to seize it. Janelle refers to studies showing that new bridges and roads will attract considerably more traffic than can be accounted for by the diverted traffic alone (1968a p. 488). If a grocery store stayed open to tap the custom of night workers, some day workers would patronize it at three in the morning just for the experience. Galbraith termed it the *dependence effect*—in which wants are increasingly created through the process by which they are satisfied. (Galbraith 1958 pp. 128–9). Colby offered the related idea of *functional magnetism*—in which the concentration of one activity in an area raises awareness about its attractiveness, and related activities are drawn in. In one suburb of Boston, for example, a drive-in movie was built in a large field that heretofore had been the domain of chirping crickets after dark. Drive-in cinemas, of course, wait for nightfall to begin functioning. This structure was followed soon by two ice-cream parlours, for people were habitually coming early and waiting around the cinema, and then by a miniature golf course. One year later a restaurant opened for business. Now that customers flock to the area in all seasons (not only summers, the drive-in movie season) an indoor cinema is being built.

This secondary inducement is like the secondary demand cited in the preceding section. A major organized activity draws a population to it. Then other satellite enterprises are attracted by that population. Dining places stay open late near universities, cinemas, and three-shift factories. Breakfast parlours open early near wholesale food and flower markets. Taxicabs line up at office building entrances at change-of-shift times. Chemists shops remain open longer near hospitals. Inns and hotels establish themselves adjacent to airports (cf. Gottmann 1972, p. 510). Rent-a-car agencies remain open to serve passengers arriving in transportation terminals. Where people use their autos for late shopping and dining and recreation, fuel and service stations attend them too.

A large cadre of cooks, waiters, drivers, desk clerks, store clerks, mechanics, porters and small entrepreneurs are drawn into off-hours employment in this way. Secondary inducement suggests that a precondition of such growth is a social organization which includes an advanced division of labour. It also implies a rather orderly expansion from primary to secondary forms, and the possibility of forecasting its course upon noting the first signs of lengthening the active day.

The secondary expansion may come full circle in a mutually amplifying process. The time expansion of one large company is enough to pull a coffee shop into its spant, but many shops and services are required to entice another large company to extend its hours. Once a number of satellite services are present in a spant, a management which had been loath to assume the added costs of providing all these services for its employees may now perceive that it is feasible to lengthen the organization's active day.

Stabilizing Feedback

Growth in any system is never unrestrained. In the case of city time there are also various counteracting forces at work. We can understand some of these as *limiting factors*, cousins of the enabling factors I described in the first section on causes. The following notes would belong in that section above, but it suited my discussion to introduce them at this point. In any case all the causes operate together.

Social barriers are sources of limiting conditions. Inasmuch as public transit systems close down shortly after midnight, many inhabitants return to their homes by then rather than stay out later. Zoning ordinances, which have been rigidly applied in some cities, were designed to keep functions separate. They therefore suppress wakeful activities at night in some areas while permitting them in others. The labour agreement between the League of New York Theatres and Producers and Local One of the Stagehands' union calls for penalty payments if a performance runs later than a certain hour.

Another reason is that each active spant in human society depends on a sustaining base which is geographically and temporally larger than its own boundaries. Whenever the point is reached at which a regularly patterned activity engages almost all of the available population, it will inhibit the emergence of similar pursuits in adjacent spants. Beyond those points the labour pool and the pool of clientele cannot support further growth. In Boston in 1974, a supermarket that was located between two others a mile apart which were open twenty-four hours a day, changed its schedule to be always open. Within six months it had retracted its hours. Apparently it drew customers from the same catchment area and there was not enough custom for all three stores. Thus cities will have incessantly-active centres supported by cyclic hinterlands.

The growth in time spurs negative feedback as well. One of the most potent suppressors of more late-phased activity is *crime*, which acts back upon the growth to quell it. As more people are up and about, those who prey on them increase their endeavours as well. Small, isolated businesses like newsstands and drugstores are especially vulnerable. The newsstand dealers in the Greenwich Village area of New York are closing earlier. They say they are scared of holdups, of harassment, and that their after-dark customers have been driven off. (Kotuk 1971). Druggists from the greater Boston area met in 1972 to discuss the possibility of closing their stores at six p.m. for a week to drama-tize their need for protection against robberies (*Boston Globe*). Some churches in a section of Boston have abandoned evening mass because elderly worshippers were being mugged. Hundreds of licensed cabs sit idle on the late night shift because drivers, fearful of robbery or assault, will not take them out then (Prial 1972). This in turn results in more citizen protest, which leads to increased street illumination and improved police coverage, which to some extent offsets the danger. So crime is both a depressant and indirectly a stimulus to afterdark activity.'

A sudden change in availability of an enabling resource may also reverse this expansion. Such a shortage befell the United States during the 1973–4 winter. It is so instructive in its impact that I have allocated a separate section in which to report and analyse the events.

Loss of an Enabling Factor: The Oil/Energy Shortage

Energy is one of the basic requirements for growth after dark and for sus-taining any given bustling level. In the waning weeks of 1973 the United States was suddenly plunged into an 'energy crisis', as it came to be called. It was due to restriction of shipments of crude oil from Arab lands and sharply higher prices for the amounts that were shipped. Individual consumers, such as car users and business enterprises, felt the shortage because of deliberate witholding of emergency supplies in the US and costlier rates for refined products such as petrol and heating fuel. So the shortage was due as much to higher costs as to under-supply. That crisis ended four months after it began, with the resumption of shipments from the major oil exporters.

During that period I studied the impact of this event upon the hours open of establishments serving the public. The nature of such establishments, in contrast to private organizations like factories, is that their operation is sus-tained by direct participation of a wide segment of the populace, much broader than the portion employed by the organizations.

In March 1974 we contacted all known twenty-four-hour organizations, and all that stayed open after midnight in the city of Boston and its immediate neighbours—Brookline, Cambridge and Somerville. As I noted earlier in this essay, there is no comprehensive knowledge about the scope and amount of extended-day activity, so that straightforward sampling was impossible. We resorted to several lists of late-night establishments and energetic first-hand enquiries. Because I had been collecting such information for several years, my conservative estimate is that at least 80 per cent of the organizations open to the public after midnight were caught in our net. We then *matched* these organizations by selecting ones of the same type, in the same neighbourhoods, whose hours were shorter or of the one-shift length.

We learned what the open hours had been before the crisis for each organiza-tion, and whether a change in hours had been made in response to it. The hours open varied from the single eight- or nine-hour shift through a range of extended-day activity such as one-and-a-half shifts (many supermarkets) and two shifts (many eating places) to incessant organizations. A number of petrol stations were included in our list. Since all of these reported cutbacks to single shifts, and since this group's response to the shortage is understandable and would distort the overall findings, I have omitted them from the analysis that follows.

Table 1 shows the distribution of the remaining 139 organizations by type and by how late they were open before the energy crisis. The categories of organizational types are arrayed in order from the most vital and least substitutable services to the least vital and most substitutable forms. How long the establishments kept open before the crisis is given across the top of the table grouped into three clusters: A-regular day, an eight- or nine-hour span beginning and ending in the daytime; B-extended day, a longer span, usually beginning near daybreak and continuing after dark; and C-incessant, open all day and all night.

The table also shows the reported cutbacks in active hours among these establishments, eight such instances (or six per cent). There were no reductions in service by the most vital (and least substitutable) organizations, categories one through four. It is plausible that this pattern would be repeated in future energy shortages. Essential services would be maintained if possible and non-essential services would be curtailed first. The retail food or merchandise outlets (category four) reported no reductions in hours, perhaps because people gave more importance to shopping for their needs than to dining out and allocated their automobile fuel accordingly.

Of the organizations that reduced their hours, there was one of the twenty-one group A types (4·8 per cent), six of the fifty-three B types (11·3 per cent), and only one of the 65 group C types (1·5 per cent). These differences yielded a chi square of 3·374 which, in spite of the small expected frequencies in some of the cells, is close to an acceptable level of statistical significance. It is noteworthy that *most of the cutbacks in hours befell establishments with intermediate-length schedules*, while the incessant organizations—open the maximum possible span —showed the lowest rate of reducing their active hours in this initial response to the shortage.

The daily single work-shift of group A is the most common schedule in the community, an intact eight- or nine-hour period ending sometime between five p.m. and seven p.m. It would be difficult to shorten because it would imply a reduction in work hours below 'full time' employment in conjunction with the widespread five-day forty-hour work week in the United States. Group A's establishments followed the minimal open-for-business time span, well-embedded in community practices and supported by its norms. Group B's organizations, open more than a single work shift but less than the maximum possible each day, reflect the customary demands for their goods and services by their clients. But apparently the norms for hours open are weak or uncertain for this intermediate group, and it is the most susceptible to a curtailment in energy supply.

Group C's organizations are always open. Since these units resisted the initial blow of the energy shortage while the *same types* in Group B succumbed to it, time itself was probably significant. The theme of twenty-four-hour activity promotes an image of access in the public mind, unending access. Administrators of emergency-service units (categories one and two) follow a moral

TABLE I

Types of organizations	A Regular day: no later than 7 p.m	B Extended day: from 12 to 23 hours[a]	C Incessant: open 24 hours	Σ	A Regular day	B Extended day	C Incessant	Σ
	Active hours before crisis				Reduced hours in response to the energy crisis			
(number of cases)	21	53	65	139	‑21	53	65	
1. Personal emergency: hot line, medical counsellor or clinic[b], ambulance, pharmacy, bail bond	6	1	16	23				
2. Business or household emergency: utility, heating fuel, pest control, Mayor's complaint office, drainage, locksmith	1	2	14	17				
3. Other urgent services: veterinarian emergency, diapers, laundry, ice	6	–	1	7				
4. Retail outlets: food and/ or merchandise	–	3	15	18				
5. Auto: service and repair, rent-a-car	2	1	4	7		1		1 (14·3%)
6. Eating places: fast food outlets, restaurants, coffee shops	6	40	14	60	1	4	1	6 (10·0%)
7. Recreation: baths, cinema, bowling	–	6	1	7		1		1 (14·3%)
Reduced hours[c]					1 (4·8%)	6 (11·3%)	1 (1·5%)	8 (5·8%) mean

[a] No establishments open ten or eleven hours were in the sample. Among these extended day organizations, closing hours varied. Some eating places closed from 3.30 a.m. to 5.30 a.m.; a Turkish Bath establishment closed from 9 a.m. to 11 a.m.

[b] No hospitals or private physicians were included in the sample.

[c] Groups A and C cells collapsed because of small expected frequencies and correction for continuity introduced.

$$X^2_{1df}7f = 3·374, \text{ for two-tailed test } p = ·07$$

imperative to be available all the time. The 'we never close' restaurant or recreational place may follow an economic imperative to stay open, for they sell *access* along with food and diversions. Their advertising emphasizes the service-all-the-time feature and they base their reputations on it. The public may confirm this by patronizing these establishments more, for as discussed in the section on Supply Pull above, people respond to the availability of goods and services by wanting them, buying them, and using them. Incessant access becomes an organizational *time role* in the same way that a 'we deliver any-where' company enhances its primary function with a spatial role. This builds a commitment to withstand an energy crisis and remain open twenty-four hours a day. To be sure, twenty-four-hour organizations may be touched by energy shortages too. Some, especially the most vital and least substitutable ones, will be protected by receiving a priority classification from the agency regulating the distribution of such resources. But this privilege may well depend upon the prior fact of their unremitting operation and the public service connotation it implies.

Did the same patterns hold in other places affected by the oil cisis at that time? Were those organizations with active hours of intermediate length (that is, more than the ordinary minimum but less than the maximum) most suscep-tible to cutbacks? The answer is a mixed one. It reflects the play of other agen-cies that also exerted influence. Governments, for example, intruded to cope with the shortage. The Spanish Interior Ministry ordered cinemas, theatres, bars, cafes, restaurants and night clubs in Madrid to close at least one hour earlier than their customary times. This happened to a city where in good weather families with small children could be seen strolling on main streets at one a.m. (*New York Times* 1975). By government decree, British television programmes ended at 10.30 p.m. to save electricity and the early shutdown was to continue until the fuel shortage ended (*New York Times* 1973b). In the United States, the California Public Utilities Commission's plan, though not put into effect before the 1973–4 crisis ended, was typical. It would have barred all athletic events at night, and all night shifts, as well as curbing night lighting (*Newsweek* 1973b). In Michigan, where auto travel for shopping is commonplace, thirty-one around-the-clock supermarkets cut back their hours to two shifts or less (*Newsweek* 1973c). Yet while suburban shopping centres were suffering decreased sales, centre city department stores reachable by public transport showed significantly increased sales. And in New York City the theatre district experienced a revival.

One year after our initial Boston survey, auto fuel prices were still high but petrol was plentiful. We rechecked the twenty-four-hour organizations to learn what had happened in the longer run following the crisis. Some enterprises had closed. This represents a loss of cases common to this type of 'panel' study. A number of others had indeed cut back to a twenty- or eighteen-hour day. Why? Since these changes were limited to public places offering non-essential services, such as dining out or recreation, it appeared to be directly related to decreased use of autos due to the high fuel prices, which in turn resulted in reduced clientele at the quietest hours of the night. Our enquiries and dis-cussions with managers of these organizations confirm the impression. For example a year earlier the proprietor of a coffee shop explained his shop's retrenched hours by saying 'It was not the energy shortage, it was the customer shortage.'

So twenty-four-hour establishments will resist cutbacks in the face of an energy shortage if they enjoy wide public support. The 'shortage', in this case, has to do with the amount of money a society is willing to spend for the energy it needs. If other values concerning the standard of living and the quality of life were shunted aside, the Rocky Mountains could be levelled and over a trillion barrels of crude extracted from its oil shale. The pricing mechanism shows its power here indirectly. Higher costs of running automobiles produced a slow-moving but cumulative change in travel practices in the Boston area. This in turn led to a loss of clientele. Thus in some cases enough public support was eroded through this outside circumstance. Without that support these organizations could not sustain their incessant operation.

This event was not the only energy shortage of this decade. Its potential impact was reminiscent of England's experience two winters before. A massive walkout of British coal miners made energy resources scanty. After a while only the most essential services were operating full time—the sewage plants, hospitals, and water works.

There is a resemblance between the forced retreat in the time dimension because of energy shortages and the forced withdrawal from geographical colonies in earlier days because of shortage hardships. The ghost towns and the dust bowls of the American West are spaces from which humans retreated when the important resources—metals in the lode, fertile elements in the soil—were exhausted.

Overtures

The appearance and spread of extended-day and increased activities signal an evolutionary step in the growth of cities. They add the permanent colonization of time to the colonization of space and the ecological structure of human life is altered. Whereas other terrestrial creatures are either diurnal or nocturnal, and though humans emerged from the same biosphere, we have transformed ourselves into an *incesssant species*.

Some work on individual aspects has been carried out through research on time budgets (cf. Szalai 1972; Chapin 1974), but it would be useful to know the nature, scope and extent of all-hours activities. The task is to document what happens, count the number of people involved, and to chart the daily social cycle of events for the community. What are the ratios around the clock by type of activity, such as production of goods, services, recreation and maintenance? How much of this growth in time reflects an *absolute enlargement* of all human activity and how much is a *redistribution* of people and their ventures? We need a *spant-census* in cities, not only a demographic census.

To what extent does continual activity affect individuals? What does it mean for one to experience lengthening wakefulness and to be aware of unending access? There are probably differences in conduct and in moods around the clock, just as we find variations in different neighbourhoods.

Consider the possibilities of a future in which many forms of unremitting activity are even more commonplace. Anticipating such happenings helps understand future urban needs and points to planning opportunities. We should review how city time might be used, with due consideration for the physiology of individuals and for impacts on families. There is ample evidence that pricing strategies could redistribute activities. But we must be careful that we do not simply drive the poor into the night. If the peak commuting loads were smoothed by such redistributions, a smaller mass transit system would be needed, It would require smaller capital investment and would be used more fully. The populace, being more dispersed among city spants, would experience less crowding. Since more people would occupy some of the now rather-empty spants, there would be more natural surveillance there and this would probably reduce some forms of crime. The colonization of time must be studied for deliberate problem-solving potential as well as to have more knowledge about what is blooming around us.

ACKNOWLEDGEMENT

I gratefully acknowledge grant MH–22763 from the Centre for Studies of Metropolitan Problems, National Institute of Mental Health (USA), through which the research and the preparation of this essay was supported.

PART 2

The Lund School

Introduction

The notion of time geography which originated in Lund requires some further explanation. The person who in many respects has been its pioneer is Torsten Hägerstrand. When Abler, Adams and Gould (1971) spoke of 'meshing space and time', they were thinking mainly of spatial diffusion theory as formulated in its modern dynamic and chorological version by Hägerstrand in 1953 and later extended by others. The probability basis in his description of spatial fields and the contemporary novelty of quantitative techniques in human geography drew attention away from the fact that his diffusion processes were just a part of a wider package deal designed to come to grips with space, time, population, activity and process. Many geographers still associate Hägerstrand with mean information fields, random walks, simulation models, diffusion, migration and quantitative techniques. But this is essentially his work from the 1950s and only part of it. Leaving aside his efforts in the field of spatial information systems based on the coordinate grid system, and his work on regional policy in the Swedish administrative system, Hägerstrand from the mid-1960s onwards has been preoccupied with building up a more comprehensive time-space structured theory, which has its roots in his population studies from the 1940s. The transition between the earlier and the later form of time-space theory was a little noticed essay on migration in which one of the first graphs of individuals as paths or trajectories flowing through time-space were depicted (Hägerstrand 1963). At this stage, the idea was only taken up by a few people, mainly as a descriptive device (Chapman 1970, Norborg 1968).

The main thrust in terms of development and broadening of the approach came in 1966 with the establishment of a research project on 'Time use and ecological organization', in which Hägerstrand shared his basic ideas and developed them together with his students and collaborators Lenntorp, Mårtensson and Carlstein. More recently others, notably Wallin, have joined the group.

What then can be said to be characteristic of the approach, which distinguishes the Lund school from other space and time studies? Already it has been called physicalistic, behavioural and what not, and like all labels these are fuzzy and misleading, and unfortunately they suggest that a new, separate field of specialization has been established. This has not been one of the intentions. One definition of time geography is that it is an *approach*, an origin and a place to start anew, although many of the ultimate destinations are as yet less clearly defined. The approach uses a *basic model* of reality that contains some elements which time geography cannot (and which any time-space approach in geography should not) neglect or forget, elements which have too long been dealt with carelessly in most social science. When even one of these elements is left out, there is an immediate danger of losing contact with the real world. This is not to say that time geography has yet incorporated all the important elements of reality. Very much remains to be done, but what has already been incorporated seems to be extremely fundamental and can carry one far, especially in the realm of meaningful deduction.

In an essay on 'Space, time and human conditions', Hägerstrand (1975b) summarized some basic conditions affecting human life and society which gave the limits to possible organizational forms, and these are:

1   the indivisibility of the human being (and of many other entities living and non-living);
2   the limited length of each human life (and many other entities, living and non-living);
3   the limited ability of the human being (and many other indivisible entities) to take part in more than one task at a time;
4   the fact that every task (or activity) has a duration;
5   the fact that movement between points in space consumes time;
6   the limited packing capacity of space;
7   the limited outer size of terrestrial space (whether we look at a farm, a city, a country or the Earth as a whole); and
8   the fact that every situation is inevitably rooted in past situations.

Hägerstrand goes on to state that, 'I believe that the interaction between these fundamental conditions could be and ought to be the object of precise theoretical research. I feel that this research *is the starting point* from which more *practical* consideration should develop concerning better or worse institutions (capitalism versus socialism, bureaucracy versus participation), concerning better or worse technologies (private transport versus public, videophones versus letters) and concerning better or worse cities (circular, multi-nuclear, band-like or no cities at all) . . . this conclusion is a clearcut value consideration. I believe that the criteria for a good socio-technical organization are not to be found along the spatial cross-section but along the time-axis and in the particular sequence of events which makes up the life of each individual human being. It is the biographies of people that should count,' (Hägerstrand 1975b, italics added). To get at the different kinds of interactions among humans and between them and their environment, the various dimensions and mechanisms of interaction must be translatable into common language. 'My hypothesis is that such a needed common language can best be developed if we start far back, with a very general kind of space-time ecology' (Hägerstrand 1975b). This language and notation system should at the same time be a *model* of society and habitat and a device which in its germ, in its genetic code as it were, should contain deductive power as to possible (and, equally important, impossible) system states and transformations.

The underlying model of individuals as paths or trajectories in time-space had been in Hägerstrand's mind for many years and was inspired by his regional geographic studies in the late 1940s of Asby parish in Sweden (cf.

his input-output study of population in an Asby farm, chapter 7 below). The excellent population statistics allowed him to trace all individuals in the parish from 1840 to 1944 (Hägerstrand 1947; 1963) and he came to order these individual data according to the scheme developed by the demographers Lexis and Becker, who viewed each individual as a *life-time* in time from birth to death. Hägerstrand generalized this notion to that of *life-path* in *time-space* which could be viewed in all temporal and spatial scales (e.g. day-path, week-path, year-path and life-path), just as he argued that the path (or trajectory) concept as well as the population concept could be generalized beyond living populations to include also artifacts (and of course organisms), having a very general ecology in mind (Hägerstrand 1974b). Both human beings and domestic organisms, tools, vehicles, equipment and indeed buildings have paths in time-space which interact and form bundles over time; all constituting a web or texture of paths having a complicated structure (Hägerstrand 1969a; 1970a; 1973b; 1974b). Just as there is a turnover of humans who form the minimum strands in the societal web, the same applies to other living and non-living entities. This turnover process is especially shown in chapter 12 with regard to the human population.

Some of the eight points above are more emphasized than others in the various chapters below, but all of the authors have borne the other points in mind. If one takes the *indivisibility* property of the human individual (confining ourselves to humans), there is hardly any theory of importance in social science which has genuinely looked into its implications, either for person-person or person-land kinds of interaction. The logical necessity of this concept cannot be over-estimated, as it gives rise to a different theory both of interaction and economy. In sociology and elsewhere the cumulative effects of indivisibility (and continuity) in time-space have largely been ignored because there was no deductive framework in which to trace their real ramifications. In economics, indivisibilities in plants and equipment have been more noticed than those inherent in the minimal economic production and consumption units—the human individuals. Some leading economists have been quite emphatic about indivisibilities. For instance, Koopmans (1957) argues that 'without recognizing indivisibilities—in the human person, in residences, plants, equipment and in transportation—urban location problems down to the smallest village cannot be understood.' One reason why this finding has been so neglected in the mainstream of economic theory is, as Macmillan points out in his chapter of *TSST* volume 3, that it ran counter to the assumptions of convexity and continuous variables made in economic optimization and programming theory. But there were other reasons making it impossible to exploit this fundamental fact in a pecuniary framework: many of the consequences of indivisibility only become evident when socio-environmental systems are viewed in *real* terms and in time-space location and allocation terms, i.e. in time-geographic terms.

The fact of limited length of life in human beings has been accepted in all demographic and general social research, but the logical consequences thereof have not. Coupling this to the other *facts of life*—that all activities take time, that individuals have limited capacity and capability, and that individuals must be continuous in time-space, i.e. form an unbroken path between birth and death—a very basic *time and path allocation problem* emerges. This sets the inner and outer limits to much of human interaction and group formation, and hence to information exchange, care and service exchange, teaching-learning and transmission of knowledge, and so on. Some of the problems of time-consuming interaction within a population system are discussed in chapters 11 and 12 dealing with the tertiary (service) and the quarternary (administrative) sectors. These two papers are just the very beginnings, however, and more research is going on at Lund which will eventually show the power of an interaction theory based on the above premises.

What characterizes the chapters by Lenntorp and Mårtensson, dealing with individuals and households in relation to the time-space structure of the social and material environment, is that the time-allocation viewpoint is fused with that of path allocation in time-space. The system of paths of individuals can be one way of entering into time-allocation and man-space interaction problems through the population system. Conventional time-budget studies start with activities rather than paths, and hence the constraints on activities emanating from the fact that human time has to be mobilized in space, that transport takes time, that the choice space of individual behaviour is affected by *prisms* and the speed constraints, simply do not enter the picture. The time-geographic model of paths in time-space ensure realism in individual behaviour as well as collective interaction. The connections between roles are maintained by the physical unity of the individuals, and stationary activities are interspersed with movement in a realistic way, rather than roles being pulled out of their sequential and locational context.

The facts that activities, tasks and projects consume time and that space has a limited packing capacity (cf. points 4, 5 and 6 above) lead to a general packing problem both in a population time-budget and in the space-time budget of a given area, domain or region. Given a population with its distribution of capabilities and qualities (cf. chapters 8 on innovations and chapter 12 on the population system), only a certain volume of time-demanding activities can be packed into it. Likewise, geographic space has a limited capacity to accommodate space-consuming activities (or rather populations, materials, organisms and artefacts.) But the time-geographic model does not look at space in static terms. What is occupied is *space over time* measured not in acres or hectares but for instance in hectare-days or hectare-years. Just as inputs of machine units or vehicle units are measured in machine-hours or vehicle-hours, and labour inputs in person-hours ('man-hours'), there is every reason why space in the form of *room* to accommodate things should be measured in square-metre-hours or other relevant *space-time* units (as applied in chapter 8 below). This is in accord with the dynamic approach to land use employed by the Danish economic historian Boserup (1965) in the guise of 'frequency of cropping', which was her basic concept in accounting for agricultural *intensification* of land use as a response to population growth. In dealing with the same topic, the anthropologist Geertz used the broader term 'involution' for Indonesia (Geertz 1963). Using the time-geographic approach, Carlstein (1973; 1975b) developed a synthetic model of shifting cultivation systems in which different activity cycles (daily, annual and perennial) are meshed with a dynamic land-use model in which room for cultivation and fallow is looked upon in space-time units (cf. also chapter 8). Both intensification, involution, density, frequency of cropping, colonization of 'spants' (cf. Melbin, chapter 6) can be seen as aspects of packing in space-time, regardless of whether the setting is rural or urban. Erlandsson (1976), for instance, uses a time-geographic approach to analyse the way in which firms occupy space(-time) and grow or decline in Swedish cities over a period of several decades. Looking at areal-budgeting in a spatial way is insufficient, and in a recent paper Erlandsson and Johansson (1976) explore the extent to which firms expand by colonizing space-time in the daily round. But the biographies studied in this case are those of firms rather than persons.

The chapters in this part of the book, which are all based on the time-geographic model, illustrate some of the fields where this model has been applied, such as historical geography (chapter 7), innovation theory (chapter 8), urban transportation and daily time use in households (chapter 9), regional differences in daily living conditions (chapter 10), firms, administration and the communication problems of the quaternary sector (chapter 11), and a futurological study (chapter 12). These chapters provide glimpses of more comprehensive studies carried out on the basis of the time-geographic model, and they have been chosen to indicate the range of topics that one can deal with and the synthetic potentials of the approach. To see time-geography as a separate field would thus be inappropriate. It is rather an approach anchored in certain basic facts of life which one can possibly ignore or neglect, but hardly deny. For those who have probed more deeply into the intrinsic and unyielding logic of viewing populations as interacting paths in time-space, and who have unwound the constraints acting on the paths of evolution that social systems may take, the model becomes a very useful tool for keeping to the real world at the same time as one develops theories about it. But the burden of proving the validity of all this still falls on those who make the claims, as well as those who are motivated to take up the approach in their own work.

Chapter 7
Survival and Arena
On the life-history of individuals in relation
to their geographical environment*
Torsten Hägerstrand

Survival and Arena is a combination of concepts which perhaps sounds a bit dramatic. That is the intention, since what I am going to discuss are serious and fundamental elements in our existence as it is conditioned by human nature, culture, history and place: birth, family-formation and death, access to home and livelihood, engagement in social cooperation and conflict. Each of these elements is of course a longstanding topic for research in a great number of various disciplines. But my outlook as a geographer leaves me dissatisfied with a disjointed approach. I am compelled to try to deal with them all for the same area at the same time in a contextual perspective and with a synthesis in view. The final aim would be—to put it boldly—to try to turn human geography into a study of the conditions of life in a regional setting.

I believe that the time is ripe for this kind of effort. There are in fact many signs showing that specialized disciplines, consciously or not, are beginning to ask questions which only a regional geography of the kind I have in mind could illuminate. Biologists with a concern for the ecological development are a case in point. Similarly, at least some engineers are wondering what place their efforts should have in the future service of society in the rich as well as the poor world. Recently I listened to a review of a piece of medical research of great interest in this connection.[1] The analysts had followed by interviews and medical examinations—also post mortem—the health history of a large sample of men born in 1913 in a chosen city. Two observations came out strongly. The first was that health and even length of life was related to external living conditious. Low income, unsafe employment, inadequate housing went along with bad health and early death. The second observation was that life style had a strong co-variation with health and length of life. Of course, one can always argue about cause and effect. But more importantly for the student of society is to note a further implicit conclusion. Medical treatment of the already sick person has almost reached its full potential now for scientific as well as economic reasons in a country of Sweden's structure and health-care system. If we take health and a full life-time as quality indicators then the major part of further improvements must predominantly come through changes in living conditions and life styles.

Thus, presently an exhortation seems to come from many sides, political as well as scientific, to deepen the understanding of the human world in distributional terms. This problem fits well in the geographic tradition. We

*Reprinted from *The Monadnock* Clark University Geographical Society, vol. 49 June 1975.

are accustomed to dealing with the distribution of phenomena in space. It is a short and logically following step to ask questions about how states and events are distributed between the members or the subgroups of a population in a community. Already a growing number of geographical studies deal with this. Next comes a still further distributional dimension. I am thinking of the kinds of individual life biographies which are taking shape over time within the fields of prevailing distributional forces.

The set of individual biographies of a population in an area is perhaps the most apparent entity which connects the past with the future. It should also be able to provide a yardstick by which we could compare the performance of various structural settings, and perhaps, also evaluate utopias as well as less spectacular political goals. In the term biography I include both the outcome of everyday life and the total life curriculum which unfolds over days and years. This dimension, although the most essential in human terms, has still to be put in place in our picture of the world.

A life biography, seen in its entirety, is made up of both internal mental experiences and events—more easily observable by the outsider—related to the interplay between body and environmental phenomena. We must assume that inner experiences and outer events are joined in many intricate ways. The most indisputable connection lies in the sequential correspondence between what happens in the two realms. We have to do with a continuous dialogue between person and environment in a clear sequential order. The major task of a biographical approach would be to look into the nature of this dialogue as it takes place in its ecological context.

It should be clear from what I said before and have published elsewhere[2] that my personal concern so far is the external part of the total problem area. This choice does not entail a dismissal of the experiential dimension. It is only a natural outcome of earlier research. And the efforts are accompanied by a hope that other workers will line up for co-operation on the other side in order to restore the balance.

It is my belief that the introduction of a biographical perspective where human populations are concerned will have beneficial effects over the whole range of geographic enquiry, because it will force us to reconsider many conventional ideas and in particular help us to deal with space and time as a unified entity better than we have been able to do so far. We need a geography today which helps us to see ourselves, our fellow-passengers and our total environment in a more coherent way than we are presently capable of doing. To me the answer seems to lie in the study of the interwoven distribution of states and events in coherent blocks of space-time—in other worlds in a regional synthesis with a time-depth.

My purpose today is only to indicate the conceptual direction of the approach I have in mind. I am not trying to make an abstract and systematic review of the matter. The comments will be related to historical data from a small region of Sweden.[3] So far the empirical work in the area is not as exhaustive as one would like to have for the purposes at hand. Therefore, what I have to offer now must remain both conceptually and empirically just a minor sketch over a territory to be more fully explored later on.

Life requires that the individual successively and without interruption associates himself with sets of entities emerging from his surrounding. Some elements are actively sought, others cannot be avoided. These entities could be classified in a number of ways. Presently four major classes are sufficient for helping us forward. These are:

1   other individuals,
2   indivisible objects (such as other living organisms, machines, tools),
3   divisible materials (such as air, water, minerals, foodstuff) and
4   domains.

(It is assumed that the two fundamentals, energy and information, are special aspects which cut through the items of the fourfold classification.) The concept of a domain as used here needs to be expounded more than the others. It refers to a specific kind of social construct brought into being in order to secure a certain amount of order and predictability in human affairs. The concept first of all refers to the intricate lattice of earthbound spatial units in which specified individuals or groups have socially recognized rights to exert control. In this sense the domain appears in all scales from informal divisions inside a home, over work-rooms, real-estate units and municipal territories up to states and confederations. The units are all geographic in a traditional sense—although curiously enough only partly recognized as proper objects of research. But secondly the concept stands for 'position' ('office') that is to say for a derived 'space' which by contrast gives its holder certain rights as well as duties. This kind of domain has sometimes, but by no means always, a fixed location. Even if not it shares many characteristics with the terrestrial domain, so do, for example, rules of entrance limit access. Likewise, in a given area only a limited number are present simultaneously.

Now, consider that a complete record is kept for each individual person as his life is proceeding, enumerating in sequence of occurrence the sets of surrounding entities of the four kinds with which he is associated. Clearly, the record-keeper must apply certain rules for defining association in a consistent way. The rules should cover variations from physical contact to legal right. The record describes the steps of a path or trajectory between points of 'contact' with surrounding elements. People will appear in each other's sets. Similarly, for example, tools and domains will now be elements in a set around one person and now around another. To a very large extent these couplings are not possible simultaneously but only by turns.

It is now close at hand to interpret all records taken together as describing a closely knit web of trajectories. This kind of understanding gives prominence to the sequential relations of events across the whole population (the time-dimension if you like). The prominence of domains in the channelling of trajectories makes us see space, first and foremost, as a provider of room (and only secondarily as a maker of distances).

As soon as this picture of the world is reasonably clear in one's mind it is easy to see that there are various levels of detail at which one can try to find the determinants that give shape to the pattern of the web as it grows towards the future 'at the edge of history'. To begin with we have a close contact level. Here we try to understand how elements come to hang together or depart with respect to their most immediate relations. In this respect there is little difference between the chemist's interest in the nature of chemical bonds and the economist's interest in the transaction between buyer and seller.

In other words we focus attention on the natural principles or the social rules and regulations at work once the set of elements is at hand. This level of analysis or operation is the research area of numerous sciences and technologies. And the results when applied are moreover the source of much of the particular kinds of stupidity which from a human point of view are current in the technological society of today. What is missing is the ability—or willingness—to see the micro-processes with respect to their conditions and consequences when put in place in the wider situation.

It should not be denied that for example political economy and macro-sociology try to deal with the second society-wide or area-wide level. But they tend to do it in ways as if the step between the two levels was a matter of simple multiplication. The world-picture disregards the many environmental realities which lie between elementary regularities and gross outcome. The web-model suggested here is believed to be able to cast light on just this little understood, in-between area. When we broaden the view over a wider field of trajectories we begin to see that all of the specific events of local interaction must take place under the influence of certain fundamental limiting conditions. The access to elements at the formation of sets comes out as an intricate budgeting process. At every next step in the process options are limited because of constraints which operate both simultaneously (as if over space) and sequentially (as if over time). Events and states become place- and time-specific in ways which are beyond the grasp of those sciences which assume away the importance of geography and history.

As an illustration of the interplay between the formation of life-biographies and limited options as they come out in a space-time perspective I am now going to use observations from a small nineteenth-century rural community. Attention is concentrated on how the members of the population join and depart from domains, seen both as terrestrial units (farms, crofts, shops, etc.) and as functional livelihood positions inside these. Concomitantly we get an impression of the formation and dissolution of families. This particular selection of elements leaves out the major part of formation of sets for social interaction as well as for production and consumption. Neighbours are not considered nor are tools and materials. We have only to remember that the omitted elements belong to the full picture and that they make their influence felt implicitly. The selection made in my illustrations is partly an outcome of what the sources have to tell in full, partly due to a conviction that family, economic unit and livelihood position are in many ways steering elements in the lives of people.

I will try to demonstrate first the general nature of the relation between a population and the structure of domains in its environment. My example is taken from one single farm seen over a hundred years—from 1840 to 1940. At the end of the period the unit was made up of forty acres of arable land, fifty acres of pastures and meadows and 140 acres of woodland. The total area did not change over the century, a smaller increase of arable land took place at the expense of meadow land. The relative value of the woodland increased considerably.

On the graph (Figure 1) each individual person connected with the farm during the period has been given his own time-channel. It is then indicated over which period he or she existed on the farm. If a person who has moved out returns later on he will resume his private channel again. Most individuals move in from the outside, some are born into the farm. Likewise most move out again but some die on the farm. In all, about two hundred different individuals have moved through. The number living on the farm simultaneously has varied around ten to twelve, the major deviations due to variations in the number of children. There might also be some errors in the yearly sums because of delays in the registration of migrations.

A Population's association with a farm from 1840 to 1945.

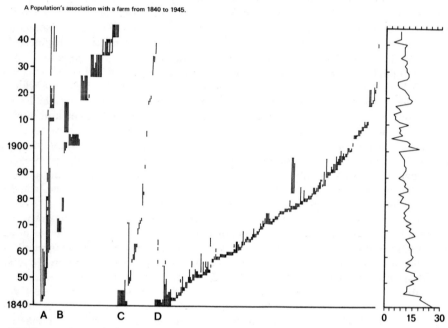

Figure 1   A population's association with a farm from 1840 to 1945. Every vertical channel represents the life-line of an individual who has lived on the farm for a shorter or longer period. Bars mark time of stay. In all around 200 different individuals moved through. The scale did not permit the rendering of information on sex, births, deaths and movements in and out. Cluster A represents owners, B tenants, C lodging persons and D farmhands and maids, in all cases with families included. The graph to the right gives the number of individuals registered simultaneously on the farm.

The channels and thus the partial life-lines have been grouped according to the functional positions of the adults. This means that wives are placed beside husbands and children grouped with parents. Inside functional groups individuals are placed in order of entrance.

The first cluster to the left represents the freeholder and his (her) dependent family members. In general these people have remained on the farm over longer periods of time than others, sometimes an entire life.

The second cluster represents tenants with families, that is to say people who did the actual farming. (A small contradiction in the grouping should be noted. A family, located further out to the right because they were returners, actually came back in order to function as tenants.) The characteristic feature of the tenant population is the relatively short periods of stay, as a rule either five or ten years.

The third cluster reflects a peculiar social institution of the time. It is made up of persons lodging and supported on the farm, frequently elderly relatives, sometimes friends who are hard to distinguish from household aids. This kind of position was filled only occasionally.

The fourth cluster, finally, represents the progression of servants employed in farmwork, a mixture of farmhands and maids, sometimes married and with small children, more often single. They came in from the vicinity, frequently several at a time, stayed one, two or a few more years, and moved out again.

So what the graph communicates is how an economic organization, the farm with its various functional positions, cut out shorter or longer slices of life-time from the total life-time of the population of the surrounding area. Owners were the only stable part of the population. The rest, also family members of owners, just passed through while involved in some sort of career. It should be easy to imagine how—if we had access to corresponding graphs of all farms over a wider area—the population actually formed a web in their search among the available domains. Farms did not have much to do with each other in terms of economic transactions but they formed a closely knit system in terms of population flow.

The most striking overall feature is the stability of the pattern of through-flow over time. The highly standardized parade persisted rather unchanged up to around 1920 when positions for farm-workers ceased to exist at least as whole-year tasks. If information of a similar detail had been available concerning equipment, we would in all likelihood have been able to see how machines went in as servants disappeared. The stability of pattern means that individuals and families had to make their successive choices within a rather rigid structure of options. The relatively constant organization of the farm meant that new people as a rule could come in only after others had left. The timing of stay for tenants and servants was regulated by traditional and standardized forms of contracts. Therefore, movements in and out occurred with a high degree of regularity over time.

In order to illustrate the generality of the pattern a second domain is chosen a couple of miles from the first (Figure 2). The period covered is now much shorter, 1880–90, and the data are presented in a more aggregate form. This particular unit was made up of a central farm occupied by the owner, plus five small crofts and tied cottages. The physical base consisted of eighty acres of arable land, ninety acres of pastures and meadows and 300 acres of woodland. The square of the graph should now be understood as a compact 'space-time' box, the vertical side representing years and the horizontal representing 'roominess'. This time the trajectories of people have been aggregated into groups in order to make the quantitative input–output relations more distinct.

As many as seventy-six individuals resided inside the chosen area some time during the period of observation. But out of these only twelve remained all the time. No less than twenty-nine just moved through, staying one or two years. One died and ten were born. Of these four moved out with parents within the period.

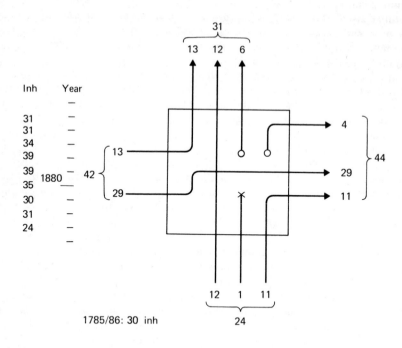

Figure 2 The box represents a farm in 'space-time' terms, observed over a decade around 1880. The vertical axis describes the length of the period of observation. The horizontal axis describes the 'holding capacity' of the farm. Arrows and figures indicate in what numbers and space-time directions people have moved through the farm. Arrows coming in from below and moving out upwards account for those who lived inside the area at the start of observation, resp. remained there at the end. Arrows coming in from the left side and moving out on the right account for residential moves in to and out from the farm. Death inside the farm and period is marked by a small cross, births by small open circles. The number of inhabitants each separate year is given in the left column. Seventy-six separate individuals lived on the farm for a shorter or longer period.

Despite this great turnover the number of people inhabiting the whole unit is also in this case remarkably stable from year to year. One hundred years earlier, in 1785, this farm had thirty inhabitants, that is around the same number. Practically no clearing of new land for new holdings took place inside the domain in the meantime. Thus it seems safe to say that the unit had a rather fixed number of positions for adults from year to year—an expression one must assume of quite definite carrying capacity from the point of view of production. Throughout the decade we observe how different individuals came in to fill positions vacated by those who had left for something else. Only the owner with family and some older crofters made up a stable population.

Given a constant number of positions inside a territorial domain, like the two farms chosen as examples, new individuals cannot move in until vacancies arise because others move out, die or retire to the more elastic class of dependent family members. In times when the adult population grows in number above the generation of ultimate vacancies (retirements and deaths) the trajectories which cannot become accommodated have to seek destinations elsewhere. A different solution for the excess population is to refuse to accept the given structure and to try to enforce a generation of entirely new livelihood positions. This was actually what had happened up to about 1860 in our sample parish. The number of inhabitants grew from 1,200 in the year 1750 to 1,700 in 1860. New livelihood positions were created during this period through division of holdings and clearing of still remaining marginal land for crofts and tied cottages. The demand for land was such that rather impossible, hilly and boulder-strewn pieces of land were made into arable patches. Still the excess of births over deaths had been 1,100 during the same period so only less than half of the natural growth had been accommodated.

By 1860 the period of internal colonization was coming to an end. The size of the population came to a standstill up to about 1930 when the modern depopulation began. The natural growth was now taken care of by large-scale emigration to America (more than 700 individuals left the parish) and by moves to the developing industry in Sweden. On the whole no new livelihood positions came into being in the parish during the remaining part of the nineteenth century. Rather the reverse process began to take place in that some small-holdings were abandoned and farms which had been divided earlier were consolidated again.

The process of abandonment gives some further insight into the relationship between the space-time trajectories of people and the underlying structure of options. In Figure 3, three different small-holdings, each capable of accommodating one family, are represented as space-time boxes over a four-year period. A movement out to America of a family of two in the year 1893 initiated a series of local moves during the following year. In this process a holding came to be abandoned in 1895, situated two steps and two years away from the one the emigrants had left. This example is just one case among a great number of similar ones.

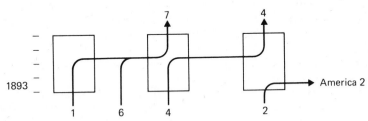

Figure 3   The boxes represent three small one-family holdings in space-time terms. Arrows should be understood as in Figure 2, except that residential moves have been placed in the actual year when they took place. The holdings were located within a range of around eight miles.

In all its simplicity this graph has a lot to say about the difficulties in drawing conclusions concerning social processes from overt behaviour. That the holding to the left became empty because somebody moved away does not say very much because moving away was a normal step to take. The interesting thing is that nobody around chose to move in to the empty position, something which up to this time had also been a normal kind of event. But suppose now that a contemporary researcher had wanted to get hold of the reasons for abandonment. To whom should he direct his enquiry? The abandonment is a non-event. An expected step did not take place and it is impossible to localize a specific decision-maker. What one can say is that the gross balance between human trajectories and positions within perceptional range began to offer more freedom of choice than had been the case earlier.

The data shown so far must be sufficient to indicate that we are viewing an economic arena made up of a rather fixed set of domains in the form of territorial units and livelihood positions inside them. In fact it would not be too difficult to enumerate the kinds and numbers of options available in the parish. More approximately stated, the main groups were *free-holders, farm tenants, crofters, craftsmen, farm labourers* in tied cottages, *servants* and *dependent persons* (wives, children, sick and retired). Only the number of servants and dependent persons varied to a greater extent and in a somewhat random fashion around an average.

Given this simple structure a young person did not have many building blocks inside the area for making a career. If this state of affairs did not satisfy him, he had to move elsewhere, but during the nineteenth century still there were few chances of finding destinations which differed radically from that of his home-area. The exception was of course offered by the wider opportunities in America.

In order to demonstrate what kinds of life biographies took shape under the prevailing circumstances, a sample of individuals has been followed from birth and onwards as long as the population records of a single parish permit. The sample of about 500 individuals includes every child born in the parish from 1860 to 1869.

A first classification was made with respect to the social position of the parents at the birth of the child. Group I includes free-holders and farm-tenants as well as a few estate-owners and officials. Group II includes crofters and craftsmen. Group III comprises farm labourers and servants. Group IV, finally, holds unmarried mothers of all social classes.

A first set of graphs (Figures 4 to 10) gives the basic information concerning each individual. The vertical 'life-line' marks the time spent within the parish from birth and onwards. A small cross indicates death, a short horizontal line, change of residence inside the parish or to and from Swedish destinations; and a dot, movement to (or from) America.

The life-lines are ordered in four sub-groups in all graphs. The first sub-group (A) includes all individuals of the cohort who died within the confines of the parish. The second (B) marks the very small fraction of individuals who survived within the parish for at least seventy-five years. The third (C) represents all those who have at some time moved out permanently to other places in Sweden. The fourth sub-group (D) contains those who emigrated directly to America.

Individuals stemming from the different social groups come to be divided up in sub-groups in essentially the same way. The only more striking deviation comes out for the children of unmarried women. All except one of these disappeared very early. Infant death rate is here twice as high as for the other groups. Clearly, it must be kept in mind that the sample is too small for really significant conclusions about differences.

Already the gross resemblance between the fate of the members of all major groups shows that there existed a fundamental similarity in living conditions over the entire population of a farming community a century ago. Apart from this general observation we will need a little more precision than the graphs can give immediately in order to get hold of the differences between the social groups.

Let us first consider how members of the different groups (group I excluded) die or leave the parish of birth at various ages (Table 1). Decade by decade we compare the added length of observed life-lines with what we could have found if everyone had survived up to seventy-five years of age and remained in the parish. The difference is expressed in percentages.

The decline in the amount of added life-time during the first decade is to a rather large degree caused by early deaths. On the whole infant mortality is strikingly high.[5] As time goes on it turns out that the farmer's children, sons and daughters alike, remain in the parish to a somewhat larger degree than

TABLE 1A   Number of children born in Asby parish, Östergötland, from 1860 to 1869 (still-born included). Division in groups according to position of parents at time of birth: group I freeholders and farm tenants, group II crofters and craftsmen, group III farm labourers and servants, group IV unmarried mothers of all groups.

	I	II	III	IV	Total
Males	75	118	70	12	275
Females	78	76	59	15	228
Total	153	194	129	27	503

Note the big difference in number between males and females in group II.

TABLE 1B   Observed time spent by all individuals within the parish expressed as a percentage of maximum possible time if every individual had survived up to the age of seventy-five and stayed within the parish all his life.

	Males			Females		
Age	I	II	III	I	II	III
70–75	14	5	2	14	11	12
60–70	17	7	7	17	14	15
50–60	20	8	10	19	16	17
40–50	20	10	11	20	18	17
30–40	22	13	14	21	21	21
20–30	33	19	22	36	23	32
10–20	52	36	45	58	35	50
0–10	74	59	63	77	62	69
% deceased before 10	23	25	30	19	21	20

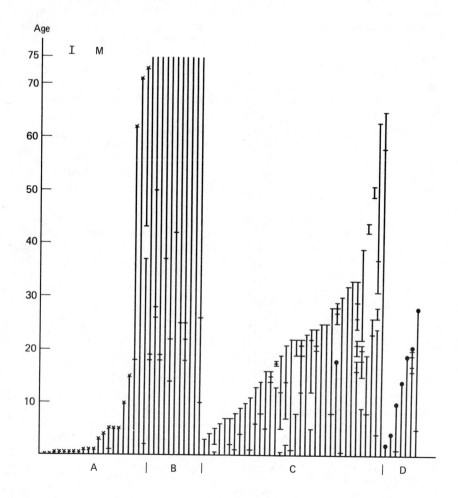

Figure 4 Life-lines representing each male individual, born in the period 1860–9, are descending from group I (freeholders and farm tenants). A small cross indicates age of death, a short horizontal line residential move (inside parish or Sweden) and a dot migration to or from America. Subgroup A died in the parish of birth, B survived there up to seventy-five years of age, C moved out definitely to Swedish destinations and D emigrated definitely to America (some may have returned to other parish in Sweden).

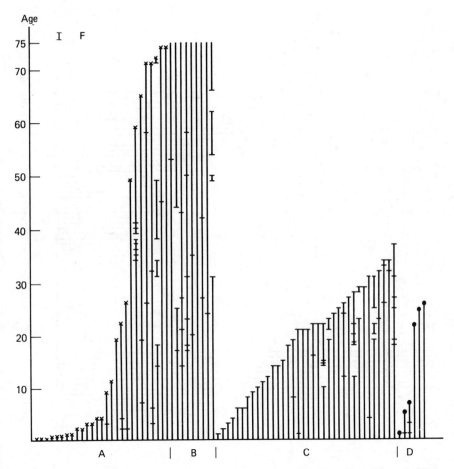

Figure 5 Females, born in the period 1860–9 and descending from group I (free-holders and farm tenants). Notation as in Figure 4.

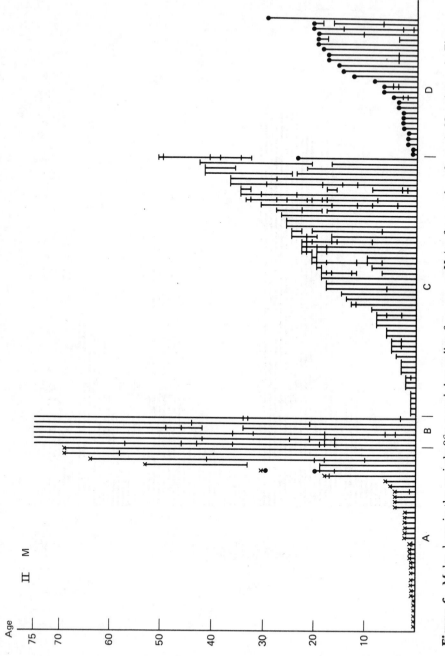

Figure 6 Males, born in the period 1860–9 and descending from group II (crofters and craftsmen). Notation as in Figure 4.

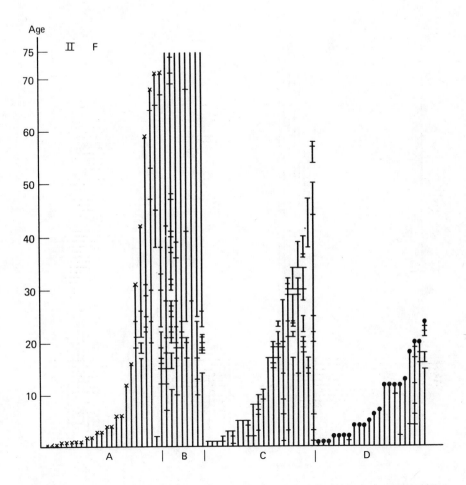

Figure 7 Females, born in the period 1860–9 and descending from group II (crofters and craftsmen). Notation as in Figure 4.

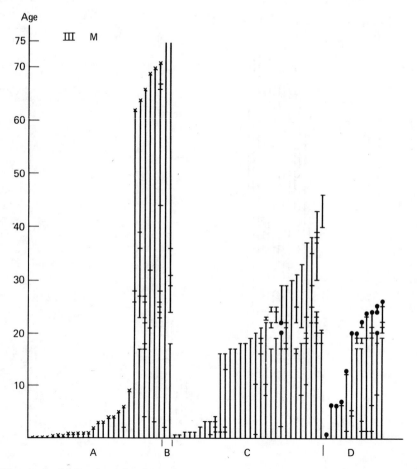

Figure 8 Males, born in the period 1860–9 and descending from group III (farm labourers and servants). Notation as in Figure 4.

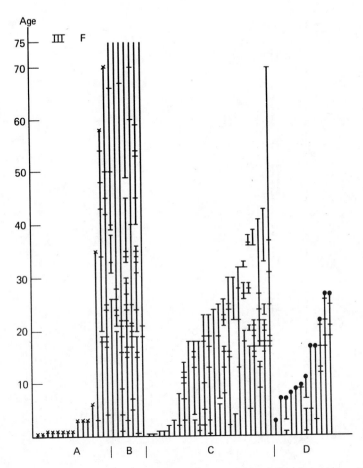

Figure 9 Females, born in the period 1860–9 and descending from group III (farm labourers and servants). Notation as in Figure 4.

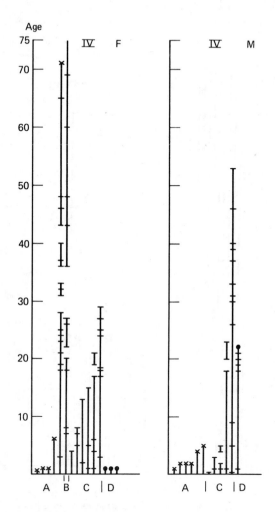

Figure 10 Males and females, born in the period 1860–9 by unmarried mothers from all social groups. Notation as in Figure 4.

the other groups. Nevertheless between the ages of twenty and thirty already two thirds disappear. Crofter's sons tend to leave first. The greatest differences between classes are on the whole among the males. Some differences among the females are discernible but they are not very great.

The clearest differences between classes emerge when we observe mobility (Table 2). The typical age of changes of residence comes between twenty and thirty. But mobility is rather low among farmer's children of both sexes. The highly mobile individuals are the daughters from crofters' and labourers' homes.

TABLE 2   Number of residential moves within the parish of birth or across its border per ten individuals still living in parish per decade.

	Males			Females		
Age	I	II	III	I	II	III
70–75	0	0	0	2	5	0
60–70	2	0	4	2	5	3
50–60	1	3	0	3	3	5
40–50	4	10	4	6	7	11
30–40	5	13	13	14	14	22
20–30	15	15	32	11	36	31
10–20	10	14	14	7	23	23
0–10	6	8	8	4	9	11

TABLE 3   Number of moves to and from America per ten individuals still living in parish per decade.

	Males			Females		
Age	I	II	III	I	II	III
70–75						
60–70						
50–60						
40–50						
30–40						
20–30	1	2	4	1	1	2
10–20	1	2	2		3	1
0–10	1	2	1	1	3	2
% emigrated	11	23	17	8	29	20

Emigration to America, finally (Table 3), was an act which in this generation took place before the age of thirty. In at least half of the cases the emigrants accompanied their parents as children. The strongest tendency to emigrate is found among the children of crofters and labourers. It should be noted that if we had been able to follow over time also those who moved away to Swedish destinations we would undoubtedly have found many more emigrations later on. So where emigration to America is concerned we do not get the full picture.

The next question to ask is to what extent steps between social classes took

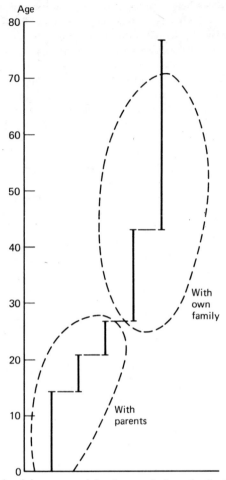

Figure 11   Residential moves and family association of a freeholder's daughter.

place during the progress of life. The available information is poor on this issue since relatively few individuals came to live a long period inside the parish of their birth. Let me first be very specific and show two individual biographies with respect to their association with domains and families. They are very different and they are representative of their social classes.

The farmer's daughter (Figure 11) moved several times inside the parish. But first, up to twenty-seven years of age, she followed her parents in their moves and then—without an independent existence as single—she started out with her own family. There is of course a possibility that she lived elsewhere for periods shorter than a year, which is the minimum unit for registration of a move. This uncertainty does not apply to her married period. The final years of life were spent with the son who had inherited the property. All her life she remained in the social class of her birth.

The crofter's daughter left home early—at the age of sixteen—in order to join the circulating population of servants (cf. Figure 12). At the age of 33, after

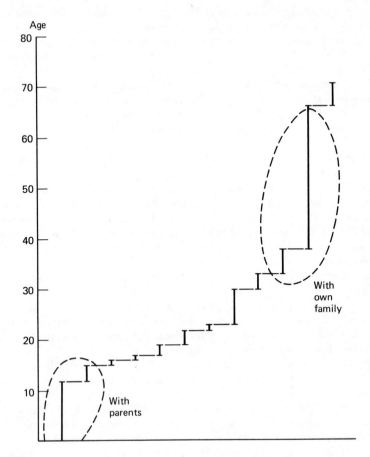

Figure 12   Residential moves and family association of a crofter's daughter.

many changes of residence, she became the wife of a crofter. Her final years as widow she spent in the poor-house. Also she lived her whole life in the social class of her birth. One could even justify the opinion that the final years meant a step down.

An overall description of the long term transitions of individuals between social classes is given on Table 4. What is compared is the social position at

TABLE 4   Steps between groups from time of birth up to the age of fifty.

		Males To				Females To		
		I	II	III		I	II	III
From	I	15	1		I	14	1	
	II	5	5	1	II	1	9	3
	III		5	2	III		5	5

birth with the position at the age of fifty. At this age further steps over class-boundaries do not seem likely. The women who are married or widowed or act as housekeepers in a brother's home have been put in the same category as the men. Now fifty years is a rather long time and it might well be possible that the same designation, say farmer or crofter, in the registers from the beginning and from the end of the period means rather different circumstances where standard of living is concerned. But it is less probable that the social rank-order should have become reversed due to the general economic development. So in this respect the transition matrix should give a reliable picture.

Individuals attached to the farms, whether as owners or as tenants, show practically no social mobility. They have been able to stay where they set out. The middle group is more mobile. The figures are so small that their distribution must be understood just as hypotheses. But seen as such they give some interesting indications. Almost half of the men have moved upwards whereas the women have remained the same or tended downwards. Among the individuals of the third group, finally, a considerable number has moved up but not more than one step. The farms were closed domains to them.

I hope that the various descriptions presented, although very scattered and incomplete, have provided some palpable content to the web model as described at the beginning. We have seen on the one hand the biological human population, viewed as trajectories or life-lines, and on the other, a structure of channels made up of domains with which individuals associate according to various rules of entrance and of durations of stay.

Other aspects of the conceptualization, not openly included here, such as production, consumption, and social interaction, are describable in essentially the same way although we would need to go down to more detail in order to do it.[6] As indicated before, stable primary groups such as families, and delimited spaces as territorial and positional domains, form the frames within which much of the other activities are contained. Although one must assume that there exists a mutual developmental inter-dependence between the frames and their content, historical evidence seems to justify the notion that primary groups and domains show a considerable stability as well as strong controlling power over other elements. There are, therefore, grounds to pay special attention to them, as has been done here.

The central analytical problem is to look into how more exactly the human trajectories, primary groups, domains, and the other items left out here, fit together. In conclusion I will briefly discuss this matter with respect to what my empirical examples have dealt with in more detail: population versus domains. I repeat once again that the expression 'domain' is used to designate both territorial space and livelihood positions in the socio-economic system (competence spaces).

The first question to ask is how the suggested way of looking at the man-environment complex, derived as it is from a relatively simple and rigid agrarian setting, is more generally useful and particularly so in a highly differentiated and swiftly changing modern society. The population side is simple to deal with conceptually. The idea of a life-line as a representation of an individual existence is fundamental in demography (and is in fact applicable to all living populations). What geographers can do with it as a further elaboration is to change the rather bare life-line concept into the more containing space-time trajectory. This entails also the obligation to view it as a distributional dimension and consider the various factors behind the sequence of states and events as they become projected over the individual trajectory. A fundamental circumstance with respect to this distribution is that for each individual the outcome is a budget specification of his most precious resource, his life-time. Every choice or—if it is not really a choice—every piece of use consumes beyond recall a part of this resource.

More open to variation is the understanding of the options offered in the environment through which the searching trajectory has to move. The purely social component of options is rather simple since all we have to deal with is the set of human trajectories which join and depart. Beyond that one can probably differentiate conceptually the physical and biotic surroundings in many ways. It seems to me that among conceivable starting points, the concept of domain as understood here in a twofold way, should have a very high degree of generality. The phenomena which the concept stands for have as principles a biological foundation. The terrestrial domain can be seen as a human elaboration of the animal territory. On purely practical grounds it is hard to believe that any human society could be livable without the imposition on space of some kind of domain structure. Livelihood positions (competence spaces) are rooted in human nature in a different way. Originally they must have come into being because every individual has a limited capability of mastering a wide variety of techniques for physical and psychological reasons as well as because of time-budget constraints. To these factors are added, in the more elaborate society, the many pressures towards organizational stability which a complex flow of information, people, things and material calls for. The working of the whole requires that there be a great deal of certainty about what kind of input needs to go where, and what kind of output one can expect from where. The obvious solution is to institutionalize positions with defined tasks, frequently tied to terrestrial domains, without regard to which particular individuals are going to hold them. It might well be an impossible task to map empirically the total spectrum of livelihood positions in an urbanized region—a population census gives only an approximate idea—but we need not doubt that the phenomenon can be identified as an ordering construct. We note for example how the number of inhabitants of an area is frequently nearly constant from year to year or changing only slowly, irrespective of the fact that a substantial proportion of the population, seen as individuals, has been exchanged through migration. This could hardly happen without a latent structure of considerable stability.

The basic point I want to arrive at with this discussion is that the concept of budgeting in the spatial direction is still as applicable in modern society as it was in the historical example. First, the population of any delimited area has always a fixed number at any fixed moment. This means that the groups (clusters) of individuals that can be formed for various purposes simultaneously are very much interdependent. Take the case of a playground. If fifteen children are present and the majority decide to play a game which needs ten participants then the remaining group has, for the time being, been cut off from playing all games which need more than five participants. In this respect there is no difference in society at large, as is well illustrated by the case of transportation where public transport is collapsing because a majority prefers private movement.

Secondly, the domains are likewise limited in number at any cross-section of time. Therefore, the fit between human trajectories on one hand and terrestrial spaces and livelihood positions on the other, is again a budgeting problem and a very complex one. So for example, dwelling and work-place must go together as a combinable pair for the indivisible individual, but in spite of that, they mostly come into being in urban society as separate sets of domains under rather separate controlling forces, largely beyond the power of the individual.

The double space-time perspective requires us to try to see the simultaneous (the spatial, the room-providing) allocation of human trajectories over limited options as directly connected with the sequential (the temporal) allocation of states and events over the limited life-time or shorter periods as the case may be. Great efforts have been made both in research and politics to deal with the entrance conditions under which an individual can become a holder of a domain, in particular a competence space, and what rights and obligations the holding entails. This is in line with the dominating weight in most scientific and political thinking which is given to the micro 'close contact level,' mentioned at the beginning. But we will never be able to understand what the open and hidden rules and regulations lead to in terms of distribution of life biographies of various content until we are willing to throw light on the quantity and quality of options which define what the individual person can actually do step by step and what the constraints at work lead to in the long run.

I do not want to give the impression that I believe the pattern of options to be absolutely rigid and not responding to the reactions of people. There is change to a varying degree. But it is also very clear, from the straying debate about the future, that even those who believe that the primary goal of human effort is to help everybody to carve out a decent life, are at a loss concerning what the distributional forces look like. But how could it be otherwise with the very small attention given to the total landscape in terms which are realistic from the individual's local point of view.

What I am suggesting seems to beg the question of supplies of data of an almost unthinkable extent and intrusiveness. But I am not so sure. Although one must learn how to respect the continuity requirements of the individual, from a research point of view, we naturally have to deal more with types than with single cases. Further, structural conditions might well be better understood from data sources other than those which inform us about single individuals. After all, the main question is to try to find out what choices and behavioural combinations are made available by the 'geographies'—I cannot find a more telling term—that people have come to be part of. A host of little understood relations between spatial, social and biographical distributions should become possible to grasp without recourse to the actual behaviour of large samples of meticulously investigated individual persons. The amount of detail which my approach seems to call for should not be mistaken as a request for pedantic empirical completeness in the description of past history or for technocratic (computer-wise) regulation in future planning. I am looking for a way of finding conceptual coherence in the geographer's understanding of the human world all the way from home to globe and from day to lifetime.

Footnotes

[1] Professor G. Tibblin, University of Göteborg, Sweden.

[2] Cf. T. Hägerstrand (1975b).

[3] Asby parish in the province of Östergötland.

[4] I believe that this material conveys a rather unique piece of information. I cannot show it without mentioning that my patient wife Britt put it on paper many years ago. For decades it has served as a structuring conception behind my view of the world.

[5] Note that also still-born children have been included. The reason for this is that in a time-perspective these influence to some extent the relation between family formation and change of position.

[6] Cf. for example T. Hägerstrand (1974a) on socio-technical ecology and the study of innovations.

Chapter 8

Innovation, Time Allocation and Time-Space Packing

Tommy Carlstein

Innovations, time and space

Any region when studied in continuous time can be looked upon as an open but delimited time-space region which contains society and habitat, population and resources. Over the years, such a time-space region is affected by innovations which contribute to structural change of the socio-environmental sub-systems found there, for instance the population, activity and settlement sub-systems. Innovations imply new kinds of human projects, activities and socio-cultural output, and they alter the daily and seasonal routines as well as the life-cycle content of the population.

Up till now, there have been few if any systemic models which relate innovations to both the spatial and the temporal structure of society-habitat or indicate the way innovations impinge on the latter. The early generation of innovation studies, applying chorological methods which Hägerstrand developed, did not really deal with the temporal organization of society at all. The framework was one of time and space but hardly time-space, and time was used as an 'aid in the study of process' and was decomposed into a row of regularly spaced and chronologically ordered points. Space was mainly a locational dimension, and it was the spatial structure of communication and innovation diffusion which was the real object of study (cf. Hägerstrand 1953/1967; Gould 1969). Although this generation of innovation studies meshed space and time and were more dynamic than most human geographic theory, neither human time or settlement space were looked upon as resources affected by innovations and in turn influencing them.

The present essay aims to outline an approach to innovation theory which is time-geographic and based on the model of individuals as paths in time-space, of time-space resources and of temporal and spatial organization of society-habitat. Once innovations are analysed in such a framework, certain new and important aspects reveal themselves, but in order to see how, it is helpful to look at the existing theory of innovations.

Some features of current geographic innovation theory

Most of the formal innovation theory in human geography seems to be focused on the spatial diffusion of innovations and the underlying patterns and processes of communicating them from one locality or region to another together with the barriers in space and other constraints affecting their spread and adoption. Many insights have been gained into the spatial structure of innovation processes as evidenced from surveys by Gould (1969) and Brown (1974; 1975). Innovation diffusion theory has further been merged with that of urban-industrial growth (e.g. in the studies by Pred 1973a; 1973b; 1975) and with the various studies on growth poles and growth centres (cf. Kuklinski 1972), as well as with studies on the transfer of technology (Thomas and Le Heron 1975; Thomas 1975). Another off-shoot of innovation studies has been the spatial modernization studies (e.g. Soja 1968; Riddell 1970).

Innovation theory covers several disciplines. While economics has tended to concentrate on product innovations, cultural anthropology has looked into the historical processes of culture diffusion. Social anthropological studies have applied a structural-qualitative framework of analysis with the emphasis on the integration of innovations in local societies and the concomitant effects on social and economic structure (e.g. Salisbury 1962; Long 1968). In sociology, where innovation theory has been a main concern for rural as well as communication sociologists, the major focus has been on the dynamics of the communication process behind the adoption of innovations (Rogers 1962; 1969) rather than their integration or contribution to structural change. The principal issues investigated relate to the stages of adoption; why some individuals and households adopt innovations while others do not, the age-sex characteristics of potential adopters and their occupation, income and wealth; the role of mass media as opposed to face-to-face interaction; the effects of perception, outlooks, norms and opinions; the influence of change agents and opinion leaders; as well as the rates of adoption as represented by curves of cumulative growth over time, the latter being a common denominator in most innovation studies. The method used by rural sociologists was generally quantitative and heavily based on statistical inference as opposed to the more structural-qualitative reasoning of anthropologists.

Returning to geography, the salient feature of its innovation theory is the concentration on diffusion and communication. It is the spatial movement of socio-cultural elements, their propagation, transmission and communication from place to place. Among other things, Hägerstrand (1953) showed the role of personal communication and contact—as opposed to mass media—in the spread of Swedish rural innovations. Later Brown emphasized how product innovations for household use were diffused through markets and central place systems (Brown 1968). The epidemiological studies of how contagious diseases spread are also heavily focused on human communication in a spatial setting (Pyle 1969; Haggett 1972; 1976; chapter 2 in vol. 3 *TSST*). The orientation towards the spatial structure of communication is also apparent from the near affinity between diffusion studies and the analysis of contact systems in industry (Törnqvist 1970; Gould and Törnqvist 1972), the structure of rural communication networks as found in marriage fields (Mayfield 1972) or various compound movement and information fields (Morrill and Pitts 1967; Mayfield and Yapa 1971).

It is interesting to note about most of the innovation diffusion studies that although a series of different innovations are spread in the same region, each innovation is studied in relative *isolation* and independence from the other. This is as true for the early studies by Hägerstrand as for many later studies by his successors. Even the modernization studies essentially follow the pattern of looking at innovations as *indicators*, although students like Soja and Riddell have a pronounced interest in innovations as inputs in regional change (in spite of the other shortcomings for which the modernization studies have been justly criticized, e.g. by Slater 1973). But generally speaking, the innovation itself has not been the main object of interest in diffusion studies, nor the effects of innovations. This has had two noteworthy consequences. First, diffusion studies have been less useful in planning for development because of the rather crude implicit assumption that all innovations contribute to development and progress and not merely change. This was the main point of Slater. Secondly, there is no comprehensive and *generic classification scheme* of types of innovations affecting regions, but innovations are not homogeneous because they all potentially spread. Surely, a region is not similarly altered by innovations such as a new political party, the foxtrot dance, a new soft drink, a new method for checking cattle disease, a new religion, new birth-control methods, a new means of transport, a new principle of voting, or a new way of producing energy through nuclear fission. Rogers noted in 1962 that 'to date there has been little integration of what is known about diffusion of innovations with present theories of social change ...' and that 'such convergence might result in increased fruitfulness for both fields' (Rogers 1962, p. 74). This is still the situation more than a decade later.

Too little geographic work has been done on how regions are cumulatively influenced by the whole spectrum of innovations they are exposed to, as well as the contributions of each kind of innovation to overall structural transformation. It is necessary to climb the step following actual diffusion and see how innovations are integrated in the population, activity and settlement subsystems of regions and with what kind of impact.

It is likewise urgent to adopt a more futurological as opposed to an historical *ex post facto* perspective. This becomes evident when one considers that in most societies today there are many latent innovations which have not yet spread but which exist in blue-print form or have been spread in other regions. To be useful, innovation theory should enable us to *assess the kind of impact* these innovations will have before their spread is induced by powerful organizations and before they penetrate society by altering routines, living conditions and life styles. Such innovations are not found merely in the realm of technology, since there is also the whole range of organizational and institutional innovations which equally require prior assessment and evaluation, such as those promoted by governments and sectoral interest organizations.

There are thus many arguments why geographic innovation theory would benefit from de-emphasizing the diffusion aspects for a while and move towards a more future-oriented approach of *innovation assessment*. This need not imply a neglect of study of empirical innovation processes, but it points towards the requirement of constructing different kinds of theory looking more at how innovations are integrated in socio-environmental systems and with what effects, and how this is related to the actual kinds of innovations diffused—how kinds of innovations affect kinds of environments.

Innovation theory from a time-geographic viewpoint

Are there any general aspects and key dimensions which can unlock the door to new kinds of innovation studies? The answer must be yes, and many of these have been closer at hand to geography than most geographers have actually realized. Yet they have been overlooked and underexploited.

What seems to be missing in the existing body of geographic innovation theory is both a *resource dimension* and a *time-space systems model* to deal with populations and resources in true process terms. Innovations affect the use of resources in space and over time. Some innovations serve to increase capacity and release a certain resource, while other innovations require additional inputs of human time, settlement space(-time), water and energy, and so on. And each of these resources is made available in certain time-space locations and can only be spatially reallocated under certain continuity and indivisibility constraints among stations or locations.

The only resource referred to in conventional diffusion theory practically, has been economic wealth, monetary assets, or resources used to overcome space through transportation. The pecuniary bias is strong. But geographers ought to look more at resources in real terms as is the custom in other branches of geography, particularly as the monetary criteria for what is workable, efficient or socially just are generally misleading. This aside, the fact that human time and settlement space(-time) are universal resource inputs in all human activities, regardless of political or ecological structure, makes them singularly important to geographers.

Empirically, it is a fact that most local communities within some wider region or nation have been exposed to a series of substantively different innovations rather than single ones. Taking a couple of examples from the Third World (in which the present author has a special interest) the Mexican village of Tepoztlán had adopted numerous innovations in the last decades, among them a new school, new roads, new government institutions, new tools such as sewing machines and maize mills and several new agricultural or domestic practices. In Tanzania, major innovations have been the introduction of new rural settlements, health services, schools, cooperatives, cultivation techniques, political councils and committees, and so on. In any modern country local populations have been exposed to numerous technological and organizational innovations which have affected their use of time and settlement space. To see the interdependence between such diverse innovations, how they promote or bar each other, how they interact among themselves and with the environment in which they are integrated, innovations must be sorted out in a way which is cross-sectoral and systems oriented rather than sectoral and substance oriented. Commonly innovations have been classified by substance logic into political, economic, agricultural, educational, religious and the like, but this does not solve the problem of *multiple innovation processes* in local societies. One way of achieving 'commensurability' between such diverse innovations is to interpret them in activity terms and see how they affect the occupation of human time and settlement space-time and the general carrying capacity in these limited resource time-budgets.

Not only do innovations affect the packing of activities in aggregate resource time-budgets. Innovations are location-specific in their resource relations and are slotted or fitted into certain parts of more or less cyclical activity systems of the region, the annual cycle of production, the daily round of household activities, the perennial cycle of shifting cultivation activities, the life-cycle of individuals in the population, and so on.

In order to make a start in this general field of innovation analysis, the strategy of the present author was to make assessments of some past in-novation processes and to narrow down the size and complexity of societies-habitats investigated before looking into development problems and impacts on the future. To this end a series of local agrarian societies were taken up for more systematic enquiry, material which will be presented elsewhere (Carlstein, forthcoming). A set of time-geographic sub-models was therefore developed to grapple with various socio-environmental sub-systems. Elements of these models have been presented in the writings by Hägerstrand (1969, onward) and his research associates (cf. chapters 7, 9 and 12). A more coherent set of sub-models on time allocation, packing and interaction that are of relevance to innovation problems has been published elsewhere (Carlstein 1975d). What will be done here is to give some glimpses of this work by illustrating a few important ideas.

Innovations and their impact on occupation of resources

Innovations influence the allocation of human time and settlement space-time in many more ways than most of our existing social science models or common sense observations convey. Some examples will therefore be pre-sented by way of introduction to illustrate how innovations cause shifts and reallocations in the use of human and spatial resources both with regard to more elementary mechanisms and more composite effects. This is in order to bring out some main points on studying what innovations *do* rather than what they are in substance terms.

Beginning with how innovations are related to human time allocation, this can initially be analysed by looking at two crude categories of innovations, time saving and time demanding innovations.[1] The effects of these must be seen in a systems context, however, and the daily round of household acti-vities is one such important *activity system* in most if not all societies. In the diurnal cycle, several activities of routine and subsistence kind have to be performed such as cooking, washing, eating and sleeping. This seeems quite trivial but is more interesting when put in a cross-cultural or historic per-spective. Taking the less developed countries, and the time consuming chores allotted to women, for instance, Reining (1970) notes that many Haya women in Tanzania spend more than one hour on carrying water every day. This is often a low figure in societies on this technological level. Getting firewood is another activity. The Nyakyusa women in Southern Tanzania studied by Wilson (1951) fetched firewood two to three times per week and this took from four to ten hours depending on the distance to the woods from the village. In total this activity could take up to thirty hours per week and

woman, which is probably a rather extreme case, but most data available
support the assessment that much time in rural Africa is expended on fetching
water and firewood in order to cook, for instance. This can be compared to
the turning on of a water tap or an electric stove in a technically advanced
country, which is done with minute time expenditure (although the water and
electricity systems require much investment time and maintenance time).
Likewise in an African rural situation, before cooking a meal can commence,
much time has had to be expended on grinding the grain or preparing root
crops such as cassava. For Bemba women to grind flour before making por-
ridge took about three quarters of an hour (Richards 1939, p. 103), but this
is a low figure compared to many other societies. In rural Mexico in the old
days 'women spent from four to six hours a day grinding corn by hand, often
rising at four in the morning to prepare breakfast' (Lewis 1951, p. 99).
Hence, merely to carry out daily cooking projects, the component activities
may be extremely time consuming in societies at this technological level when
compared to modern societies.

It is in a similar context of the daily round as an integrated activity system that the role of many time-saving and time-demanding innovations must
be understood. When comparing a metal pot with a clay pot, it is easy to see
this in terms of the former being more durable, less fragile and easier to clean.
But that metal pots may be quite a time saving innovation when introduced
in an African society is only apparent when one sees them in an activity and
resource perspective. Metal pots are time saving because they require less fuel
to cook in compared with earthen pots (hence less time spent on gathering
fuel) and so they hasten the cooking process, as described for instance by de
Schlippe (1956) for the Azande people of the Sudan. In a similar fashion,
grinding mills have been time-saving the world over, something which is often
mentioned casually in historic or ethnographic accounts. 'Those ... who have
sufficient cash prefer to take their grain for grinding rather than pound and
grind themselves, a lengthy and arduous task' (Long 1968, on Zambia). In
an Indian village it took a woman many hours to make *ragi* into flour by hand
pounding, whereas the same activity was performed in a few minutes by a
labour-saving flour mill (Epstein 1962). Hence many time-saving innovations
cause substantial shifts in the habitual daily time-budgets of household
members.

The introduction of a village school in an agrarian society is a typical
time demanding innovation. When the previous informal education of children
is partly replaced by formal schooling, the time demands of the latter attain
considerable proportions, since children generally start working in production
at an early age. Long before puberty they are competent to help at home by
fetching water and fire-wood, tending younger siblings, taking animals to
pasture, weeding fields, or guarding fields from vermin. A village school if
totally adopted thus makes a substantial imprint on the population time-
budget as well as the temporal organization of village activities. The time
requirements of village schooling can be illustrated schematically in Figure 1,
which covers one week and the total population affected, pupils and teachers
and others. The time of the children is thus not some kind of 'free good', and
school activity competes with all other time consuming activities in the
population time-budget (Carlstein 1970; 1975e). The integration of village

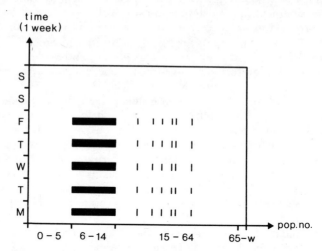

Figure 1   The time demand of a school during one typical week. The population is ordered by age, and the total volume of demand (black) is described in relation to the time supply for one week.

schooling activity thus leads to time allocation conflicts with traditionally performed activities, both in the daily and weekly activity cycle and in the annual production and ritual cycle. The school year, which is often centrally decided upon in the capital city, may be very ill adapted to the local variations in seasonal labour input in agriculture, for instance. Or it might clash with the religious or recreational cycle. The impact of an innovation is thus not homogeneous over the daily, annual, or life cycle and it fits more or less well into the preexisting temporal structure of activities. (Figure 2).

The above examples readily illustrate that innovations affect the packing of activities in a limited population time-budget. Innovations such as a school, a cooperative, a further-education programme, or a new forum for political participation are time demanding for different age-sex-skill categories of the population. Time-saving innovations by contrast reduce the time requirements for various tasks and projects and thus generate slots in the habitual time-budget, gaps which are then filled by other activities. Seen in this perspective, even the most substantively different innovations are interdependent by either competing for the same finite time resources or by contributing to the re-allocation of time in other respects.

There are thus innovations which restructure the temporal organization of activities without necessarily being either time demanding or time saving by shifting the constraints on activities. For physical, biotic, technical or institutional reasons, some activities are heavily constrained to certain times and places because necessary activity inputs are only available and accessible there. This naturally affects the synchronous input of human time. Likewise, the capability constraints on individual path allocation in time-space may change with consequences on how individuals in the population can supply time to various activities.

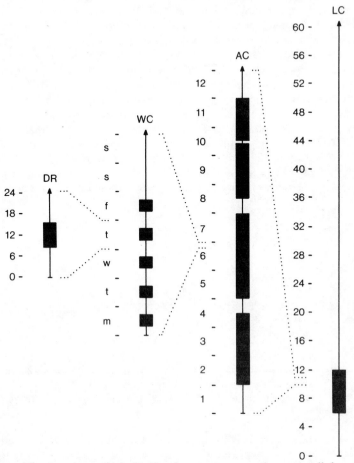

Figure 2   The time demand of schooling for an average student or pupil throughout the day, week, year and life-time and its temporal location. (The example is based on data for the Mexican village of Tepoztlán described by Lewis, 1951).

Take the example of the daily round of household activities in a technically simple agrarian society. Many activities in this setting are severely restricted by the temporal location of daylight. To look for firewood, clear bush and trees, manufacture fencing, prepare the soil, plant, weed, or harvest, or keep an eye on grazing livestock is generally not feasible at night! Even when there is a busy season of ploughing or harvesting, the volume of time which can be used for this task is often constrained by the maximal duration of the day. Many domestic and handicraft activities cannot be very effectively performed without light either. In this way, light is an input which affects the input of human time as well as the output of time spent. Artificial light is a kind of innovation which extends the day, as it were, and facilitates a repacking of activities in the diurnal cycle and seasonal cycle. Activities which otherwise would have to compete for scarce time during daylight hours can be shifted till after dark, when light is made locally available as opposed to the widespread availability during the daytime. Electric light makes it possible to use evening time for new projects and activities in the field of education, politics or recreation, for instance, and it facilitates adult education which might otherwise conflict seriously with daytime work.

This touches upon what Melbin (chapter 6) has called the colonization of time or more specifically of the daily cycle, since the 'spant' or time-space region for which he studies the packing of activity is the city-day. A minor analytical fault is that he does not separate the locational properties of 'spants' from the resource properties of population time and settlement space-time.[2] Howevery, colonization can be seen at an annual and perennial time scale as well, for instance the temporal expansion of agricultural activities into the former dry season or the intensification and shortening of fallow periods in a shifting cultivation system. All these terms cover different aspects of packing activities, populations and artefacts in time-distributed resource budgets.

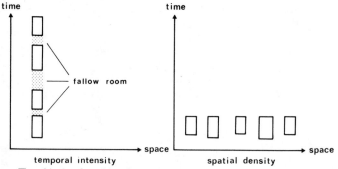

Figure 3   Two kinds of packing in settlement space-time along the temporal versus the spatial dimensions.

Having previously dealt with occupation of time (i.e. of a time-budget by time-demanding activities), let us look at occupation of terrestrial space. The traditional concept of land use is well adapted to cartography but is static, in that there is a difference in the consumption of room between occupying a piece of land or a building for one minute and for one hour, or in whether a crop occupies a field for one month or six months. Hence what is really used as an input in human activity is space-time and building time, just as we use machine-time in factories. For a farming population, their occupation of land by crops can thus be measured in, for instance, hectare-weeks, just as the colonization of a bathroom can be measured in square-metre-minutes (in reality a bathroom is an indivisible entity, one occupies all or nothing, and hence it is measured in bathroom unit-time). When land or buildings are not occupied by human populations (or populations of cultigens or artefacts, if one wants to extend the concept of population as Hägerstrand (1974b) does), it is empty or 'fallow'. The occupation of settlement space-time and building space-time can thus be looked upon in terms of packing, spatial density and temporal intensity, as in Figure 3. In this way the intensity with which agricultural land is used or occupied by crops can be illustrated as in

Figure 4, for different systems of cultivation. Boserup chose to call this 'frequency of cropping' in her study of agricultural intensification (Boserup 1965), which was a kind of colonization of space-time at the perennial, annual and seasonal time scale. The causes for this kind of intensification are those of resource expansion.

Irrigation as an innovation thus performs the same facilitating function in the annual cycle of agricultural production as electric light did in the daily cycle. Both are 'enabling factors' in Melbin's terminology. Irrigation removes

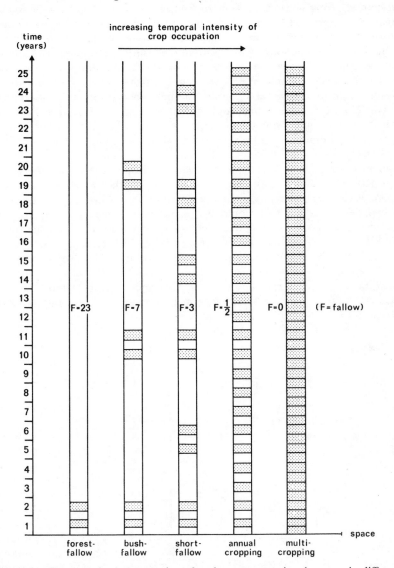

Figure 4 The intensity in occupation of settlement space-time by crops in different cultivation systems. (Carlstein: 1973a, 1975b)

the constraint (or 'limiting factor') of water and allows its redistribution in a more continuous or 'incessant' way over the year. It should be noted, however, that many enabling factors in reality are other and complementary resource inputs. This implies that intensification or expansion in the occupation of human time or settlement space-time is often a function of the *synchronization of inputs* and the synchronous accessibility of other resources such as energy or water. From a temporal organizational viewpoint, it is very important to incorporate the phenomena of synchronized occupation, use and economizing with resources in order to see how activities can be packed into time-budgets. The same thing applies when assessing how innovations can be integrated in the population, activity, or settlement sub-systems.

But the syn*chron*ization of resource inputs and the substitution between inputs must also be seen in a spatial context of how the various inputs are syn*chor*ized in space. *Chronos* and *choros*, time and space, must be viewed together to grasp *coupling* of resources in time-space. Confining the analysis to two resources, human time and settlement space-time, electric light and irrigation as technical innovations have two interesting features in common. Both allow temporal *expansion* in resource occupation, but both also result in a parallel *contraction* in spatial distribution and accessibility. Temporal expansion is constrained to those spatial areas which are covered by the irrigation network and electricity network. Spatially, in other words, it is a matter of *local* rather than *global* expansion (Figure 5).[3] This is because the reduction of capacity-capability constraints on the extent to which human time and settlement space-time can be occupied with the aid of some complementary resource, can only be done within the framework of the *coupling constraints* associated with the physical coupling of that resource to the other resources.

Therefore, resources must not be looked upon in the abstract sense of quantitative occurrence within a time-space region, but in material terms of localized quanta and bodily existence in time-space. Only idealist sociology

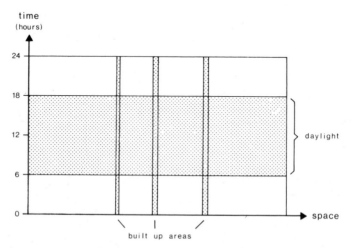

Figure 5a   The figure shows how activities demanding day-light can be extended beyond the time of natural light by the use of artificial lights in limited areas.

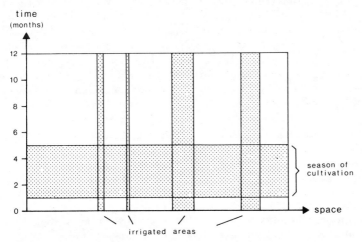

Figure 5b   The figure shows the same kind of temporal extension but of the cultivation season in four local areas by means of irrigation systems.

(to which even much work on historical materialism ultimately belongs) or pecuniary economics can afford to neglect these constraints on how resources are physically located and reallocated in time-space. This is why time-geography looks upon individuals supplying human time as indivisible and continuous entities in time-space (as described by trajectories or paths) and upon other resources in similar real corporeal (tangible, bodily) terms. The synchronization of resources and the substitution between resources must thus be seen in a spatial context of how they are synchorized in space and coupled in time-space.

While some innovations are time demanding as well as space demanding, such as the introduction of a new crop or a manufacturing plant in a region, other innovations may save both human time and settlement space-time by allowing a more condensed form of activity. The automobile as innovation (taken in conjunction with modern roads) shows a different pattern. Unlike the train, the car allows much choice in the times of departure and arrival and it reaches effective speeds that are greater than those of trains. In space it is also less station-bound and there is much greater freedom of choice in direct destinations—the net effect being saved time and the generation of time gaps to be filled by alternative activities. However, roads and the automobile are not room-saving; quite the contrary. Roads take much space and cars take more space than the slower bicycles. With the car, the saving of time has been accomplished at the cost of an increased occupation of and competition for settlement space-time. And by crowding certain cities from the pre-automobile era to bursting point, it has made the car less time-saving than it could be. To complicate the matter, however, the car has paradoxically also generated more accessible space-time within 'prisms' (Figure 6), where a prism centred upon two base stations circumscribes the portion of a region's space-time that can be maximally accessible for any kind of occupation by an individual in a population (cf. Hägerstrand 1970a). At any rate, the car is an example of

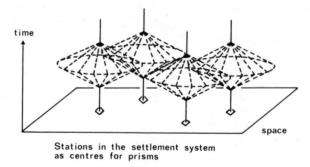

Stations in the settlement system
as centres for prisms

Figure 6   Stations in the settlement system as centres for day prisms.

an innovation which saved time but was more expensive in the occupation of settlement space-time, and as such is an interesting example of a mechanism for substitution between the two. It is also a kind of innovation which requires lavish use of energy, and hence it is obvious that changes in the energy economy will lead to alterations in the economy of human time and settlement space-time because of the impact on travel activity and spatial mobility.

Human socio-ecological history provides endless examples of how innovations affect the two resources of human time and settlement space-time. Returning to the structure of agrarian societies in the tropics, systems of shifting cultivation are very extensive in their input of settlement space-time due to the long fallow periods (Figure 4) while rather thrifty in labour time input. The intensive irrigated agriculture of Monsoon Asia by contrast is thrifty in the space-time occupied by crops per capita of the population, while very demanding in terms of human time requirements. It is not surprising, therefore, that population growth is generally accompanied by innovations which cause shifts and repacking towards room saving solutions (cf. Boserup 1965). Settlement space becomes more densely and intensively occupied over time, and the fallows of shifting cultivation systems become 'colonized', while obversely, the input of labour time per areal unit is lavishly increased. So without going into the various mechanisms of structural cause and effect, time-space packing and innovation processes can be observed and analysed at different levels of aggregation and complexity. At the extreme macro-level, two obvious major directions of packing response to technical evolution and population growth are agricultural intensification and urbanization *cum* urban intensification in time and space use.

Some dimensions of a new time-geographic innovation theory

Innovation processes should be placed in a much broader socio-environmental perspective than has been the case in current diffusion theory. Many innovation processes are both in part and in total adaptive responses to ecological predicaments (cf. *inter alia* Wilkinson 1973). This is the case with the response to population growth in terms of agricultural intensification, to take one major instance. Other innovation processes are associated with resource mobilization within the broader framework of religious, ideological and political resurrection and expansion. Whatever the case, innovation processes should be related to the use of resources and to the natural and cultural environment in which human projects and activities are carried out.

One way of understanding this is to see how innovations act as mechanisms of packing and repacking activities in time-space, taken in relation to the limited carrying capacity of the population and settlement sub-systems. This general theme is the object of a study on agrarian systems to be published by the present author (Carlstein, forthcoming). But before closing this subject here, some further points must be made with regard to the limits to action, interaction and the capacity to absorb innovations by socio-environmental (i.e. human ecological) systems.

There is every reason to be cautious when discussing *limits* to socio-economic input, output and performance, as limits can be absolute or relative, short term or long term or they can be seen statically or dynamically. Up till now, the major 'limits to growth' have been discussed with regard to resource consumption in industrial societies and limitations to carrying capacity of land for agriculture and the like. However, the limits inherent in the human population have been less often elaborated on in social science theory. Intuitively and pragmatically we know that no human being can accomplish *every*-thing or can perform activities at *any* rate. On the contrary, we all act under strong capacity-capability constraints. An interesting time-geographic task is to construct models and theory on the extent to which constraints at the individual level can or cannot be overcome through collective action, couplings and bundle formation at the societal level by collective forms of resource exploitation and socio-technical organization. No doubt many capability constraints at the individual level can be overcome. One watershed in this direction was when language developed as a basis for further cultural evolution, where language is a supra-individual thing with great capability increasing effects. But given this, there is still a limit on how much of language we can use per time unit.

Hence, at least in the 'short run' there is *limited carrying capacity* in three major ways of interest in the study of innovations:

1   The first is with regard to the packing of materials, artefacts, organisms and human populations in settlement space-time;
2   the second pertains to the packing of time-consuming activities in population time-budgets; and
3   the third is a function of the packing of bundles of various sizes, numbers and durations in the population system, i.e. to group formation because of the indivisibility and continuity constraints of individuals.

Any local region and society can thus be modelled as a kind of input-output system in which there is a limited carrying capacity for innovations at each point in time. This carrying capacity is not a static thing, however, since it is altered as a result of innovations entering and displacement effects arising. The carrying capacity of the population system can be increased both extensively and intensively, e.g. by reducing the time spent on travel (by faster vehicles or spatial concentration or urbanization) or by using equipment and energy which allows humans to perform a given activity in less time. Expanding the population size increases carrying capacity in terms of human time by providing a base for more complex and efficeint specialization, but need not in relative terms increase capacity at all, as a population has the dual roles of producer and consumer. Also, the facilities to perform activities at a greater capacity and faster rate are themselves a function of the capacity with which prior projects and activities have been completed and to what extent they could be fitted into limited time and space budgets.

Because carrying capacity is limited in the short term while some innovations that are resource demanding may be introduced at a faster rate, as well as for other reasons, innovations cause *displacement effects* in the population time budget and settlement space-time budget. Hence as many innovations are introduced, there is a corresponding outflow of what I have termed *exnovations*. These also deserve special attention. The factory system of production displaced many previous forms of craft activities and artisan forms of production, for instance, and the introduction of new projects and the associated groups and collective activities may displace old institutionalized groups and activities. Any expression of culture in the field of art, religion, economy or recreation is based on human activity and hence takes time to create and maintain. Looking at the 'life-cycle' of institutions and organizations, there is always a birth, life and death, so to speak. Innovation studies have so far dealt with inception and birth, but also ought to include the maintenance, viability and turnover of input and output, and exnovations are elements of decline, displacement and disappearance. Whether one is dealing with life-cycles of the population(s), of organizations, and of institutions, or with product-cycles in industry, the whole cycle should be treated within the same theoretical framework, including the exnovations, which are the new ways in which old elements disappear. Intensification and capacity expansion is one mechanism by which societies are able to keep a lot of the old cake while eating new cake at the same time. But no society is able to keep the whole cake and eat it, and there are certainly limits to relative carrying capacity within a population system, considering the interaction between supply and demand for time within it (Carlstein 1974a; 1975c; 1975d).

There are even limitations to the capacity with which human communication can be effected. Communication and interaction was the classic theme underlying most modern diffusion studies. It does take time to meet other people, however, and if time is allocated to some, it cannot be allocated to others. It also takes time to transmit and receive, as well as process, information, once people are in contact with one another or with the media they are using. The way in which these time-consuming activity components affect the diffusion and communication process is far from clear in previous studies, so even the more conventional innovation studies could gain by reinterpretation within a time and space allocation framework which is not simply *dia*chronic but *holochronic*.

Footnotes

[1] Actually innovations can 'save' time in a good many ways, e.g. by speeding up the gestation period in completing a project, by increasing capacity in performance of an activity, or by reducing the time input for a given activity. These distinctions will be made in a more comprehensive study by the author (Carlstein, forthcoming).

[2] In my own time-geographic studies, I have taken the liberty of talking about *time-space* when I refer to a locational coordinate system and view time and space as existential dimensions. The term *space-time* I use to denote a room resource in the settlement system, isomorphic to other resources such as human time and machine-time.

[3] Compare the phenomenon of urbanization as local rather than global expansion and intensification, being a function of coupling constraints in order to expand capacity.

Chapter 9

A Time-Geographic Simulation Model of Individual Activity Programmes

Bo Lenntorp*

The aim of this essay is to present selected parts of the time-geographic approach, especially a computer simulation model, which allows the simulation of daily activity programmes in urban environments and regions. This and some of the general theory and philosophy behind it will be discussed and illustrated with some concrete applications of relevance to urban planning.

The research work presented here is a part of a broader research enterprise in the field of 'time-geography' conducted within a group at Lund University. The endeavour, inspired by Torsten Hägerstrand, has been aimed at developing a broad analytical and conceptual model on interrelationships between social, technical, economic and human ecological factors (cf. Hägerstrand 1963; 1969; 1970 onwards). This work has now progressed in a number of different directions, as is indicated by other chapters in this volume and references to the time-geographic approach supplied there.[1]

This essay presents a few fragments of a particular direction of time-geographic analysis. It examines the possible behaviour of an individual in time-space environments. To do so, a formal computer simulation model, PESASP, has been developed by the author (Lenntorp 1970) to model urban regions and simulate individual activities. This general effort has been published in a more comprehensive study (Lenntorp 1976b), so what will be done here is to give an outline of the PESASP computer model. Mårtensson (chapter 10 below) uses the same kind of model approach for a different purpose, *viz.* for comparing living conditions of households in city regions. But before taking up the simulation of daily activities in urban environments, some time-geographic preliminaries are essential.

Human individuals as trajectories in time-space

In essence, the time-geographic approach is based on modelling individuals in populations as trajectories or paths in a three-dimensional coordinate system where two dimensions represent geographic space and the third dimension time (cf. chapter 7 by Hägerstrand). This system in all its ramifications makes

* Translated from the Swedish by T. Carlstein.

it possible to study human action in space dynamically and to analyse a series of spatial and temporal location and allocation problems. Individuals and other indivisible entities are depicted as continuous paths or life-lines in constant movement through time and sometimes also through space. So long as the individual is stationary (or stationed) in geographic space, this path (henceforth referred to as the *individual's path*) is parallel to the time axis. Travel produces a deflection of the path away from the direction of the vertically described time axis, the slope of the path increasing proportionally with the speed of travel (Figure 1). The individual's path must be continuous and unequivocally defined at every point in time. A person cannot cease to exist and later reappear again. Nor can anybody be at two or more places at the same time.

This time-space mode of description makes it possible via the individual's path to study how *stationary activities* in the home, at work etc. are *linked together by travel*. But it also allows the environment in which the individual lives and acts to be modelled in the same time-space terms. Work places, department stores, post offices and such like can and must be pinpointed, not only with respect to their location in geographic space but also by means of their time coordinates describing, for instance, business or working hours. Depending on the spatial and temporal scale chosen, specific places and areas can be delineated for which within-movements are insignificant in relation to between-movements. In this study of daily activities in cities, and journeys between work places, homes and service facilities, the spatial movements within those places may safely be disregarded. These places can be generally referred to as *stations*, i.e. places where the geographic position is defined constant.

The description of the physical environment also includes an account of the structure of the different transport networks in a time-space region, where public transport is particularly amenable to time-space studies. Mapping the geographical extent of the different routes often conveys little information about the possibility an individual has to make use of public transport services unless it is accompanied by a timetable. With the time-geographic approach, a systematic effort is made to incorporate timetables for all activities, e.g. business hours and working hours in the environment or mealtimes and sleeping hours for the individual.

A major emphasis in the time geographic approach has been placed on analysing the *possibilities* open to the individual and not merely his actually chosen and *observed behaviour*. This entails charting and measuring constraints operating in city environments and thereby elucidating the possible choices or alternatives available to the individual. To facilitate a study of such possibilities open to individuals in a particular environment, various activity programmes are postulated and contain conditions as to when and where different activities are to be performed. These postulated programmes are empirically based and realistic for different categories of individuals. The properties of the environment (transport systems, number of stations, their positions and their accessibility in time) then decide whether (and in how many ways) a programme is feasible or not. All these activity programmes must satisfy the constraints implied by individuals being continuous and indivisible paths in time-space.

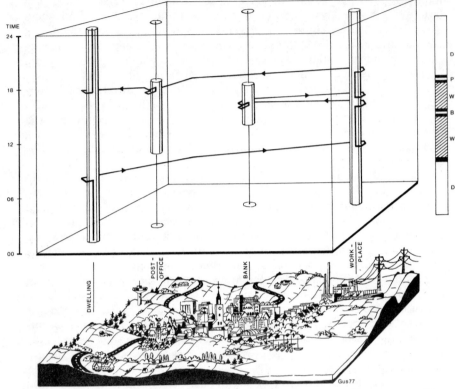

Figure 1 Example of an individual's path in a time-space coordinate system. The three dimensions of geographical space have been collapsed into two in order to make room for a time axis. The movements of the individual in space and time are depicted in a continuous and indivisible path. In the example, the individual starts from the home and visits his work place, a bank, his work place and, finally, a post office, before returning home.

To illustrate some of these basic ideas, a graphical example is provided in Figure 1 which gives concrete form to the method of approach. An individual activity programme containing a few simple errands and a resulting path will be followed throughout a day. This programme is of the same general character as those which are tested in the subsequent sections.

As is shown in the graphic presentation, the population and its environment can be described in a three-dimensional kind of time-space 'map' in which paths always move upward along the time axis. The environment in the figure is simplified; it includes one individual only and is confined to those stations which he uses and comes into contact with during the twenty-four-hour period, together with the road network. The dwelling station is represented by a pillar extending throughout the entire period to show that the individual is free to enter and leave the station at any time. The post office and the bank, on the other hand, are both stations which are open during a limited period of time. Their extent in time, therefore, has been depicted solely during their hours of business, although they do not at any time relinquish their demand for space, of course. The fourth station—the work place—is of a different type from those previously mentioned. Access to it is not free: this station is surrounded by regulations as to who can be admitted, and there are also rules concerning times at which employees can come and go. It is clear that many stations have a dual function: to certain persons they are work places with certain rules of admission, while to other persons they are service facilities with different rules of access.

The individual's path is followed from the beginning of the twenty-four-hour period, starting from the home. The period just before seven o'clock is devoted to various activities within the station, so that the path moves on the same axis only. The journey from home to the work place begins before seven o'clock. In addition to moving on the time axis, the path now moves in space, and its projection in the spatial plane depicts the journey on the road network.

Recorded spatial travel ceases at the work place, owing to the scale of depiction—the entire work place being regarded as one station. During the lunch hour the individual visits a bank and then returns to his work place. On his way home from work, after 17:00, he calls at the post office before concluding his twenty-four-hour programme with activities in the home.

A number of remarks can be appended to the simple activity programme of this picture, which takes the individual from his home to his work place and the post office and back home again. The primary purpose in presenting this picture is to impart physical realism to the structure of daily activity programmes. In many cases the rather simple and apparently trivial assumptions associated with the individual's path are sufficient for a meaningful study of the possibilities open to the individual in environments of different kinds. In the simple example given above, we find that the restrictions which distance and hours of business impose drastically circumscribe the possible sequential orders in which the different stations could be visited. Neither the bank nor the post office opens before seven o'clock. The lunch hour does not give the individual time enough to visit both the bank and the post office, because they are too far apart. After working hours the bank in this example is closed, thus precluding a combination of post office and bank visits at this time and also preventing the bank and post office from changing places in the sequence.

The PESAP simulation model

The main features of the model

Departing from the time-geographic base model of populations as paths in time-space, a computer simulation model was constructed and designated PESASP, Programme Evaluating the Set of Alternative Sample Paths (Lenntorp 1970). This model simulates the possibilities of performing daily activity programmes in environments which can either resemble actual environments or else be completely fictitious. Basic to the model is that it deals with the day programmes of a human individual, which explains the fundamental importance of the path concept. Briefly the model evaluates the confrontation between an activity programme to be carried out and the time-space structured conditions of the environment. The simulation provides an answer to the question whether the individual's path is physically compatible with the constraints in the programme itself and those imposed by the environment in the form of the spatial locations of the stations sought, their opening hours and the time-space structure and design of the transport system.[2]

Activity programmes

The procedures of the simulation model can be illustrated with the aid of a simple activity programme formulated as follows: The individual studied can only leave his home at twelve o'clock. Between 13:00 and 17:00 he must be at his place of work. He can arrive there earlier or leave later but he is required to be there between the hours mentioned. He must also arrive at home before 18:00. During the interval between 12:00 and 18:00 he is further obliged to make a post-office visit, for instance to pay a bill. This visit, comprising both service and waiting, is assumed to take 12 minutes. Since he is restricted neither to any particular post-office nor any given time, the errand can take place at any time between 12:00 and 13:00 or 17:00 and 18:00.

The assumptions made above can be given a more explicit time-geographic exposition when supplemented by an assumption relating to the speed of

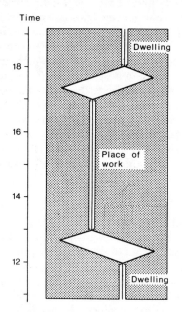

Figure 2 *Time-geographic description of an activity programme*   The following assumptions are made in the programme. The individual cannot leave his dwelling before 12:00 and he must return home before 18:00 hours. Between those times he must remain at his work place between 13:00 and 17:00 hours, and in either of the two free intervals, depicted by so called *prisms*, a post office visit must take place. (Source: Lenntorp 1973)

movement in time-space (Figure 2). The two one-hour intervals of more discretionary time can be depicted as so called 'prisms', which circumscribe the portion of time-space which is accessible to the individual given the above constraints. Had the figure been three-dimensional as in Figure 1, the prisms would have the shape of two sets of skewed cones with the circular base joining.[3] Within at least one of these prisms, there must be an open post office in order for the visit to come about.

This activity programme, described in time-space terms, can then be rotated among various spatial locations in a region to sense the environment by computing the number of alternative ways in which the programme can be performed from each location. This can be illustrated by a few simple experiments in real regions, the first of which is Örebro in Sweden, a city with about 90,000 inhabitants. Before any simulation is possible, however, the region must be modelled in the computer both with regard to the set of relevant stations and the transportation systems connecting them.

The environment

A square grid coordinate system is placed over the chosen region of investigation with a cell size of 250 by 250 metres. This size can be adjusted to any desired scale and level of detail. (The same cell size is used for the Karlstad investigation below.) Everything found within a cell is referred to its central point, and all stations of potential interest in the tested activity programmes are determined with regard to their grid location and opening hours. In the examples below, all activity programmes are performed using the home (dwelling or residential station) as both origin and final destination in the day. (Hence dwellings will also be referred to as test points). Dwellings are systematically sampled in the region using a triangular grid in which each triangle cell side was 1,500 metres. Each vertex in this grid which coincided with a residential area was chosen. Upon this selection seventeen residential stations remained. Work places were also systematically located within the city but only six places were chosen, while the nine post offices of relevance were placed in the coordinate grid system according to their observed location.

Movements

In the simulation, four different modes of travel are distinguished: walking, cycling, car travel and travel by public transport (bus). In an activity programme testing, what is important is that the *total travel time* between two stations can be accurately computed, since this is the factor affecting the time which will remain for stationary activities prescribed in the programme and whether it can be carried out or not. Pecuniary or other costs such as discomfort to the individual are not looked into.

The individual's journey on foot is described as follows. The distance between starting point and destination is measured as-the-crow-flies, this distance is then multiplied by a constant, the value of which has been put at 1·2, which implies an elongation by 20 per cent. Travelling time can then be calculated by means of the computed distance and an assumption regarding average speed (invariably assumed to be 5 km per hour). If the individual is to travel between two stations within the same cell, his journey is always assumed to be 150 metres, which corresponds to the average distance between two randomly chosen points within the cell of the given size.

When travelling by bicycle and especially by car, the individual is much more dependent on the road network than when travelling on foot. It is consequently unrealistic in either case to calculate distance as-the-crow-flies. The model therefore provides for depicting the main structure of any road network. A series of points—*nodes*—are located in the area at the major route intersections. Distances between nodes are then measured manually along the routes whereby the distance between pairs of nodes are unequivocally determined and used as input data. These nodes further serve as interchange points for journeys from stations to the road network and *vice versa*. All stations analysed in the region are linked to these nodes in the network of routes or roads before the actual simulation can begin. A station can at most be linked to three nodes. The speed of travel can be varied between any pair of nodes. It is further possible to introduce a general reduction or increase in basic speed during a couple of intervals, for instance, in order to calibrate for traffic peaks.

A journey, then, is simulated in the following fashion: First the individual travels to a node that is linked to the station of departure, whereupon the journey proceeds along the measured routes to the node which is linked to the station of destination. Finally, the individual travels from that node to the actual station. The shortest route of travel amongst at most nine routes between origin and destination is chosen. This procedure can be used to simulate a journey by bicycle or automobile. In the latter case it is possible to introduce delays at terminals; time for movement to and from the vehicle and for parking for instance, can also be added to the actual travel time in the car.

Finally, it is possible to simulate journeys in conventional public transport systems. Since the important thing is the complete travel time between two stations, this time is not subdivided into time for walking, waiting and actual transport. Neither is the number of changes in mode of travel recorded. This simplification makes it possible to speed up calculations drastically.

The geographic distribution of the transport network is described by determining the locations of bus stops or train stations. One requirement is that the distance between all stops on one line is the same. For each line there is also a uniform average speed. This rather inflexible assumption has consequences which are avoided by subdividing bus lines into shorter homogeneous segments. In this way, for instance, one can calibrate for differences in density of bus stops between outlying and central areas in a city.

The frequency of services is recorded for each route and can be varied any number of times per twenty-four hours. Determination of the first departure time then governs the departures of the buses so that the model is true to reality. Consequently, the model does not calculate *statistically estimated* waiting times at bus stops. The stations and the public transport network are linked up in the same way as with pedestrian journeys, and every station can be linked to several stops in the immediate vicinity.

To sum up, a journey by public transport is simulated in the following way.

The passenger leaves his starting station and goes to one of the bus stops linked to it. This part of the journey is simulated as if it were undertaken on foot. The passenger waits at the stop until the bus arrives in accordance with the timetable. The bus trip ends by the passenger getting off at the station of destination. Since the stations are usually linked to several bus stops, travelling times are calculated for all possible combinations. The alternative with the shortest travel time is the one that counts in the actual simulation of the total activity programme. Travel on foot is a basic alternative which is always computed to avoid absurdities which compulsory bus travel would have given rise to should the starting point and destination be close together.

A simulation experiment

The model now has all the necessary information for the simulation, and it can now calculate all the possible combinations of stations and permutations of activities in a programme. The procedure begins by the individual seeking his way from the dwelling to one of the six work stations. On the arrival at the work place, it is checked that the time is correct and is not later than 13:00. He then leaves his work-place at exactly 17:00 (when according to assumptions made he was first allowed to begin his homeward journey) and he seeks his way to a post office. On his arrival there, it is checked that the post office is open. The errand is performed and the individual departs for home. If he arrives before 18:00 the simulated path conforms to the conditions set in the activity programme. The simulation then takes charge of events at the point in time where he finished his work, but this time a new post office is looked up, where the errand is again performed before the person moves on home. For one work place, each of the nine post offices are tested for whether they can be integrated into his path. Consequently, a maximum of nine alternatives are feasible for each work place. The *sequence* 'dwelling-work place—post office—dwelling' can, however, be permuted into 'dwelling—post office—work place—dwelling'. The simulation model automatically investigates also this possibility. Hence there is a total of 2×9 possible alternatives for the individual's path to pass through each work place and from all dwelling stations there exists $6 \times 2 \times 9 = 108$ possible alternatives since the activity programme is tested for six work places, nine post offices and two sequences.

In a first series of experiments, the possibility of carrying out the programme was simulated under conditions corresponding to the real ones in the city. The individual was assumed to travel either on foot, by bicycle, by car or by public transport (bus). The speed by bicycle was given as 12 km per hour, which is an average speed for several categories of individuals. The average speed of the car traveller was set at 40 km per hour within the whole city. The possibility in the model to differentiate speeds among various road segments was consequently not used.

Once empirical data on the environment have been collected, it takes little effort to alter the parameter values in the model to conduct various experiments. In the Örebro investigation, a series of small tests on the public transport system were made which will now be presented. In these, different trip densities and average speeds were also laboured with while the activity pro-grammes and sets of stations studied in the region remained the same.

In the first attempt, all bus lines were assigned a mean speed of travel of 20 km per hour and the buses departed at twenty-minute intervals. (For some of the bus lines this trip density was lower than the actually observed one.) Keeping this bus service density, the effects of changed mean speeds to 30 and 40 km per hour were investigated.

In the next series of experiments, the trip density was doubled so that buses departed at ten-minute intervals. (For some lines this density was now higher than in reality.) This new trip density was also tested for three different mean speeds. In the last series, the trip density was again doubled and the effects evaluated for all three speeds.

But the set of alternative actions of individuals in time-space are not simply influenced by changes in the transportation systems. In many instances other solutions, for example alterations in the working hours or opening hours, may be more effective and may also be in many cases more economic to society. To this end, flexible working hours were introduced in order to assess the impact of such measures on the performance of this specific activity pro-gramme. The individual was assumed to be able to start his work whenever he wanted for half an hour around 13:00, while the duration of work re-mained the same. It was further stipulated that the individual had to use the actually observed public transport system.

It is not possible to draw any general conclusions from these simulations, since they merely comprise one single activity programme tested in only one city. But for this unique type of programme, certain results emerged which it would be interesting to subject to a more comprehensive investigation.

If a person travels on foot, the number of alternatives are few from the majority of the dwelling stations. From four of the outlying residence stations, the programme is impossible to carry out. Few alternatives implies that the individual has only few work places to choose among, that he is restricted to very few post offices and that it is in many instances not possible to vary the sequence. When, on the other hand, the individual is allowed to travel by public transport, the situation is somewhat improved.

The bicycle, however, is an even more efficient mode of travel if measured in the same terms. From all the residential stations, the cyclist has more al-ternatives to choose among than a traveller by public transport. The car driver, finally, is so privileged that he can freely choose over the whole region places of work and post offices as well as the sequence. He can thus carry out the activity programme in 108 different ways regardless of which stations of residence he departs from (although there may be other factors of accessibility which prevent him from choosing among work places).

Travel on foot versus by car can thus be conceived of as forming the ex-tremes on a ranking scale (as in Figure 3), in which the observations are ordered according to the average number of possible alternatives. The widest range of dispersion among the number of possible alternatives from the different residential test points is encountered for travel by bus. This is evident in Figure 3 by the great difference between percentiles 30 and 70, showing the minimum number of alternatives and the maximum in percentage terms for this particular mode of travel.

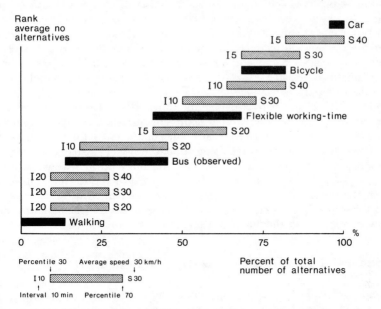

Figure 3 *Number of alternative possibilities of performing a specific activity programme under given conditions*

The postulated activity programme is as follows: An individual is to leave his station of residence and commute to work and back home again. During the trip to work or homeward journey, for which he has one hour each at his disposal, he has to visit a post office (cf. Figure 2). From every given station of residence the programme can be carried out in a maximum of 108 different ways (which are the combinations of different work places and post offices and sequences). The possibilities of performing the programme in a medium-sized city has been simulated with regard to various modes of travel.

The figure shows, for example, that a person travelling by bus in the observed public transport system has, from more than 30 per cent of the dwelling stations, a set of alternatives of about 14 per cent of the total number and that 70 per cent of the dwelling stations have a set of alternatives comprising less than 45 per cent of the total number of possible alternatives. Flexible working hours imply that the individual can start working within a half-hour interval, while the duration of work is unaffected. (Source: Lenntorp 1973).

The results of the first five simulations (indicated by black bars in Figure 3), which showed the number of alternatives for the four modes of travel plus flexible working hours, form basic points of comparison on the ranking scale for the subsequent simulations that all involved public (bus) transport. The latter experiments with changed trip densities and average speeds (depicted by grey bars in the figure) fall in between the previous results in terms of their range of minimum to maximum number of alternatives.

The effects of bus departure intervals every 20 minutes is only somewhat better than travelling by foot. The difference in number of alternatives between the three experiments with different postulated speeds is negligible. It is trip density, not average speed, which must be increased to one departure every tenth or fifth minute in order to get better turn out than in the bus network as observed, but then an average speed of 20 km per hour is quite sufficient.

A better effect than flexible working hours is obtained only when average speeds of buses reach 30 or 40 km per hour and the departure intervals are at most ten minutes. Such high *average* speeds (that include stops) are probably not attainable in urban areas unless these are designed to give special priority to public transport.

Only a high trip density of five-minute intervals in combination with high average speeds of at least 30 km per hour generate sets of possible alternatives which are on the average better than those computed for the cyclist. The inherent weaknesses of the conventional public transport systems consisting of coupling to certain routes and timetables are quite obvious from the above example. Comparing this last example with the car driver, the main difference lies in the choice of route in restricting the number of alternatives of the public transport passenger, since the mean speed of travel and the trip density was so high with the bus that it differed little from the car.

Public travel possibilities in the city of Karlstad

This investigation was carried out under the auspices of a government commission looking into various aspects of public transport in urban areas, studies which were confined in the City of Karlstad. The main principles of the investigation were decided upon in consultation with the secretariat of this commission. The emphasis was to be placed on the possibilities of actually using the public transport system as it stands today, and any alterations in the system should not be so comprehensive that their financial costs would be prohibitive.

Otherwise the basic objective of the Karlstad investigation was the same as in the present essay, *viz.* to present certain parts of the time-geographic analytical approach and *introduce a method* facilitating enquiry into the current and future efficiency of the public transport system from the angle of the user-consumer.

Activity programme and test points

The activity programmes tested below have not been selected because they are to be given special priority in the planning of public transport or because they are typical of any population category. They have rather been chosen because of their every-day general importance both at present and in the near future.

Two of the chosen programmes included a service visit as well as a visit in somebody else's home, but the most important programmes were those involving a visit to a work place. This was in one case combined with a post office errand after work and in another with depositing and collecting a child at a day nursery before and after work. It is the series of tests of the latter programme that will be described below. There is reason to believe this programme to be of special significance to households with children where one or both of the parents are gainfully employed. In such a household at least one of the parents is often dependent on public transport.

All activity programmes start and finish in a residential station in the same way as in the previous investigation. The tested residential locations or test points were also systematically selected across the city surface. The centres of a grid of square cells of 500 by 500 metres constituted the first selection, subsequent to which all points which were not within or in proximity to built-up areas were excluded, leaving a total of sixty-two locations tested. An alternative method of selection would have been to delineate residential areas and then to select points within them. This method was not applied since the selection of residential test points was to be independent of the structure of the current transportation system.

Some results

The first of the simulated activity programmes contained one journey to the centre of the city. From each of the sixty-two chosen test points, the possibility of carrying out the programme was calculated under the constraint that total travel time was not to exceed 70 minutes and that the time for errands in the centre was not to be less than one hour. But situations were not ruled out in which the trip to the centre took 50 minutes while the return journey only took 20 minutes. The simple construction of this programme in conjunction with the fact that all bus lines converge on the city centre made the programme feasible from fifty-seven out of the sixty-two test points.

The next activity programme merely probed into the feasibility of making a simple visit, but the destinations, of which there were now nineteen stations, were scattered over the entire built-up area and consequently required travel which was less compatible with the radial structure of the bus network. Above and beyond this, the journeys were to be undertaken in the evening, when the service frequently was lower than during midday. The maximum travel time was postulated as 70 minutes and the visit in somebody else's home could begin immediately upon arrival there. This programme was much more difficult to perform than the previous one, since the structure of the public transport network made central locations more accessible than peripheral ones, and from residential test points located in the city centre the possibilities of reaching other residences were the best. In sum, this programme was feasible in nearly half the number of cases.

The two most important activity programmes contained an extended visit to a work place. As mentioned, one of them included a post office visit on the way home from work and the other a visit to a day nursery for children before and after work. The six largest work place areas in the city were selected as destinations for the journeys to work, and the most common hours of work were recorded and used as input in the simulations. About 50 per cent of the employment opportunities in the city could be found in and around these places. As for day nurseries and post offices, the real locations and opening hours were used. Travelling time per journey between home and work was consistently restricted to at most 35 minutes. The programmes were tested under current city conditions but also with some minor alterations in the form of increased density of bus service and the addition of a new bus route. The latter changes were studied in isolation from one another and not in terms of their compound effects.

Journey to and from work including a visit to a day nursery

In the postulated activity programme, the individual leaves his home 40 minutes before work begins. Five minutes of this time are spent depositing a child at a day nursery. After work the child is collected during the journey home. The same maximum travelling and stopping time of 35 minutes applies here as during the outward journey.

The sixty-two test points are combined with the previously recorded work places and the six existing day nurseries. The locations of the latter are shown in Figure 4. All of them are open between 06:30 and 18:30. The feasibility of performing the programme was investigated without postulating a particular

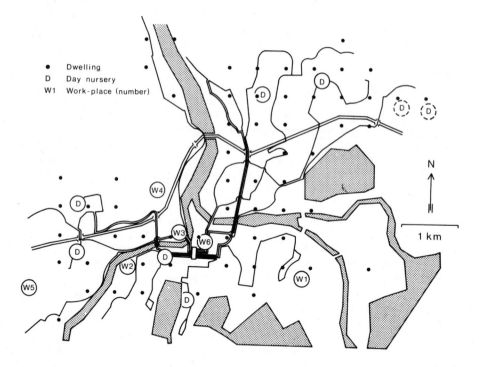

Figure 4 *Locations of day nurseries, work places and the sample of dwellings plus the public transport network in Karlstad* The figure shows the total of 62 dwelling locations and starting points from which the activity programmes were tested. The number and locations of day nurseries correspond to the actual ones. (Those encircled by dashed lines were planned at the time of the investigation, but are included only in the last series of simulation experiments.) The six places of work were the largest in the city. The motorway and the areas of water have been filled in for reference. (Source: Lenntorp 1975)

day nursery to be used, though of course the same one had to be visited both in the morning and the evening.

With the time limits assumed here, no traveller by public transport could from any test point reach work place *W1* in Figure 4. Work place *W5* is peripherally situated and can only be reached from a very limited number of points. This state of affairs is very much due to the location of day nurseries and work places and the structure of the transportation system, among other things. Two work places, *W3* and *W6*, could be reached from around fifty out of the sixty-two residential test points. These work places had the most favourable location in relation to the nurseries and the nodes in the bus network.

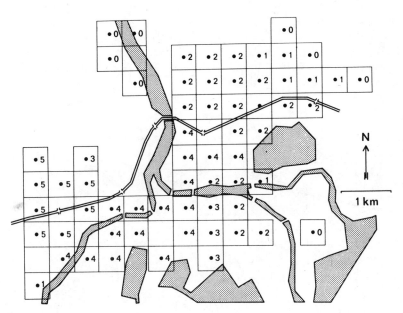

Figure 5 *Journey to and from work and visit to a day nursery* The figures denote the numbers of work places accessible from the various test points if a day nursery is to be visited on route to and from work. The public transport routes and trip densities are those actually observed in the city. (Source: Lenntorp 1975)

Figure 5 shows the number of work places that can be reached from each test point. Five out of six work places can be reached in the western parts, due not least to the existence of two day nurseries in that area and to the distance to the centre being short. The capacity of the nurseries was not looked into, which may give the presented situation too favourable an appearance. The poorest access is found in the northern parts of the city. This situation is most pronounced in the northwest, where the activity programme cannot be performed at all.

In the next trial, the trip density of buses was increased in order to assess improvements in accessibility. The density was changed on all routes which previously had two or three departures per hour to four departures per hour during 06:00 to 09:00 and 16:00 to 18:00. During the rest of the day the old timetable was maintained. The simulation was carried out exactly as before. Accessibility only improved for four work places ($W2$, $W3$, $W4$ and $W6$). Altogether only ten additional activity programmes became feasible. This minor increment may be due to the fact that the day nursery programme is difficult to carry out and that a greater increase in bus service frequency is necessary for substantial improvements to materialize. The test points for which the situation is ameliorated are shown in Figure 6, and half of these locations are found in the northeast part of the city where previous accessibility conditions were inferior (cf. Figure 5). Apparently trip density had some influence on this.

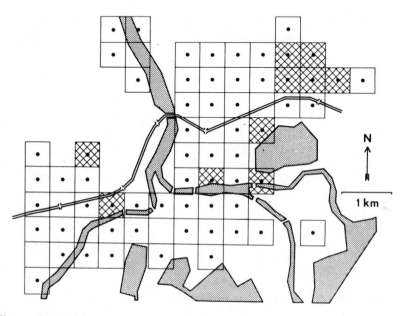

Figure 6 *Work journeys and visits at a day nursery with changed bus service frequency* The figure shows the additional number of work places accessible from each test point if service frequencies are increased. Hatched cells denote additional work places accessible from the residential test points. (Source: Lenntorp 1975)

The next round of simulations entailed the addition of a completely new bus route to the existing network, while the trip densities were changed back to those actually observed in order to isolate the effects of various improvements. The new route forms a tangential link which departs from the present radial bus-route structure, linking the northeastern areas with the western parts of the city. The buses on the new link were given a high average speed since the density of bus stops was low on certain sections and the road quality was high where the new route coincided with the motorway. The route had four departures hourly between 07:00 and 20:00. With these departure times, it had no effect on work places where work begins at 07:00 (as in the case of two work places) or earlier. Both the route and the timetable had been suggested by the municipal bus company.

The addition of the new bus route increased accessibility to two work places (W_3 and W_4), but the increment was modest and only four more programmes became possible from the test points shown in Figure 7. As expected, the residential areas and work places affected were those in the vicinity of the new route.

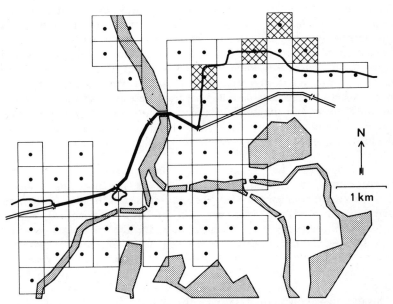

Figure 7 *Work journeys and visits at a day nursery in extended bus network* The figure shows the additional number of work places accessible from each residential test point after a transverse route (as indicated in the figure) has been added to the bus network. Hatched cells surround points from which one more work place has become accessible. (Source: Lenntorp 1975)

The introduction of the transverse bus route has also placed a larger number of day nurseries within reach of many residential areas. The present account has been confined to the set of work places, but from the outcome of any simulation it is also possible to select particulars which illustrate conditions in terms of day nurseries rather than work places.

In a third and final experiment the number of day nurseries is increased by two which are planned for the northeastern residential area (cf. Figure 4). The observed bus network is retained for this experiment (the service frequency and bus routes thus being the same as in the first simulation).

Owing to the peripheral positions of the scheduled day nurseries, an improvement could be discerned in the test points near them, but only in so far as residents there work in the city centre ($W6$ in Figure 4). There were nine residential test points from which it was possible to visit at least one of the new day nurseries provided one's work place was in the city centre. Thus the new day nurseries had a very slight effect in making it feasible to visit more work places from the various points of residence.

Some final comments on the Karlstad study

Despite its limited scope, the study shows that the city requires a well developed public transport system. It is only in the central parts of the city that walking provides an equivalent alternative from a time-allocation viewpoint. But the results also indicate that it is doubtful whether the travel times of the bus passenger in the outlying residential areas are satisfactory. Tests of programmes combining journeys to and from work with highly frequent visits showed that individuals in some areas had very limited hinterlands (i.e. prism size and content) within reach at reasonable expenditure of time. The boundary between acceptable and unacceptable travelling times is of course a debatable issue, but the maximum of 35 minutes per journey assumed here is quite a considerable length of time for a medium-sized city. A motorist from any residential location could have completed one hundred per cent of the programmes tested.

The restriction of the present public transport system to fixed routes and departure times impedes utilization, and this becomes particularly apparent when visits to different stations have to be combined in the daily programmes. If the conventional transport system is to be fundamentally retained, *co-ordinated intervention* will probably be necessary both within the transport sector and in the station (work and service-place) sector. The feasibility of carrying out activity programmes is not simply a function of the transport system. The spatial location of stations in the city ('land use') and their temporal location and accessibility in time have a decisive influence on programme feasibility.

This interplay between mobile and stationary activities is such that one-sided changes in the transport sector are unlikely to have more than marginal effects. In many instances, these effects are so small that they provide no incentive for car drivers to change their mode of travel. There are probably certain threshold values which must be exceeded before there is any effect in this direction, and these values are likely to be very high since even full-scale experiments with very efficient transport systems such as 'dial-a-bus' have failed to attract car users.

The presentation of the simulation results from the above study were focused on the accessibility to work places from residential stations. The model, however, provides a good many other opportunities which were not used. Other issues such as describing how different day nurseries would be affected, how many nurseries could be visited from a given residential test point, what the possible combinations of work places and day nurseries are, and so on, could also have been investigated.

Conclusion on the PESASP computer model and the simulation of paths and activity programmes

The above analysis has been an attempt to give a concrete presentation of the time-geographic approach as it can be applied to the field of person movement and public transport. More specifically, the PESASP computer model was demonstrated and applied, and the possibilities of individuals of carrying out certain activity programmes in given urban settings were assessed. This was done under the explicit assumption that individuals had to form continuous and indivisible trajectories in time-space. The basic time-geographic view of individuals as paths in time-space (Figure 1) brings out the conceptual difficulties in cutting out segments of individuals and treating them in different sectors. To focus only on the segments of movement activity while disregarding the interspersed stationary activities in fact implies that continuous paths are chopped up. This entails great loss of information (and realism) about the sequential constraints in human activities. It is also contrary to the way in which an individual perceives his environment—as a physical whole in time and space that is not fragmented into sectors. This explains why the present kind of work is based on continuous daily activity programmes of individuals as measuring instruments, why the model considers the composition of journeys in activity chains, and why there has been a connection between individual programmes and the temporal organization of society.

The PESASP simulation model maps the set of alternative ways in which a particular activity programme can possibly be carried out. The number and kinds of these alternatives are a function of the *combined* qualities of the individual and the environment. The individual has to make choices which fall within the set of possible alternatives, although the model does not predetermine which choices will be made. A person's behaviour is controlled both by the structure of the existing environment and by individual preferences of which the latter are less known.

From a planning viewpoint, however, the important issue is not to make behaviour conform to some imposed norms, but rather to make room and give leeway for various possibilities of action within city-regions. These options can be provided without making a total inventory of the characteristics of individuals and groups inhabiting the area. The advantages of this planning approach are obvious in the long run, since in each area there is a turnover of population and a change of its structure, giving rise to new demands and new forms of behaviour; something which planning must be flexible enough to provide at least part of in advance.

The simulation model PESASP described here was originally designed for use in more theoretical contexts. It was principally intended for the analysis of possible combinations and permutations of activities in time-space and as a means of recording differences of another magnitude than many practical investigations require. The present model should therefore be regarded as a prototype which can be modified to suit a range of problems of how individuals are able to carry out activities in different environments.

One limitation of the PESASP model, as designed at present, is that it deals with an individual rather than groups or populations of individuals. It is thus a model of interaction between man and environment than within a population. This limitation can partially be overcome, however, by testing complementary programmes for individuals belonging to the same household; for example where there are certain points of coordination in time-space between household members (e.g. that certain meals should be joint, or other activities). Individual programmes can also be designed which correspond to membership in certain household categories such as those presented in Carlstein, Lenntorp and Mårtensson (1968).

It is also possible to place the PESASP-model in a wider context by coupling it to a more aggregated time-geographic model of the population and activity systems, as was done in a study on activity organization and the generation of daily travel in the year 2000 (Ellegård, Hägerstrand and Lenntorp 1975). In this study two future alternatives of activity (time) organization, population structure and the kinds of daily household activities this implied were assessed, especially with regard to daily travel. To this kind of study, a model like PESASP can be coupled in order to evaluate the effects at the individual level of specific kinds of spatial environments.

One of the basic ideas behind the time-geographic approach is to evolve an instrument for the integration of knowledge. This requires the operational development of auxiliary instruments in order to obtain additivity between studies. The individual path is a fundamental concept in this context. The development of the simulation model PESASP, which can be seen as one method for handling individual paths operationally, is a contribution towards this general goal.

Footnotes

[1] See the other chapters in this book by Hägerstrand, Carlstein, Mårtensson and Olander.

[2] Unlike the studies of human time allocation behaviour in the form of time-budget and activity surveys, the major data input in this kind of analysis is data on the environment, the stations and their opening hours and the transport system and its timetables.

[3] A more elaborate description and measurement of prisms is available in Lenntorp (1976b).

Chapter 10
Time Allocation and Daily Living Conditions: Comparing Regions
Solveig Mårtensson*

Access to gainful employment, services and recreational facilities is of vital importance to individuals and households in their daily life. This essay will analyse the possibilities of carrying out *daily activity programmes* in three Swedish sub-county regions with an emphasis on comparing both inter- and intra-regional differences.

When main research activity was initiated in 1966, a very important area of application of the time-geographic model consisted of assessing the extent to which households could utilize or were constrained by their social and physical environment in daily living. This analysis, applied to cities and regions of varying size and location, was to serve as a basis for the design of Swedish regional policy. Our objective was to develop general theory as well as analytical tools and test instruments, of which the PESASP computer model was one (cf. Lenntorp, chapter 9). The overall approach not only required data on time use but also it demanded a heavy input of environmental data. The research team has over the years collected data for a number of regions such as Hässleholm, Västerås, Örebro, Linköping, Lycksele, and Stockholm as well as for certain smaller settlements where sectoral studies of shift-work and the like have been carried out. A major objective was to compare somehow living conditions both in the densely populated southern regions of Sweden and in the sparsely inhabited north. Consideration also had to be given to the effects of urban and regional size and to systems of different sized agglomerations in a region in which relations of proximity varied. This present abridged version of a larger study published in Swedish (Mårtensson 1974a) thus compares three Swedish regions containing a medium-sized city as the focus of the regional activities (in one case a small town), but in which there are also a number of smaller settlements or agglomerations of town to village size that are linked to the focal city or town by a route and transport system. The regions compared are those of Hässleholm, Örebro and Lycksele, the size and structure of which are indicated on Map 1.

Activity programmes

It has been shown in empirical investigations of time use that there are great similarities in *content* of daily programmes of individuals who belong to the same

* Translated from the Swedish by T. Carlstein.

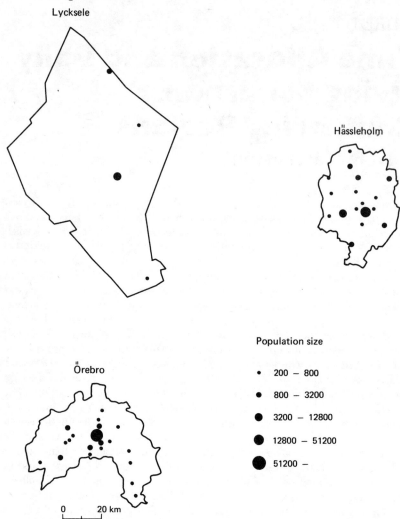

Map 1   The investigated regions and their agglomerations of population.

household type. Thus many activities are non-discretionary and must be performed on an every-day basis. With the aid of available time-use data for Sweden (of which some was collected by the Lund team), a standard daily activity programme could be postulated with regard to time demands. First, the period of continuous rest required by an adult was taken as eight hours and in immediate conjunction with this, half an hour was added both before and after for personal care. This interval of nine hours was assumed unavailable for alternative activities and the whole is designated simply as sleep. Time for a morning meal in the dwelling was also discounted, and the time remaining for other activities in various stations thus comprises 14 hours and 40 minutes. In all discussion of the daily time-budget further below this will be the period referred to. This time can be allocated to such activities as work (or gainful employment), meals, service contacts, recreation, and so on.

The *durations* of component activities in the postulated activity programmes were designed to be as congruent as possible with those of empirical studies showing time use in general for large groups in society. A programme therefore contains activities of very variable duration, some of which are performed at home, some outside. Likewise some are delegatable to other potential household members, while others are not. The meals and their preparation were thus allocated a minimum of two hours together with other non-discretionary activities of maintenance character such as house care and the consumption of daily news and similar information. Those in paid employment were also assigned eight hours of work.

When time has been allocated to these categories of activity, which are all necessary in the daily perspective, five hours remain for the individual working full-time. This time span is to be filled by activities which are not necessary on a daily basis but which become so in a longer time perspective, together with other discretionary activities. The postulated activity programme is thus constructed in such a way that all fourteen hours and forty minutes is put to some use. Should time be needed for any additional activities, an item in the initial programme must automatically be changed, either so that an activity is totally displaced or else so that it is reduced in duration. As soon as an individual has to change station during the day in order to perform a certain activity, a similar reshuffling will be made but it will only affect the discretionary activities. When in some cases so much time is required for travel that the non-discretionary activities are encroached upon the programme will be regarded as infeasible. However there is no predetermined preference order for sorting out the discretionary activities.

The environment

A postulated activity programme is constructed in such a manner that it can only be carried out in total in the home station. But any normal daily programme requires people to visit stations outside the home as well, which implies that the physical organization of the environment (i.e. its time-space structure) will also influence its performance. The various stations are found with variable density and their opening hours also vary over the day and the week. These time-geographic characteristics of stations imply that the time input to reach certain types of stations varies for individuals in different residential locations. Since the results in the computations below partly reflect this, it is necessary to describe the relevant stations with regard to location and opening hours. The postulated activity programmes have further been partly designed to provide examples of the consequences of different situations of accessibility to stations, a picture which changes for the individuals as shops are closed down, new service stations are added or service hours are changed. The time-geographic assessment of accessibility can thus provide a picture of the effects of such changes in the environmental structure for the individuals.

These accessibility conditions are also obviously related to the transportation system, the structure of the road network, the effectiveness of the public transport system, and so on. In each area the inhabitants have differential transport possibilities in another respect, since there are great disparities between those who have access to cars and those who do not. The latter category is very heterogeneous and comprises both the youngest and the oldest age groups as well as people of intermediate ages who belong to households without cars or where only one member can benefit from its use. These two traffic categories are therefore accounted for separately. In computing the opportunities for the car traveller, the mean speeds have been distinguished for three levels of road quality within the region, whereas it has not been considered essential to differentiate speeds for different hours during the day in a survey such as this. It has also been assumed that forward and return journeys are of equal duration in spite of certain peaks in traffic. A similar general travel time cannot be assigned to the public transport passenger however. For him there must be conformity with the specific timetables for ordinary weekdays.

Apart from this physical aspect of the environment, the rest of the population also forms a part of an individual's environment and affects his choice possibilities. Every person is a member of one or several groups which affect his daily activity programme and facilitate or prevent its performance. The constraints that affect the feasibility of a programme in this way can take several forms. A single gainfully employed person has few ties to his household but is instead tied to a work place at certain hours in order to cooperate with others or tend a machine. The multi-person household requires joint activities by its members and the individual must adapt his timings to the activities of others. Should he also be working somewhere outside the domestic sphere, he becomes subject to many coupling constraints which reduce his possibilities of making free use of his time. When individuals form a household, this has effects in two opposite directions. Some tasks at home such as preparation of meals, tidying the house and the like are on the whole not more time-consuming for two persons than for one. Similarly, some errands such as post office and bank visits can generally be delegated to the member who can most readily fit it into his or her programme. In this respect, *household formation* allows the *saving* of time. By contrast, specialization and cooperation in the multi-person household requires mutual consideration in timing, as some activities are performed jointly and time must be set aside for them. Consequently the rule has been stipulated in the activity programmes used below that the evening meal should be taken jointly and that all household members should spend at least two hours (over and above the sleeping period) together at home. Whether this opportunity for household interaction is actually used or not in real life is a different matter outside the scope of this study. The period of togetherness stipulated was a way of normatively testing whether constraints in an environment of a certain time-space structure militate against this or not. There is thus a strong normative element in the tested activity programmes although, at the same time, they are based on common real-world situations.

Unlike the so called time-budget studies of urban settings that give empirical accounts of actually performed activities with special attention to activity durations, the present approach presupposes a much more detailed picture of the environment in which these activities are carried out. The problem in analysing actual behaviour is the well-known one of encountering behaviour which is already adapted to the idiosyncrasies of the environment. This makes it difficult to reveal the extent to which actual behaviour is a function of genuine choice as opposed to compelling circumstances built into the environment and beyond the immediate influence of the actors therein. The daily activity programmes tested here are thus instruments to measure the degrees of freedom as well as the limitations on choice inherent in regional environments of a given time-space structure. When these measuring instruments are confronted with real environments (in model form), it is possible in various ways to measure and describe daily living conditions. First, *overall action possibilities* can be determined. It can be assessed which programmes are feasible at all in a certain area and which are unfeasible due to environmental structure or coupling constraints. As a complement to this, the *number of feasible alternatives* can be computed for a given programme. This can be extended to include *how many stations* of the same kind that can be chosen among as well as the various *alternative sequences*. Both of the latter are an index of the flexibility in the environment and indicate whether there is just one choice or several. The various alternatives can further be computed with regard to *total required duration* of the programme and, as an extension thereof, the duration of single activities are seen in relation to the effects of one errand or activity on a whole programme.

Three activity programmes will be demonstrated here. In each case the results will take the form of whether the special errand or activity can be performed in the various residential towns and agglomerations in the region or not, given the constraints postulated in the programme. The total time requirements for each feasible activity will also be measured and in all cases the effects on remaining activities in the programme are accounted for.

Since this study was intended to reveal conditions of interest to the makers of regional policy, the regions in this case are much larger than the city tested by Lenntorp in the preceding chapter. The municipal regions chosen here are nearly of county size ('commune blocks') and are focused upon a major city in the region which occupies an intermediate position in the national urban hierarchy. The residential locations chosen thus consist of one in the major city plus one in each of the urban-like agglomerations focused upon this city. Variations can thus be determined both among all the agglomerations and between the three regions in which they are located (the municipalities of Hässleholm, Örebro and Lycksele).

When living conditions for inhabitants in different regions are to be investigated and compared, the computations must be made so that the results show the conditions affecting as large a portion of the population as possible. They have therefore been carried out for residential locations which catch as many of the real residential sites as possible.

How much the various possibilities provided in each residential location are actually made use of is beyond the scope of the present essay. This is a choice left to the individuals. What is taken as important here is the search for a means by which the absence of opportunities can be identified and possibly lessened or removed. Improving the environment to increase its workability and usefulness by reducing detrimental constraints and adding better facilities is a proper task for urban and regional planning, of major relevance to the quality of life. This study will focus on those components of the quality of life which relate to the performance of ordinary household activity programmes on ordinary days.

Results of testing a programme of going to work

This programme aims at testing what the travel times to and from work and the temporal location of this travel implies for other activities during the rest of the day, i.e. for the various discretionary activities. Since commuting to the major or central city in the region improves the range of choice for employment considerably, it is important to evaluate the impact of such commuting on remaining items in the daily programme. The situation for commuters employed from 08:00 to 17:00 will therefore be shown in diagrammatic form. These commuters live in the peripheral agglomerations (towns and villages) and travel to the major city. Figures 1 to 3 illustrate how much time remains having discounted time for sleep etc. They also indicate the temporal location of this remaining time which is equally important. It is above all the routes and timetables of the public transport system which limits disposable time in the home. In this respect, the intra- and inter-regional variations are considerable. Sometimes persons arrive home at seven, which makes meal-time and television news collide, and the possibilities of having time left over for

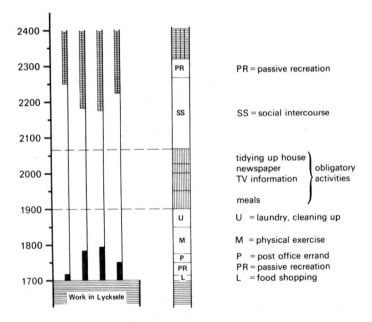

Figure 1   Disposable evening time at home of a gainfully employed person working in the central town of Lycksele between 08:00 and 17:00 hours. The left-hand part of the figure shows the situation for those living in agglomerations of descending population size from left to right. The column to the left is thus the major city or town in the region. Each column is further divided into two parts, of which the left shows the car user and the right the public transport passenger. (Lycksele region had no public transport for commuting workers.) The right-hand part of the figure indicates the activity programme and its components.

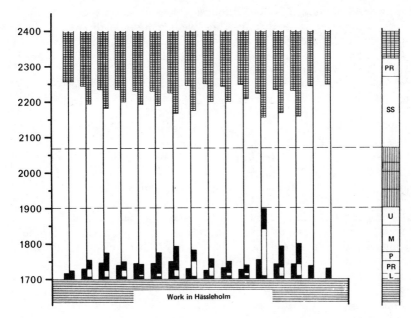

Figure 2 Disposable evening time etc. (sic) for Hässleholm region. cf. Figure 1.

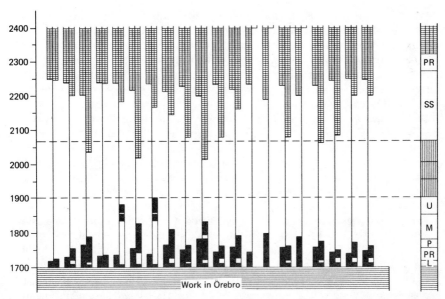

Figure 3 Disposable evening time etc. for Örebro region. cf. Figure 1.

either physical training or hobbies diminish. The early departure in the morning reduces disposable time the preceding evening also, if daily sleep is to have its stipulated duration. Should, for instance, the morning bus leave at 05:30 or 06:00, which is the case in certain places, the commuter must begin his rest at 20:10 or 20:40 the preceding night.

It is evident from the diagrams that several evening activities are displaced, especially for the user of public transportation. For several agglomerations in the Örebro region this category of person is not given occasion for any but the everyday non-discretionary activities, and enterprises like social activities, physical exercise and various maintenance tasks must be postponed to days free from work. This kind of reallocation of tasks between days will be discussed further below. Two problems arising from this are worth special mention, one being the adverse consequences for individual fulfilment of only being able to engage in certain activities just a few times during the week, the other is the difficulty in finding time for all the tasks that have been saved for the weekend. It is not only the duration of staying at home which is important but also the temporal location of this stay. There are great differences in the possibilities of consuming cultural programmes on radio and television, since these programmes are usually only shown later in the evenings.

Not all time for travel is effective travel-time. Much may be spent waiting for a bus or train in the afternoon. The extent to which this time can be used fruitfully is a question of the availability of premises. Is there access to a place which is not a cold and noisy railway or bus station, where one can do things otherwise done in the evenings such as practising one's hobby, studying, sporting activity, or the like? In some places the public libraries have become something of an activity centre for this population category, in other places such a lack of premises has led to the waste of many person-hours in inhospitable waiting rooms.

Most gainfully employed individuals are members of households. It is therefore misleading to trace the above effects only on the individual's programme. The other household members are also affected, for instance by the encroachment of a long work journey on the time that can be spent together. It was previously stipulated that at least two hours of the waking day should be spent in the company of other members. Where the latter are at home all evening this causes no problems. Even the person commuting by public transport can spend at least three hours at home and dinner can take place before 19:30 as postulated. The problems arise when more than one household member works outside the home, particularly if they do so at different places while having only one car. Figures 1 to 3 show the links between the peripheral agglomerations and the regional centre, and these are the best transport links in the region (except for certain links to the immediate neighbour settlements). Public transport to other villages or towns can be much more time consuming and make passengers arrive home around 22:00. One kind of household which is particularly affected is that consisting of all adults employed full-time plus pre-school children. These adults may then return home as late as 18:30 or 19:00, which is just in time to put their children to bed. This solution leaves no time for contact between parents and children other than during the weekends.

This programme only served as one example of how work and commuting to work affected more total daily programmes, while similar tests can also be made of programmes including other activities such as schooling–education. The programme can also be tested for those who are employed on a part-time basis for instance. Likewise this programme can be tested in conjunction with a visit to a food shop after work is finished (cf. Mårtensson 1974a). In testing this programme it was found that shopping for food was possible everywhere without a clash with other necessary or non-discretionary activities in the daily programme. In several cases there were also a great number of alternative sequences, mainly due to the long opening hours of some shops and their dispersed spatial location.

Testing the programme of going to work and visiting a physician

Contrary to programmes like that above, shorter opening hours or a station structure with fewer units of the type that are only found in cities reduces the degree of freedom in a daily programme. This should lead to fewer station alternatives and activity sequence possibilities. For the person employed the accessibility of service stations during very limited hours may cause a collision with the hours of work as well. This will be illustrated by the programme of being at home—going to work—visiting a doctor—and being at home again. The effects of concentration of service stations in a few cities and towns will also become evident.

Although a doctor's visit may be postponed to another day in many cases (leaving the most acute cases aside), it may often not be moved to a better time during the day if surgery hours coincide with those of the patient's work. Since visiting a doctor (unlike shopping) cannot be delegated to someone else either, the conflict can be resolved only by allowing medical care to displace part of the work activity. The tested programme pertains to persons with office working hours (08:00 to 17:00) as these coincide totally with the hours that medical care is supplied.

Since time for a medical visit and the associated travel can be taken away from working time, this kind of errand can take up much of the day. A programme containing such a visit is thus feasible from all the different villages and towns by various means of transport but in some cases this entails considerable time spent on travel. It is therefore interesting to test the effects of such a visit for people in different kinds of regions of Sweden, representing the spectrum from dense to sparse habitation. Gainfully employed individuals will be considered in particular but other categories are not forgotten. The visit is assumed to take place in the afternoon between 15:00 and 15:30, which is perhaps too favourable a time as the patient is then able to use some of the school buses in operation at about this time.

For a car user the differences between the settlements and the regions are not very great. A total travel time of more than 40 minutes is unusual in the Hässleholm region, 50 minutes is about maximum in Örebro and 1 hour 45 minutes is maximum in the Lycksele region. The whole errand in the two former regions thus consumes less than an hour and a half for a person able to use a car (cf. Table 1 and Figures 4 to 6).

TABLE 1   Total time use for medical treatment between 15:00 and 15:30. This time includes treatment, travel and waiting time. The table shows the number of settlement agglomerations affected.

total time	*Hässleholm*		*Örebro*		*Lycksele*	
hours	car	public trpt	car	public trpt	car	public trpt
0– 1	13	5	10	4	1	1
1– 2	3	1	10	2	1	–
2– 3		5		4	2	–
3– 4		3		6		–
4– 5		1		1		–
5– 6		1		–		–
6– 7				3		–
7– 8						1
8– 9						–
9–10						–
10–11						–
11–12						2
Number of agglomerations in the region	16	16	20	20	4	4

The situation is completely different for the other travel category. For the user of public transport who must go to another town or city, the full errand will in the best case take longer than it did in the worst case for the car driver in the same region, with a few exceptions in the Örebro region. The reasons for this are obviously the waiting times in the town of medical treatment, mainly before the actual visit but also to some extent afterwards. Medical treatment in the Lycksele region (which is the largest and most sparsely populated) implies the loss of an entire working day for the person living outside the major city, at least three work hours are forfeited for most places of residence in the Örebro region and correspondingly two to three hours for Hässleholm. It should be noted, however, that most of the waiting time is located in the central city, and this time can therefore to some extent be used for other errands. This is a case where discretionary activities can be carried out during time normally reserved for obligatory ones. The data presented in Figures 4 to 6 are also able to show the situation for pensioners or housewives who often have to resort to public transport. It is important to study their service opportunities in time-geographic terms rather than focusing on spatial distance or the time that the actual medical treatment takes. The total errand including travel and waiting time must be seen in relation to a full daily programme both of the individual and also of the household.

Testing the programme of going to work and to an evening meeting

Attention in previous sections was called to the evening hours and their utilization, i.e. the time remaining for a wage-earning person when work and commuting are over. The possibilities of using this time for social intercourse, active recreation, social participation and the like will now be discussed in relation to the average weekday. It can reasonably be assumed that the structure of the environment with regard to available premises and travel possibilities to a great extent determines whether it is feasible to fill non-work time with a varied content. Both time use for travel and the spatial location and opening hours of various leisure establishments vary regionally.

Those activities which become interesting in a daily programme of this kind could be the following:

the two hours of joint presence at home of all household members, evening visits of variable durations in various agglomerations of the region, and organized leisure time activities (at given hours) in the evenings.

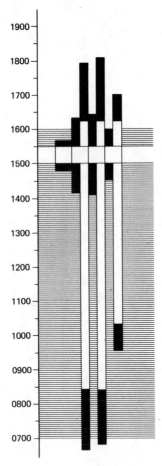

Figure 4 Total time use for medical treatment between 15:00 and 15:30 for the four agglomerations in the Lycksele region. The agglomerations are ordered in decreasing size from left to right. The left part of each column shows the situation of the car driver and the right part that of the public transport user. Black denotes travel time, white waiting time and hatched area denotes assumed working hours.

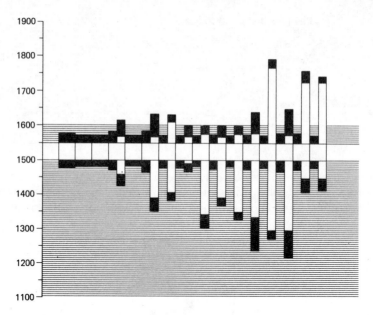

Figure 5 Total time use for medical treatment etc. for the 16 agglomerations in the Hässleholm region. Cf. Figure 4.

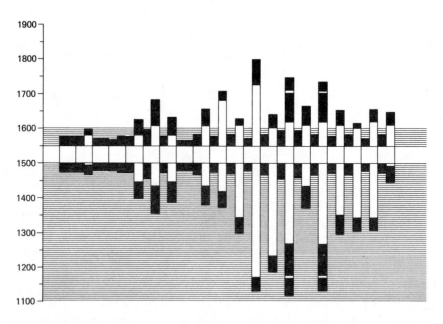

Figure 6 Total time use for medical treatment etc. for the 20 agglomerations in the Örebro region. Cf. Figure 4.

For those who live in the same village, town or city as they work, the amount of free time at home varies very little for different places and regions or travel categories. The necessary time for travel can readily be taken from the time for passive recreation in the test programme, and if more time is needed one of the remaining activities can be shortened one day, another activity the next day, and so on. And obviously, when leisure time activities take place at home, there are no regional variations to speak of. It is for the gainfully employed who live in peripheral settlements but work in the central cities or towns that the situation is more difficult.

As pointed out above, a car driver who commutes within the region is able to carry out most of the activities that are desirable on a daily basis, and to the extent he is unable to do all, one activity can be sorted out the first day and another the second. In a weekly perspective all activities can be given room on at least one or a few days. The situation is totally different in many places for the public transport passenger, since his remaining time at home is so short that many activities in the programme must be sorted out and postponed every day. The risk is overwhelming that more time consuming activities cannot be fitted in during any normal work day.

In households where several members are gainfully employed but without access to cars it is often not feasible for all to spend the stipulated two hours

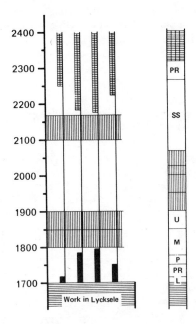

Figure 7 Possibilities for participation in collective activities outside the home in the evening between 19:00 and 21:00 for gainfully employed persons in the Lycksele region. The left part of the figure shows the different agglomerations in descending population size from left to right. For each column, the left part shows the car user while the right part shows the public transport passenger. The right part of the figure shows the daily activity programme and its components. (cf. also Figure 1.)

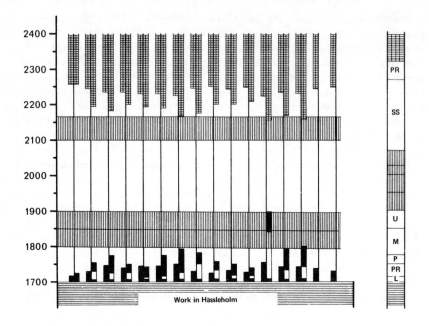

Figure 8 Possibilities for participation in collective activities outside the home in the evening etc. cf. Figure 7.

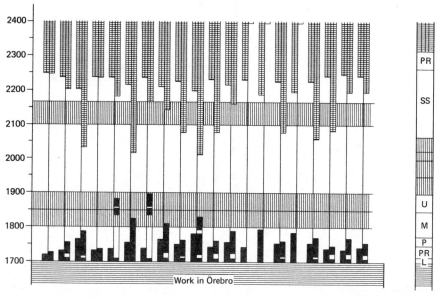

Figure 9 Possibilities for participation in collective activities outside the home in the evening etc. cf. Figure 7.

of time together (something which was possible in most other cases). This possibility is further reduced if one wishes to meet at some place other than one's own residence, to visit friends at their house, for instance, something that entails extra time for travel. In half the number of settlements investigated in the Örebro region it is apparent that the commuter using public transport is not in a position to make an evening visit lasting for two hours. These possibilities diminish considerably if the visit takes place outside one's own village or town. Thus this possibility for evening visits seems infeasible for all public transport commuters and also for some car users in certain settlements in the Lycksele and Örebro regions.

Finally the possibilities for organized free time activities can be demonstrated by Figures 7 to 9. The joint or collective activity tested in this programme can range from a study group, organized hobby activities, physical training, or sports to a political or a voluntary association meeting of some kind. All these concerted activities generally start at a common time and have a given duration. The timing is assumed to be from 19:00 to 21:00. The non-discretionary daily activities thus have to be located both before and after the meeting. The figures show the following conditions: All car users have opportunities to attend the meeting if it takes place in the home village, town or city. For the public transport passenger it is impossible in half the settlements in the Örebro region and in a few villages of the Hässleholm region. Similar meetings can be attended by car users in Hässleholm regardless of which town or village they live in. A scrutiny of the public transport system in the evening shows that it does not allow anyone to make a visit outside the home village or town. In the Örebro region, which is larger, distances are greater and even for the car driver travel time between certain pairs of settlements is too long. He can choose between approximately half of the settlements in the region. It is important here to note that even the central city is beyond reach from certain towns and villages. Even when the time stipulated for the consumption of important news and other information on television or radio is encroached upon, this is only of benefit to the car users, while it has no positive effect for the public transport user for whom the main time conflict is one between the two-hour meeting and the diurnal sleep.

Conclusion

Calculations made in a pilot study of this kind can serve as a point of departure for more comprehensive investigations of daily living conditions in relation to environments. This time-geographic study stressed certain systemic aspects by regarding any activity that might have been singled out for closer examination as part of a whole sequence and programme. The view was held that in testing environments it is inadequate to study a given activity (such as shopping, using a service, etc.) in isolation. By placing activities within daily programmes operating under time-allocation constraints, the effects of time demands for one activity on the way it can be slotted in among others was emphasized as a crucial aspect. Likewise the view of the individual as a member of a larger population system was employed, particularly with regard to the individual as a member of a household coordinating its activities, individuals adapt themselves to other members who in turn are influenced by their programmes. In all the cases tested, it was the feasibility of performing various activities which was the object of the enquiry. The results, however, are *only valid* for the kinds of postulated activity programmes that were tested and for the *assumptions* made in them. Other kinds of programmes may display other main traits. Some of the findings, however, seem to be general enough and should also pertain to other areas as well as to other categories of the population. This is true both at the intra-regional and the inter-regional level.

In some of the computations above, the PESASP computer programme was used while others were done manually in much the same fashion as the computer programme, since the alternatives in some of the tested instances were so few (i.e. the environmental constraints were so severe) that the computer became an unnecessary aid. Many fundamental points made by Lenntorp in chapter 9 therefore apply to this study as well.

A final point on theory and method should be made on the difference between this kind of study and conventional time-budget studies. This study does not begin with the time 'budgets' of actual behaviour as an input, in order to get aggregate time-use tables as an output for environments that are often undefined in spatial, temporal or structural terms. The present model uses specified activity programmes (not time budgets) as an input, together with specific environments structured in time-space terms, and the different *possible* time budgets are the output instead. These are not aggregated into abstract wholes but are seen as they vary with the environmental structure (temporal *and* spatial) so that one comes to understand the interrelation between time allocation and the time-space environment. This knowledge can be used to adjust the environment through planning to facilitate certain programmes and their daily performance.

Summing up the substantial findings of this pilot investigation, there exist considerable differences in the living conditions of individuals, between locations in a larger region as well as between those using public transport and those having access to private cars. This is a compound consequence of the settlement structure, the time-space structure of employment and service supply, and the timetables and routes of the public transport system. The location of outlying settlement agglomerations in relation to the central city (or town) in the region is of major importance, even when the feasibility of simple everyday programmes is tested. These differences in living conditions become pronounced when the car traveller is compared to the public transport passenger. Certain patterns in the location of services and opening hours reinforce these differences in mobility. This is particularly the case when service stations are strongly concentrated in the central city of the region.

However, in a limited study such as this, it is more difficult to abstract any general similarities or differences between the three regions. The intra-regional differences seem to be of similar character in all three regions but express themselves to a greater or lesser degree. Within the central or focal cities of the region, the conditions in terms of everyday programmes are very similar.

The intra-regional contrasts (between residential locations and between traveller categories) are most marked in the sparsely settled region of Lycksele and are somewhat greater in Örebro than in Hässleholm. Commuting to work in the central place is possible everywhere for the car traveller, while it is impossible for the non-car traveller in two settlements around Hässleholm and Örebro and for all settlements around Lycksele. For such commuting few differences emerge for car travellers in the observed regions when considering the effects on other activities in their day programmes. By contrast, public transport passengers are subject to substantial limitations on the remaining time; the total time for utilization of medical care facilities varies somewhat for car travellers in the three regions, but exhibits extreme differences for the public transport users. In Lycksele they require a whole day away from home compared to a maximum of six hours in Hässleholm region and seven hours in Örebro region. The possibility for two hours of leisure activity in the home area is present everywhere for the car traveller but it is absent in two of places in the Hässleholm region and for half the settlements in the Örebro region.

Chapter 11
The Study of Activities in the Quaternary Sector
Lars-Olof Olander and Tommy Carlstein

Introduction

It is a well-known fact that the conventional division of economic activity into the three sectors—primary, secondary and tertiary—is becoming deficient even in those situations where one wishes to give a superficial description of the activity system of a modern society. Parallel to the case of raw materials production, manufacturing and service provisioning, there is a rapidly growing sector which Jean Gottmann (1970) has called the *quaternary* sector. Within this sector is found the greater proportion of private and public decision-making activity, administrative service and research. The tasks carried out can be designated as advanced administration and they differ substantially from tasks in other sectors. Instances would include formulation of ideas, exchange of information, information processing, planning, management and coordination. These activities are all characterized by their 'abstract' content and by their demands for different forms of theoretical competence.

There is no doubt that this sector plays an essential role in developed economies. Its influence on the development in remaining sectors is considerable. While the production of industrial commodities, for instance, is still basic to most countries in the economically advanced nations of the world, success in this field is to a great extent dependent on administrative expertise, particularly in the development and marketing of industrial goods. In this context, substantial contributions to so called 'invisible earnings' within these economies are given by the administrative services of a wide range of specialist firms. Moreover, the production of public goods and services is on the increase in these countries and to a growing extent requires specialist (administrative) guidance and coordination.

The quaternary sector cuts across the organization of a given activity system, and can either constitute a minor fraction of the total employment in a company or else totally dominate it. It can further be grouped into organizational units together with other forms of employment or else exist within a totally independent unit. With the increase in specialization in a society and its overall activity system, information and ideas are to an increasing extent being circulated among its different administrative units.

Part of all this information flows between formally independent units, while another part serves as a means of monitoring and coordinating units within large companies. Much of this information can readily be transferred using modern telecommunications, but the qualitatively essential parts of it still require individuals to travel and meet. *Information* and *interaction* are thus key concepts in analysing various activities in the quaternary sector, a sector whose importance for material welfare and employment distribution (both positively and negatively) is increasingly being looked into in geographic research.

This research is mainly conducted within the domain of economic geography, and several social science disciplines are continuously supplying new knowledge which must be accommodated within a geographic frame of reference. Examples of such disciplines would be economics, organization theory, sociology and psychology. It is rather rare that scholars from these disciplines collaborate directly with geographers. Up till now the problem has been that there have been a good many geographers taking the initiative in collecting bits of knowledge here and there in adjacent disciplines which promise to cast light upon variables affecting the location of and interaction between administrative units. So far it has not been possible to fuse these pieces of knowledge together into a coherent body of geographic theory. And it is increasingly felt that geography lacks models which facilitate the weaving together of such different strands into a synthesis—a problem which is not unique to research on the quaternary sector.

In this perspective, the aim of the present essay is to give a short review of findings and approaches in current research on the quaternary sector and to proceed from there to discuss some problems of synthesis of geographic theory in this field. Next, some suggestions will be made as to how the time-geographic model can be used as a basis for modifying some existing concepts as well as for providing new ones, so that some of the existing independent approaches may be partially inter-linked and fused. Of course, very little can be accomplished in a short essay such as this, but the objective of this presentation is to supply some broad ideas of possible steps that can be taken in the geographic study of administration and the quaternary sector.

A brief outline of research on the quaternary sector

Particularly in the older geographical literature, administrative activities are studied mainly as a feature of the city landscape and as a component in the morphology of the city region. There exists a comprehensive literature on the location and distributional changes of such activities in individual city regions. As a rule these studies are aimed at analysing changes in the structure of the core of the city, a place where administrative activity is of central importance. It is seldom, however, that these CBD-studies are able to link their observations to a theoretical paradigm of the organization of the economic activity system. Some general observations do deserve attention; it seems, for instance, that a general trait is that concentration in the city core increases, the more specialized and interaction oriented the activity observed is. Another trait is that decentralization to suburban regions increases with time and with the size of the city region, tendencies borne out in a series of studies from the United States and other countries. One of the most comprehensive reports is that by Armstrong and Pushkarev (1960, 1973).

In later literature more all-embracing attempts dominate the studies on location and activity redistribution. What is studied as a rule is the change and distribution of employment and organizational units in the whole city system for different countries. The most conspicuous finding in such studies is the extreme level of concentration on a few dominant regions in each system. The more specialized work functions and organizations are in the sphere of private and public administration and service, the stronger this tendency towards concentration becomes. In the Swedish case, similar studies of regional development have been carried out on the basis of very exact data (Engström 1970; Törnqvist 1970; Engström and Sahlberg 1973). Westaway has described similar developments in Great Britain (Westaway 1974) and Armstrong and Pushkarev have taken up the situation of the United States (1973). These approaches have proven to be considerably more appropriate as points of departure for theoretical generalizations on the activity system of a region than the previously mentioned CBD-studies.

Wärneryd (1968) has thoroughly studied the connection between employment distribution, organizational structure and regional structure. He has described both theoretically and empirically how the hierarchical structure of different organizations can be projected onto a system of regions as well as how different administrative functions, e.g. main offices, divisional offices or the administration of production, are allocated to different regions in such a system. Between these organizational units in different environments there exist linkages and dependencies which reflect that distribution of administrative responsibility. But there are also dependencies between formally independent organizations, of course (Wärneryd 1968). Pred has continued this line of research on the relations between the structure of organizations and regional development (Pred 1973).

The aforementioned organizational interdependencies are naturally paralleled by actual flows of information between the organizations. A number of studies have focused on this information and mapped the flows spatially. In Sweden, for instance, Hedberg has investigated the functional and regional distribution of personal contacts between different work functions for a number of organizations (Hedberg 1970). Sahlberg correspondingly carried out a study of the personal contacts which are mediated by the Swedish domestic air transport system (Sahlberg 1970). For the greater London area, Goddard studied how information flows (personal and telecommunication contacts) interlinked different organizations into one contact system (Goddard 1973).

A general observation throughout these and similar studies is that the bulk of contacts of individuals and organizations as a rule occur with counterparts within the region. The remaining contacts are mainly distributed among a limited number of regions and particularly affect the most dominant administrative centres in the hierarchical system. However, the inter-regional dependence seems to increase with the size of the organization and the proportion of specialized work functions. Another finding in these studies is that time use for travel and external contacts occupies a very large portion of the work time of these individuals. It appears that time use and physical accessibility play an essential role in shaping the contact networks and spatial locations of these organizations. These aspects have formed the theme for comprehensive studies of how actual or potential contact possibilities vary for organizations in different environments. Persson (1974) has investigated, with the aid of a computer model, how physical contact possibilities vary for different real organizations, which in the simulation are moved about to different regions within a national system of cities.

General contact and transport possibilities in a regional system have been studied in the form of so called 'contact landscapes' by Engström and Sahlberg (1973) and Törnqvist (1973).

These studies emphasize above all the quantitative contact possibilities and transport constraints. It is obvious, however, that the qualitative properties of information are also very important. Thorngren has in a number of studies discussed the role of different kinds of information for the development of organizations and regions (Thorngren 1967; 1970; 1973). Depending on the information content of personal contacts, three categories of contacts emerge, programme, planning and orientation contacts, the importance of which covers anything from daily running issues to more radical changes of activity. Thorngren has shown that the actual and potential supply of these three forms of contacts vary among regions, and that organizations consequently are able to allocate parts of their activities to different regions in order to benefit from 'external economies'. Goddard has applied these ideas to an interesting investigation of how contact activities change in organizations which are decentralizing from London to other regions in Great Britain (Goddard and Morris 1975). Thorngren and Goddard make clear references in their work to the connection between these qualitative aspects and the quantitative, physical aspects referred to earlier on. It should be emphasized, however, that these two aspects have not so far been explicitly interrelated by both being analysed simultaneously.

It should be mentioned that Thorngren and Goddard stress the important connection between information from the environment and the organization's internal activities and general orientation of activities. This touches upon a main research tradition in organization theory on the time-use and activities of different administrative organizations. Carlsson initiated this line of enquiry as early as 1951 by studying how chief administrators allocated their time to different activities. The key role of information and interaction was pointed out (Carlsson 1951). One of the most comprehensive studies undertaken in this research tradition was that by Stewart, who investigated the time and activity distribution for 160 individuals on different administrative levels within organizations (Stewart 1967). Mintzberg continued work in this field and was better able than his predecessors to map the connections between kind of enterprise and time-use for activities (Mintzberg 1973). There exists at present in this research tradition an approach to organization theory which strives to introduce an activity-oriented physical realism into a subject which has been dominated by very abstract kinds of generalizations, and it seems likely that this approach eventually will be capable of interconnecting the observations of organization theory with traditional geographic ones. So far, however, this link is missing, one reason being the lack of interest in organization theory in placing the organization in its environment, another reason being the propensity of geographers to analyse almost exclusively the external side, i.e. only the relations of the organization to the environment (thereby ignoring internal structure and relations).

Some problems of synthesizing current approaches

The foregoing discussion of literature is by no means exhaustive. The various approaches have been very superficially treated with empirical findings accounted for in too summary a fashion. Yet, by and large, the approaches mentioned were taken in an order that makes them interrelated and supplementary to one another, and although a great number of researchers were not referred to they can, with a few exceptions, be identified with the approaches discussed. The intention in this brief review of the state of the art was to paint a background to a discussion of problems arising when different pieces of knowledge are put together as a more comprehensible and coherent whole. It is a necessity, particularly on the part of geography, to be able to arrange these diverse observations and ideas within one and the same paradigm and attack the current state of theoretical fragmentation.

What will be discussed are some general problems encountered when linking together the currently used approaches. Each of them is limited in its scope, quite naturally, but they are in themselves also *limiting* in the aspects of the problem they make amenable to treatment. This limiting quality of an approach with regard to its possibility of merging and forming a synthesis with other approaches is in itself a very interesting phenomenon. Generally speaking, any approach consists of a concentration on a particular *object* or a particular *theme*. A concentration on the object is evident by the focus on either the individual, the organization or the regional system. The problem then is that it is seldom very clear how the level of resolution or scale chosen is related to other levels or the way in which the parts constitute the whole. A thematic concentration usually consists of selecting some interesting relation or variable which is then detatched from a more complex whole. In some instances it may consist of studying the relevance of different organizational principles and structures; in other cases the main task may be to isolate the role of transport systems and interaction possibilities. Contact forms and contents may be a third kind of theme in a general list that can be made quite long. Whilst the concentration on certain objects by now may seem exhausted, there still remains great scope for finding new and untried themes.

In practice, research is often conducted so that one approach at a time is explored in order to find out how much of reality it is capable of explaining. When the potential of one approach seems to be drained, it is replaced by another. These constant shifts lead to a lack of recognition of the fact that the important knowledge is often to be found in the border areas between the specific approaches. What is sought here are the contours of a synthesis which is capable of interconnecting different objects and themes in clear and real terms. What is *not* sought is the kind of synthesis which draws on elegant tricks of heuristic arrangement, i.e. which lines up thematic approaches into apparent order. In fact, the previous outline suffers from this default by mainly being a list on which the different aspects so far produced are checked off in due order.

A time-geographic conceptualization of the quaternary sector

One way of achieving a synthesis over a wider field is to reduce and translate earlier findings into a new paradigm or model, which has the capacity both to absorb established work and to promote further investigation and understanding. Since the quaternary sector cannot exist in a vacuum, it also follows that the new model should be much broader than this particular sector. The time-geographic model and its basic concepts can serve such a purpose, if it is further developed to deal with the specific activities and processes found in the sector. Some headway has already been made, while much work remains to be done.[1]

What will be done here is to emphasize specifically some of the concepts strategic to the development of study of the quaternary sector, as well as pointing out what is the unique actual and potential contribution in the time-geographic conceptualization. Some of these concepts are already in use and are not in themselves new, while all of them have been defined or redefined in order to achieve logical coherence on a wider front.

Some of the criteria for successful time-geographic modelling have already been stated by Hägerstrand (1974c) as follows:

1   It should be easy to identify what the counterparts of the model are in the real world. This precondition excludes many of the conventional verbal and mathematical expressions from being directly applicable. The rule of projection relating observation to model must be clearer than words but less abstract than numerical signs. So it is essentially a matter of a generalized 'video-recording', the nearest analogy to which would be musical notation or similar notation systems of process.

2   The model must have a wide field of application. One should be able to move back and forth between micro and macro levels without losing the connection between them. The model should also be capable of extension and elaboration in such a way that one can move from that which is simple and obvious to that which is aggregated and complex with information retained on what simplifications have been made in the process.

3   The model should have the capability of *generating* questions, which one would not have otherwise thought of (i.e. it should have its autonomous and intrinsic logic, which brings one beyond manifest reality to the deeper structures, to use structuralist terminology).

4   Hence, the model should permit conclusions and calculations to be made which are adequate to reality without having to be verified by corresponding real world observations. (This implies that the model should deal not only with actual worlds realistically but also with possible worlds. This also means that the model should go beyond inductive generalizations.)[2]

These requirements are rather far reaching, since they serve as guidelines for basic research. The existing descriptive techniques are still not developed to cope with the many relations between levels of aggregation, nor are the conventional methods for collecting data adapted to the situational requirements in time-geographic depiction. However, one need not look upon the above requirements as absolute prerequisites. In fact, in many contexts the time-geographic model of viewing activities, events, objects and processes in time-space is useful in modelling one's own thinking and reinterpreting earlier work as well as one's own material and observations. This is because this particular model has certain fundamental qualities in capturing reality and channelling thoughts about it in a way which furnishes more faithful images of the real world. The emphasis upon trajectories or paths of individuals in the population, for instance, leads to a different kind of dynamic theory of interaction between people. It fuses aspects such as time allocation, group formation, human communication as well as both the temporal and spatial organization of society into one body of theory rather than several separate ones. This and many similar features unfold the 'deep structure' behind many administrative processes, for instance. It also avoids unnecessary specification of substance in the sense that one can deal with interaction in a human population at several levels of specification of the properties of the actors involved. At a very general level, for instance, one can deal with interaction and group formation amongst individuals of whom we 'know' only that they are indivisible, have a limited life span, and certain maximum speeds of travel. This gives rise to certain limitations on group formation and the performance of collective activities. At the next level, it can be further specified that the individuals are engaged in certain kinds of activities such as verbal communication as opposed to the processing of materials. At yet another level, it can be added that the population is clustered into interacting sub-sets of individuals, some of which are allowed to have external contacts with other clusters while some are not. One can then analyse what is the differential capacity for interaction, to take but one problem. Finally, very detailed specifications as to actors, roles, activities, contacts, forms of communication and so on can be given, as well as specific descriptions of environments in which these activities and processes take place.

The time-geographic model can operate at all these levels of substantive specification but the question is, in terms of deductive power, how much specification is necessary in order to get at the deep structure of how a particular system works? Another important consideration and issue to be probed into is whether or not a good many existing studies are overloaded with substantive specification which does not really yield additional information and insights. These may remain open issues, but a time-geographic working hypothesis could be that many studies have become sectoral and overspecialized because of unnecessary specification of superficial properties which conceal more than they reveal. Should this hypothesis be true, the resulting strategy should be to start by working from the bottom up with a general conceptual model at the base. This is the argument of the present essay, which will hence proceed to list some of the concepts needed and give some brief suggestions as to how they can be used.

Activity   It is convenient to depart from our initial description of the quaternary sector as that involving activities such as decision-making, exchange of information, formulation of ideas, administrative service giving and taking, information processing, planning, management and coordination of different individuals affected. These activities are dominated by two forms of interaction, first that between individuals in direct contact through verbal intercourse or mediated exchange of information via telecommunications, and secondly inter- action with information in written or recorded form (reading, writing, drawing) as well as using and processing information stored in one's brain in the process of thinking. The processing of materials and manufacturing, construction or other forms of physical production is a third kind of interaction which is little represented in the quaternary sector. Yet, the use of artefacts imposes many crucial constraints.

One important way of resolving the different approaches to this sector would be to look at activities both within and outside it as belonging to the general sphere of *human activities* comprising all sectors, however classified. Human activities are quanta of action, generally purposive in that they are aimed at goals, achievements and some kind of output. Activities as quanta are also measurable in a very important way, since they are *time demanding* and materialize through the resource input of *human time*. This places all different activities in a network of causal interdependence, as all activities compete for the limited time supply of a regional population or the sub-population con- tained within the domain of an organization or organizational sub-unit. Hence, qualitatively different and functionally otherwise unrelated activities interfere with one another, promote and bar one another in various ways which affect overall capacity and performance. For this reason alone, there exists a relation between the quaternary and other sectors of society, since the individuals playing roles in the former are also taking part in the latter, and the same is the case between different roles within the quaternary sector, as roles exercised in practice entail the performance of time-demanding activities.

The advantage of focusing on activities as time-demanding is not only that functionally different activities become dependent on the same resource, but that activities can be *measured* in time amounts. Moreover, they can be located —not just in space—but in terms of relative location to other social events in the temporal coordinate system based on clocks and calendars. This opens up a fresh perspective for a new allocational framework and a new relative locational analysis, analogous in many ways to that of space. The structuring of time use within and between organizations is not only a problem of manage- ment but more broadly one of understanding how they operate (cf. *inter alia* Moore 1963).

The individual There is nothing new in the concept of the individual as such, but time-geography has a special view of the individual, as has been described elsewhere in this book, by looking at each individual as a unit *existing* in time and space, describing a continuous and indivisible path. The facts of limited duration of life and indivisibility impose many constraints on existence in space over time as well as on the forms which interaction between individuals can take. The individual is the minimal unit with a time income and thus the smallest entity which can supply time for individual and collective activities. Human time is allocated both at the individual and the collective level, and only a certain amount of activity can possibly be performed in a given time span, depending on the various capabilities distributed in the population.

A second aspect of the individual is that he is the smallest unit *experiencing* himself and the environment during a limited life time. If we accept the superficial distinction between what is 'physical' and what is 'mental' or 'psychic', it is noteworthy that mental processes of cognition, perception, thinking and internal processing of information and impressions are also time consuming and involve time allocation. We call it *concentration* when we think of one topic to the exclusion of others, but in reality this is a clear form of time allocation. By virtue of being anchored in a biophysical body, mental processes are 'psycho-somatic' and hence also localized in time-space. In short, all the aspects of how an individual perceives, thinks, stores and processes information about and from his environment, also have a time-space structure.

The reason for emphasizing this is that the time-geographic approach does *not* recognize mental-cognitive processes going on inside the bodies of individuals as belonging outside its scope. It rather advocates bringing *'physical realism' into the analaysis of cognitive processes*, for instance by regarding them as time consuming, as forming discrete quanta or activities, and as being intimately coupled to more overt kinds of activities that are equally time consuming. Activities have a *simultaneous* 'mental' and 'physical-somatic' component, and hence borrowing the term 'psycho-somatic' from medicine, this fundamental unity can be stressed. Only then is it possible to see how mental capacity affects mechanic actions of the body, or how somatic capability constraints influence mental activity.

When studying the quaternary sector, this philosophy is quite important. Much work within the sector involves *auto*communication, i.e. time consuming thinking and *intra*-action. However, even these mental activities can be constrained by the material inputs necessary. A whole set of implements exist which are necessary for various forms of thinking and calculation (papers, pens, typewriters, desk computers, rulers, drawing boards and so on), which place mental activity in a biophysical setting and make it an externalized process, just as signals and markers in the environment provide mental impulses and channel thought.

The mental and physical symbiosis becomes particularly obvious in communication processes. Talking to someone involves the simultaneous process of thinking and giving material form to those thoughts by expressing speech and listening to speech. What limits our capacity for communication may lie both in our capacity to think, to use speech (compare the effect of a handicapped person stammering), and the capacity of others to listen. But this alone does not decide how much information can be communicated because it also depends on the extent to which we can form proxemic groups, i.e. bundles of individuals. This in turn is a function of how paths can be allocated in time-space and how one kind of collective activity excludes another by virtue of time allocation.

Communicating via media, which to many technologists has been such a capacity boosting innovation, still implies that bundles are formed between paths, this time between individual-paths and the paths of indivisible artefacts. There are rules of bundle formation here as well. A person can talk into several microphones at the same time, but he can only listen to messages from one speaker at a time. No person can actively both read a newspaper, gaze continuously at television, listen to the radio and talk in the telephone at the same time. Our mental capacity prevents us from making use of any number of media (just as auditive and visual capacity may do), and this, of course, is just as true for a person in his domestic role as in his role ad administrative service giver or service taker. (Hence many of the administrative rationalizations involve the displacement of human activity by computers replacing book-keepers and clerks, rather than augmenting these individuals with gadgets that increase their capacity.)

Interaction in a population system   Administrative activity can be looked upon as one special form of interaction which in part can be reduced to a more general problem of time allocation to collective activities and the formation of *bundles among paths in time-space*. This view unfolds a different kind of logic by which interaction can be analysed within a *population system*. This term used by Hägerstrand (1972a) stresses the autonomy of the set of individuals in a given societal system relative to the time demanding project and activity sub-system of that society (cf. chapter 12). Population *system* also points to the systemic properties of a 'web' of interacting paths regardless of the specific activities that people perform.

To take one simple example of such interaction interpreted in terms of the time-geographic model of individual paths, one can take the simple routine of attending meetings, which can be taken as a special instance of group (bundle) formation. Two aspects will be emphasized: One is the *time* allocation aspect that when people meet and do one kind of collective activity, they are unable at the time to do other activities. The other relates to *path* allocation: their paths must coincide in space and time during the meeting. The participating individuals become *inaccessible*, both to other activities and other people and locations. However, because of the 'horizontal' integration in a population system, such inaccessibility gaps have transitive effects: they spread 'sidewise' and restrict the number of possible alternatives for the actors as well as for the larger sub-populations of which they are parts. If individual *A* (Figure 1) is an administrator, for instance, and *B* wants to see him, *B* in turn becomes inaccessible to *C* during that time (and the time for travel). *C* then adapts the time of his meeting with *B*, but this in turn means that *D* cannot visit *C* while he is away, but has to choose a later time. This cumbersome

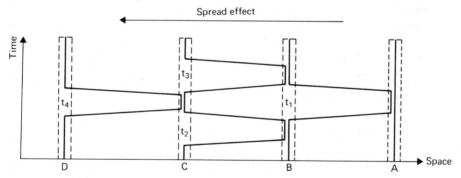

Figure 1   The horizontal spread of effects of inaccessibility gaps in the population system. (Source: Carlstein 1975d)

B's visit to A makes him inaccessible during time t_1.
C's ,, ,, B ,, ,, ,, ,, ,, t_2 and t_3.
D's ,, ,, B ,, ,, ,, ,, ,, t_4.

verbal description is much more obvious in its graphic form, which shows the relative temporal and spatial location of these meetings.

The pre-ordering of the time-space locations of bundles/meetings is one way of ensuring that unnecessary waiting and delays are not caused through sheer lack of information about potential collaborators. But then there is a time cost and corresponding coordination problem (e.g. via artefact media such as letters or phones) in obtaining information of future plans from others. In principle, there is a point at which the time saved in procuring additional information is offset by the time expended on getting it. Dumping this time cost on a secretary is the way in which business managers solve their problems. But this does not reduce the time costs, it only shifts them to another individual in the population. (It is remarkable in administrative systems how many ways there are of saving time for some by imposing new time demands on others.) But this should only be seen as a snap-shot illustration of one of the multitude of similar processes of interaction in a population system or in the sub-population system that forms the 'task force' in an organization.

Indivisible artefacts   A deeper understanding of the quaternary sector also requires a more explicit understanding of the way in which humans interact with artefacts. This is generally well understood in the primary and tertiary sector, with its emphasis on man–material or man–organism interaction. However, a good many factors affecting structure and performance in the tertiary and quaternary sectors are related to the use of indivisible artefacts, especially in the field of communication and travel. Most telephones can only be used by one person at a time, a conference television studio can only be used by one project group of engineers at a time, and so on. Just as there are limits to group formation (bundle formation) among human individuals, there are limits to the formation of bundles with artefacts. Time sharing, queueing and rotation systems are methods of overcoming these indivisibilities, but it means that performance is correspondingly constrained. If one wishes to understand bureaucracy, administration or organizational structure of firms and government agencies, it is important to be able to have basic concepts which allow one to see how similar constraints at the micro level affect the aggregate level. This is particularly relevant when trying to assess the impact of an innovation, such as the introduction of conference television or the use of electronic computers, or some new principle of allocating facilities to individuals occupying different positions in an organization. Many effects should be quite predictable if only the basic theory used incorporated basic mechanisms for interaction between humans and artefacts-facilities.

To these concepts can be added those which are already well incorporated in geographic thought and related to the *settlement system*, such as the set of *stations* serving as work places, the infrastructural *systems of communication*, such as the telephone system, and the *transportation systems* facilitating person movement. All these systems or sub-systems must, however, be seen in their time-space configurations and not merely from a static spatial viewpoint in order to be commensurable with previously described concepts.

The study of administrative projects

As a first step towards infusing temporal and spatial realism into much of what has so far been done on administrative systems, studies of the kind of projects carried out within them would be useful. This would be one way of bridging the gap between organization theory, on the one hand, and spatial-geographic theory on the tertiary and quaternary sectors, on the other hand. Such an endeavour need not entail much redefinition of concepts such as organization, role, position (job, occupation, office), competence, domain and the many allied concepts in use. It rather involves filling them with additional content that would permit getting at the deep structure of how organizations operate and can possibly operate, e.g. what they have capacity to perform. Any activity which falls outside the capability of an organization cannot materialize, for instance, and hence the introduction of time as a resource dimension is one way of deducing possible from impossible performance. The same objective can also be met by reconstructing the temporal and spatial conditions under which actors operate in particular historical and geographic settings.

This introduces the concepts of *scenario* and *project*; neither of them are new as concepts, but they should be analysed in new ways from a time-space perspective. Behind every human action there is generally an idea or concept of what is to be achieved and how one can reach predetermined objectives. If this road from idea to final result is looked upon as a temporal sequence of operations or activities, one can speak of the *scenario* of the project as the plan or blueprint for action and the whole *project* as the physical process of realizing it. The distinction between project and scenario is essential in order to separate the current image of how different steps in the plan should or can be taken from its implementation. The scenario relates to initation, planning and monitoring of, for instance, the production of goods and services. In principle it can be said to have the following properties: It is assumed that some (in itself time consuming) process of thought gives rise to ideas and goals. In an idealized scheme, the next activity consists of analysing possibilities for and consequences of a project if realized. All these activities are really the first episode of orientation of the project. The next episode consists of a long row of activities which are general consequences of decisions that have been taken. This second episode contains a number of planning, coordination and resource mobilizing activities, while a third episode comprises executive and monitoring kinds of action. The tasks of administrative organizations and sectors in principle consist of carrying out similar scenarios and projects, first mainly within the sector and later in conjunction with the sectors operating the actual production of goods and services, in the case of firms and the like.

It will not be argued here that this kind of process is predictable or fully amenable to planning. This is obviously not the case for the administration of projects in which the actual physical materialization of output lies in the fairly distant future. In reality, scenarios come and go during the performance of the project and each episode of it becomes clear only as its realization comes closer with time. One must also take into account that one scenario gives birth to another during this process of implementation, since more comprehensive projects tend to give birth to off-shoots on their way towards completion. What the original project was becomes harder to delimit the more off-shoots it has, but it is the leading ideas and objectives, the core of a project, which tends to determine which activities become inevitable. These activities then govern the basic organization supporting the project. However, every project has its component activities which are resource demanding and here again it is of the greatest interest to study the various aspects of project implementation from a time-geographic viewpoint of how resources are available and accessible for recombination and transformation in time and space.

In addition to the above general time-geographic concepts, a few basic ones found in organization theory can be given a time-geographic interpretation. The concept of *role*, for instance, can be seen as the way in which activities are allocated to individuals having certain capability or competence. Time allocation is the way individuals allocate their time to activities, whilst conversely, *activity allocation* (related to 'division of labour') is the fashion in which kinds of activities are allocated to categories of individuals. A role is a particular allocation of activities to individuals, and various stages in both the conceptualization and realization of projects requires the time of individuals with specific capability. Generally speaking, the larger, the more complex and the more specialized a project, the greater the number of specialized roles it will involve. Exercising a certain role is always time consuming, of course. Clusters of roles may be allocated to particular individuals, thereby defining the content of his specific *position* in an organization.

Up till now, most of the concepts presented belong only to the material and behavioural realms of social systems. This makes the approach seem overly mechanistic. Obviously, there also exists a symbolic-ideological realm of culture and society which includes meanings, values, norms, symbols, laws and institutions that all form cognitive instruments which guide and regulate human actions. To this realm further belong goals and interests, contracts and agreements, rights and duties and so on. Before analysing project performance and implementation, then, some additional key concepts might be the following. *Position* can be taken as the *de jure* or legally defined concept of how tasks are allocated among individuals who by contract are made responsible for performing certain activities and tasks. Likewise, an *organization* can be *de jure* defined as a combination of or congeries of positions which obligate individuals to allocate their time to the performance of some projects and activities as opposed to others. Organizations are thus legally defined entities, generally juridical persons, which means that they are treated as one entity by the law (e.g. for ownership and taxation purposes) regardless of the number of individuals belonging to the organization. It is important here to note that this is a juridical as opposed to a 'physical' definition. *Contracts* in the sense of agreements (more or less imposed) and *rules* (rights and especially duties) form regulatory constraints, 'steering' or authority constraints in Hägerstrand's terminology (1970a), and the whole system of rules and guidelines, born out of decisions and contracts, channel the allocation of time in specific directions. However, nearly all the legal-normative-symbolic concepts have a physical-somatic counterpart and existence. They not merely *are* something but they *do* something in space and time.

A major problem in most analyses on the quaternary sector stems from the fact that practically all concepts dealing with the symbolic-cognitive-ideological realm of culture-society are so *static*, let alone the fact that they are nearly always *a-spatial*. Although they *apply* to the behavioural and material realms of culture-society, they cannot be well connected and interrelated to it because of their lack of 'physical', i.e. time-space, realism. Many studies seem to depart from an abstract state of an eternal present which is referred to as the *structure* of an organization, for instance. In this, even activities can be abstracted from time and looked upon in a static fashion. For example, the scenarios can be taken as merely existing at that unspecified time state and are at best regarded as a product of a process of a prior time period. The component activities in the organization are looked upon as exercised by individuals in certain positions of the organization, something often indicated in structural charts of who is sub- or super-ordinate to whom. But roles are not seen as clusters of time-demanding activities, nor are the communication links between the positions regarded as time consuming forms of interaction. In the social science literature, there is a wealth of jural or juridical approaches to organizations character-ized by outlining legal-normative structure without seeing this in relation to process and transformation of states in time and space. This symbolic super-structure is not regarded as anchored in biophysical realities that strongly impinge on symbolic, cognitive and institutional *processes*. While it is always considered that there is a turnover of personnel, materials and machines in a production organization such as a factory, there is likewise a turnover of rules and guidelines, for instance. The latter have not always been there, nor will they always be there. Nor will the behaviour and technical systems they are supposed to regulate. In general, there is a process of birth, death and intermediate life time of the rules that circumscribe various activities, as is the case with the rules on the occupation of space for various projects, i.e. those delineating the spatial domains for people, artefacts, materials, constructions, machines or vehicles. Individual symbols, systems of symbols or cognitive systems in this respect exhibit the same 'demographic' characteristics as organ-isms, particularly when symbolic systems become 'objectified' and put into recorded form such as books, written notes, tapes, drawings, maps and the like.

Any 'formal' symbolic system of rules and regulations does not merely have this 'life-span' quality, but it also has an innate 'physical-somatic' content in terms of the behavioural and material referents the course of which it is supposed to steer or guide. Even in a simple case of who is allowed to do what to whom for how long and to what extent, the system of rules makes all kinds of assumptions about the material and behavioural realm of society. A law saying who is allowed to carry out a particular activity in certain environments on given occasions does have a time-space structure, just as the legislation regarding employment conditions does.

It follows then, that in order to understand the workings of a sector such as the quaternary, both in terms of symbolic-ideological superstructure and its material and behavioural base, it is necessary to consider a total reinterpre-tation of the former in terms of its *action* and *process* components. This in turn implies unveiling its 'physical' structure, i.e. how the time-space structure of the symbolic realm ties in with the time-space structure of the behavioural and material realm.

Bearing this dual time-space content of man's internal and external world in mind, and taking Hägerstrand's (1973b) discussion of projects as a point of departure, some main time-geographic themes in studying and reinterpreting work on the quaternary sector can be listed. These themes are interrelated and mutually supporting. For one thing, a major process to study is the turnover of projects and project and product cycles, i.e. the conception, implementation and decease of administrative projects. This can be related to the generation of scenarios as well as the input requirements of projects in terms of human time, settlement space-time, machine time, energy and so on. It can also be related to output as well as productivity, efficiency and the use of capacity. The way inputs are hierarchically ordered and the structure of backward and forward linkages between projects plus the gestation periods of component projects are other factors influencing turnover and capacity. Gestation lags, delays and more or less time saving procedures are part of the temporal structure of project effectuation. The principles of mobilizing resources, of keeping them mobilized and in preparedness in different spatial and temporal locations are interesting from a time-geographic and logistic viewpoint, as is the way in which organizations 'book in' resources for future use in order to obtain flexibility and decrease the effects of various environmental constraints. Different kinds of domains and organizational units enclose various resources and store them for use at the right times and places, and contracts and agreements between the organization and the outside world order the flows of inputs and outputs to assure performance as the 'now-line' of the present moves forward and transforms future into past.

Looking at organizations in relation to their environments, the differential effects of various projects in terms of other projects which are displaced because of a lack of resources is a feature which deserves more attention, as economists have for too long calculated costs merely financially, and this is only one way of tracing opportunity costs. Another way is to do so in terms of population time and differential effects on a population system comprised of all the different categories (age, sex, skill, etc.).

This finally raises the issue of who formulates projects and benefits from them and how politically autonomous or dependent on a wider environment major administrative projects are. The time-allocation aspect of participation in decision-making and feed-back of effects of output is a comprehensive area of study. So, at the ecological level, is how the mechanisms of life and death of projects can be found at both a purposive level of decision-making and, at the economic-ecologic system level, how projects are fitted into 'niches' in a wider system of resource competition and adaptive efficiency.

Conclusion

In an effort to explain the tertiary sector, one can make empirical observation, try to explain the range of variation and the working of the system and arrive at various inductive generalizations. This is useful, but often inadequate for understanding new situations, devising alternative systems or evaluating given systems in terms of something untried. A powerful supplement and alternative to this method is to try to explain the limits of the possible and see what happens to these limits when additional factors are incorporated. To do so for the quaternary sector involves making various assessments of innovations and the capacity for action under realistically interpreted constraints. It has been assumed in this essay that this becomes more feasible when one looks into the preconditions for action from a time-space locational and allocational viewpoint.

Chapter 12
A Note on the Quality of Life-Times
Torsten Hägerstrand*

Introduction

An important way of assessing the performance of a socio-environmental complex (city, region or nation) would be to try to find out what kinds of life-biographies it defines for its human population taken as a whole (cf. chapter 7 above). If we could know what happened to everybody and what everybody thought about it we would have a great account of history. If we then used this knowledge to find out about determinants behind events, then we would have a fine instrument for making judgements forwards in time, for example in connection with major institutional or technological changes.

Now, of course, we do not know what happened to everybody and we will never be able to find out. (Sometimes we can take samples.) But nevertheless, as soon as we have grasped what the problem is, we might very well be able to find out a lot about determinants on the basis of rather scanty information. What is needed is a frame that allows a good amount of deductive reasoning. Human time-use provides such a frame. The purpose of the following short remarks is to direct researchers' attention to such more long-term potentials of time-use studies. And note that I mean time-use studies in connection with space-use studies because all time is spent in environments and strongly tied to what is there.

Time as a framework within which budgeting takes place has several attractive properties that can serve useful purposes when studying the future. For one thing *time* is the main dimension in future-oriented studies. But from the viewpoint of the individual it is not merely a descriptive dimension, it is also a limited resource. This resource is often less well used whether seen from the individual or the social perspective. Time is further a suitable vehicle for analysing the association of humans with machines, considering that much technical development has been aimed at making time-use more efficient, a process there is every reason to believe will continue. The effects of techniques on society can consequently often be well interpreted via changed time relations. Finally, certain physical preconditions that are neglected in practically all of social theory make their appearance in a true time-budgeting or time-allocation framework. These conditions are valid regardless both of how individuals subjectively perceive them and of how society values different action alternatives in relation to one another (or some hypothetical optimum).

But the plea for greater and more consistent attention to the temporal dimension in social analysis and technology assessment is not a proposal for

* Translated from the Swedish by T. Carlstein.

statistical 'time-budget' studies of the conventional format. The point of departure here is not the daily perspective that most time-budget surveys operate within. Nor is it a matter of making empirically founded index constructions describing the performance characteristics of overall social organization (e.g. social indicators). The main task lies at the deeper level of how to grasp the determinants which distribute life-biographies of different kinds among the members of a population.

One of the motives for developing the study of the future as a research area—perhaps the most important one—is to make assessments of events which under various hypothetical conditions will affect a population in the future. Although, in theory, market mechanisms and electoral procedures are supposed to provide the necessary channels through which the needs of individuals should become known and catered for, it seems to be commonplace in many contemporary societies that the interests of individuals are not that well taken account of. Particularly, the legitimate interests of individuals are not respected in a uniform way across the *total* population. A source of special worry to many people is the consequences of technical developments to come. An indiscriminate acceptance of innovations which by themselves appear to be improvements may, cumulatively, achieve a general societal environment which is qualitatively far below that which corresponding resources and competence might have added up to if the very selection of inputs had been done in a broader perspective than our present conceptualizations of social organization allow. The time is ripe to try to work constructively with improving our understanding of how the system-wide structures of technological organization and the distribution of power and influence should be designed to safeguard the life qualities of every individual (Hägerstrand 1973a).

Conventionally, *individual-oriented* research has a very weak methodological base. The social sciences have either been less interested or incapable of constructing a theoretically solid bridge between micro- and macro-perspectives or between technology and other spheres of society. One of the very few disciplines which come close to a true individual-orientation in the macro-assessments and which maintain a link between biography and aggregate, is demography. This discipline has a series of models, for instance of how educational systems change over time with respect to cohorts of students. But even in demography, the link between society and biography is often rather weak, as is nearly invariably the case in macro-economic models. While the latter satisfy the criterion of system-wide coverage, they fail in relating this to the component individuals.

If one is interested in examining societal performance with respect to the component individuals, one must reasonably proceed via some method which projects social organization onto the component individuals in the population. It is here that the procedure of demographers furnishes a model, in spite of their somewhat limited interest in a few critical events such as birth, formation of households, migration, illness and death. But what is exemplary in their analysis and carries great developmental potential is that their *description includes all individuals who constitute the population* and that it consists of *every individual's entire life span or at least an unbroken portion thereof*.[1] This is important for at least two reasons. First, it is a useful normative element in that it forces one to consider a total population with all its age-sex-skill and other categories, something which is seldom the case in most current conceptual models of society. Secondly, this continuous analysis of unbroken portions of lives of individuals is a precondition for calculation in budgeting and allocation terms. A whole population seen as a flow without gaps for a given time period makes up the population time-budget, as the time covered in a daily or more long-term sense constitutes a finite amount, both for individuals and the population.

Using time as a basic dimension, description of society in budgeting terms will permit assessments of how much an extension of resource demands in one place will entail a contraction of action possibilities in one or several other locations. A clear picture of available choice or action space from the supply side will emerge, and for the time being this seems to be the only reliable method of deductive reasoning in social science, at the same time as it provides a factual basis for political considerations and negotiations which trend-extrapolations and predictions of a cause-effect kind do not.

Many of my basic ideas on the population of indivisible individuals and other time-geographic concepts have already been presented in this book, and hence require no further elaboration here. What I will do here, however, is to indicate a perspective with regard to the population system and to the way the future is, to a fair extent, programmed into a population through the various capabilities and exposure to events in the environment which affect individuals, but also in relation to the interaction among individuals and between them and their man-made and nature-produced environment.

Discussion can with great advantage be based on the use of graphic notation, where each individual is represented by an unbroken life-line (or life path, a trajectory in time and space). The life paths of all individuals in the given population can be lined up next to one another (preferably by increasing age but for other purposes a different ordering may be better). The result will be a block which for every arbitrarily delimited time period will represent the total available time supply in a population. This is the time-budget frame to be allocated to different activities. For simplicity of representation migration is disregarded.

Every individual is always occupied by some time-consuming activity or task. He further perceives a continuous sequence of events produced by the stimuli from his environment where he must be in order to carry out his tasks. The whole complex can with advantage be looked upon as an interwoven budgeting problem: a stream of individual time—a strictly limited time income—is through various mechanisms channelled into packages of activity and pockets of operation in space-time.

What will be presented here is an outline of some relevant aspects of this budgeting process in a population system seen in a long-term life-cycle and future-oriented perspective rather than in the short-time perspective prevailing in much of time-budget and time-allocation study. Of the many relevant ones, only two major aspects will be dealt with.

The programming of capabilities and characteristics into a population system

The characteristics and capabilities of the individual determine what he seeks in his environment, how he perceives its content of opportunities and what he chooses to compete with others for. Conversely, his capabilities and characteristics also determine what he is willing and able to contribute in order to meet demands from his environment.

Certain innate characteristics imply needs of an indisputably compelling time structure in the daily round that act as a strong constraint on other forms of time use. The need for personal care at the beginning and end of the life cycle is of similar compelling nature during longer periods of time. Puberty and the fertility period in women are likewise on the whole fixed in time. Other highly time-structured traits in the biography of an individual are some culturally derived ones, for instance those related to choice of occupation, the formation of family, the entering into the labour market, and the age of retirement when the link to the work environment is severed and the social contact network of the individual is beginning to wither as a function of increasing mortality among one's old friends and relations.

The capabilities and characteristics individuals acquire through life situations and formal education are not given by birth but can be influenced. But at a somewhat more general level certain invariant traits are found if one focuses on the way this acquisition is distributed over population and time. The characteristics imposed on the individuals by various means become fixed in a population and are then moved forward in time with each cohort. Characteristics imposed early in life can thus make themselves felt over periods in the order of seventy to eighty years. These characteristics also relate to the way in which individuals cooperate with others. It is not only the cohorts themselves which move forward in time but also the relations between component individuals. It is therefore inevitable that the way individuals with various characteristics are sorted out in society at the present casts a long shadow into the future. It is possibly also the case that an individual's capability to alter or broaden his assorted characteristics lessens with time. This relates to professional competence, habits, interests, political sympathies and various attitudes.

Taking the previous graphic representation of a population system (Figure 1), the different influences to which a population is exposed can be divided into a few main types. The graphic illustrations which follow below are much simplified, for instance by not taking into consideration that the density of newly born varies from year to year along the diagonal birth axis or that the population is gradually thinned out through deaths.

Certain kinds of events are projected onto a whole population at the same time right across all age groups (Figure 2). The pollution of air and water is approaching this situation (and it is therefore not surprising that it is easier to reach political consensus about what measures to take than in other distributional matters). A period of isolation and food rationing (as during a war) is likely to have a similar effect. Traffic risks have likewise acquired much the same structure. The broadcasting of sound and picture via radio and television in principle has similar effects in terms of exposure, although the reception

varies between individuals and age, sex and social categories, which means
that the fallout effects are differentiated.

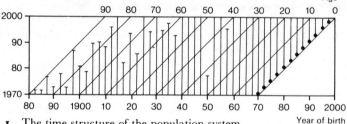

Figure 1   The time structure of the population system.

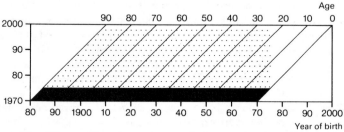

Figure 2   The fall-out effect of a temporary influence that is uniformly distributed
in a total population.

In the second main case (Figure 3) a given influence was selective already
at the beginning of life. Every new individual is introduced into an environment
with special social and physical characteristcs which to some extent mark him
for the future. Language and dialect can generally be observed as stubbornly
persisting traits but many other qualities imprinted at an early age belong
to this category. Much of this variation is inevitable and to a great extent an
asset since it generates different directions of interest which are of advantage
to societies in need of recruitment to multifarious occupations. But this social
inheritance can also have effects on the later capabilities of individuals which
serve to reduce his range of choice of activities and environments. It seems
that a sorting out of individuals into categories of likely biographies begins as
early as the pre-school age. It therefore seems of major importance to look
at the social organizational arrangements affecting individuals in early childhood in a long-term perspective (Frankenhaeuser 1972; Mårtensson 1977).

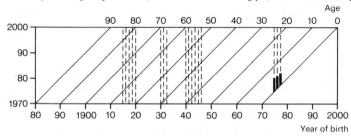

Figure 3   The remaining fall-out of a temporary influence which is selectively
localized to certain time periods and certain individuals belonging to the youngest age
cohort. The social inheritance of cultural traits is of a similar but individually variable
kind.

A third type of influence on the population is that represented by school-ing, which imposes one form of compulsory time use for a certain age period in every individual's life (Figure 4). If education is extended, the en-suing distribution of qualifications between age cohorts at each cross section in time becomes very uneven during a very long period of transition. This depends on whether the increment is placed as an extension for everyone during their childhood and youth years (Figure 5) or whether it is taken as a voluntary input of time in middle age (Figure 6).

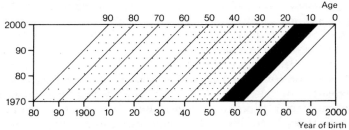

Figure 4 The remaining fall-out of a constant source of influence on one age cohort (school education). Extension of compulsory schooling is assumed to have been intro-duced around 1900 and 1945.

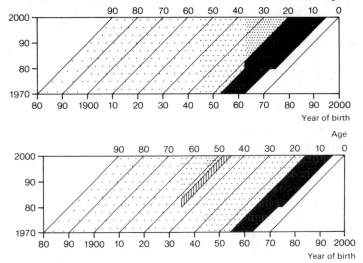

Figure 5 and 6 The remaining fall-out of an educational period which has been located to age cohorts in various ways.

Schooling does not merely entail a differentiation between groups. It also implies a homogenization with long-term effects in some respects. It is thus inevitable that the direction which language-education receives, especially choice of languages taught, will for a long time influence people's image of their external environment and their capacity to communicate with it, and thereby the economic actions of firms in the international arena or the orienta-tion of cultural life is also affected.

If, finally, one imagines Figures 2 to 6 placed on top of one another, one receives an impression of how variously channelled influences and qualities in the population interact cumulatively in sorting the population into categories with different characteristics and capabilities.

A population system as it presents itself at a given point in time is consequently a system with a considerable degree of future conditions programmed into itself. It is a biological system which in many respects has a predictable future is conditioned by the distribution of capabilities and attitudes[2] (providing it is not exterminated in some environmental catastrophe). When the contention is sometimes made as to the impossibility of making reliable prognoses, *inter alia* population prognoses, this is because the emphasis is placed on comparatively marginal quantities, *viz.* the exact number of individuals at a certain future date within a nation or smaller region. Especially the latter is, of course, difficult to foresee with precision several decades ahead. Similarly the variations in fertility rates are hard to forecast. But this should not overshadow the fact that the overall mass of the population can be regarded as one resource with rather clearly given limits as to how activities with different competence requirements can be distributed in the future. It is above all the picture of these characteristics and their changes that one could grasp by means of some suitable demographic accounting system (Bjerke 1970).

Interpersonal time demand

The goals and projects which are set up by private individuals and all the groups and coalitions that exist, from the family upward in size to the state, the multinational corporation and international organizations, all jointly define the demand for time of individuals.

To meet this demand, a defined gross available time is set by the size of the population. The competence requirements placed on individuals form one obvious constraint on the way demand can be matched by supply. But before such a matching is possible, the often neglected constraint associated with the limited movement possibilities of the individual must be considered. (These have already been discussed in the chapters by Lenntorp and Mårtensson elsewhere in this book.)

Apart from the way in which time spent on travel is a function of the local structure of the environment, the sequences in which an individual must place demands on one or several other collaborating persons, is strongly dependent on the exact way in which surrounding local resources and arrangements place available time-supply at his disposal. These local demand-supply relations deserve thorough investigation, and some cases of importance to living conditions will therefore be presented.

For the future, one inevitable part of interpersonal time demand is associated with what could be called the *care cycle*. While there is a certain amount of personal variation, of course, the main principle of it is that everybody generates a demand curve which has its maxima at the beginning and end of life. A child can hardly be left without attendance for even a short period before it reaches the age of three or four. Up till then it ties up person time in the elder age groups (Figure 7), time which cannot to any great extent be simultaneously used as an input in gainful employment.

The exact extraction of time from one or several individuals can be arranged in several wyas. The possibilities for large-scale operation are limited and for mechanization non-existent. Some conceivable arrangements require more transportation time than others, but rationalization in the industrial sense is difficult to implement, only shifts and relocations of tasks within the population system are feasible. It is of course an erroneous cliché to think that the time-demands on the primary group by children disappear when the children start school. New tasks appear, involving fewer coupling constraints perhaps, but they still demand time.

The care requirements in the final phase of the life cycle are more elastic. Care becomes more confined to purely physical care, above which a certain amount of social intercourse with others will suffice. But even here this demand for care must be extracted from the time supply of younger generations by means of various arrangements. It is easy to see how a relative increase in the number of aged has a corresponding effect of increasing these time demands for personal care.

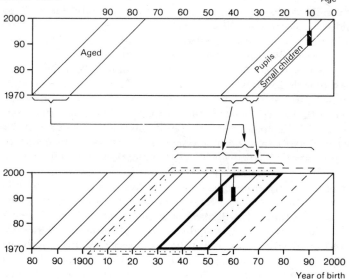

Figure 7   (a) Three age categories which, with respect to the future, generate a fixed or growing time demand aimed at other age categories.

(b) Age categories from which demand at each point in future time must be satisfied. The relation between child and adult illustrates the connection between demand and supply.

In between these foreseeable demand quantities in the life cycle comes ordinary medical care. It constitutes one of our more curious kinds of social activities as it is difficult both to survey it and to determine the total demand relations in the population system. To a certain extent the care requirements are generated by friction between other social arrangements (e.g. traffic, drugs, abortions) and even by progress in medicine itself. The choice of illnesses that one invests technical resources into curing half way will have a great effect on subsequent demand. Since there is no reason to assume that every individual can have his own private physician, which is unreasonable from a supply view-point, it is a vain hope to pretend that the problems of medical care can be solved without painful political deliberations.

Apart from other conceivable difficulties in matching different volumes of demand and supply, there exists another latent contradiction in the structure of demand and supply. The former is geared towards stability of personnel over time. The child needs permanent personal relations with a small set of adults over a long time. It is an activity of artisan rather than industrial character to rear a new individual. There is every reason to assume that the need for stability of relations for the aged is of a similar nature. And even among the seekers of hospital treatment there is a widely felt desire that the same staff should be in charge of an entire sequence of care. Investigations conducted in the United States reveal the difficulties associated with ephemeral doctor-patient contacts (Korsch–Negrete 1972). The supply side, by contrast, is marked by an ever stronger tendency towards industrial organization with specialization and division of labour, having its strongest manifestations in the hospital sector. The conflict between demand and supply would become most blatant if child care was to be placed totally in the custody of institutions. Then the children's need for stable personal relations would clash totally with the stipulated rights of the personnel to have regular working hours and freely change employment with exclusive views to their careers.

Reflecting on developments in ordinary gainful employment with respect to mutual time demands is another exercise with points of its own. It is habitually assumed that the traditional coupling of employee to machine will decrease in extent in the future. But in return the service sector will start bulging, its main mission being to process information and administer personal contacts (cf. Fuchs 1968). It can also be foreseen that 'conference technology' will be increasingly applied when workers' participation and collective decision-making (joint determination) becomes institutionalized in an increasing number of sectors. In time-allocation terms this means that the gainfully employed individuals will make ever greater demands on the time of others (i.e. on one another's time). It will also imply a growing amount of time spent on travel to facilitate requisite personal contacts, as it is hardly likely that participation in joint decision-making can be taken seriously if it is to be mediated by telecommunications. Regardless of the extent to which the latter comes to be applied, no technology can do away with the time demands inflicted by negotiations and decision-making.

In an article on the rising costs in the service sector and their impact on living standards (Baumol and Oates 1972), the conclusion is put forward that one has to live with the fact that much service production cannot be carried out at a greater pace in the future than it is at present. Judging from available facts one comes up against an unyielding invariant of human interaction here. What the above analysis neglected, however, is the condition that many personal services preoccupy both producer and consumer for an equal time period. This sort of service thus extracts twice its production time from the totally available population time (cf. Hägerstrand 1972a). An increased amount of personal services thus implies a decreased potential input into other forms of production. If this is added to the increased contact requirements between officers within private and public activity sectors, one gets the impression that the tail is beginning to wag the dog.

Two particularly burdensome bottlenecks can now be identified. One is the queueing situation around certain key individuals with special capabilities (such as physicians) or those who occupy decision-making positions in large organizations, who together determine the rate and extent to which dependent activities can be performed in their environment. The other bottleneck has nothing to do with overall time scarcities but is rather a function of the detailed temporal organization of supply. Nearly all service transactions are concentrated to the same short period in the middle of the ordinary weekday. In a situation of full employment in conjunction with a very high intensity of employment, as in the case of Sweden where there are a decreasing number of housewives or similar persons to whom errands can be delegated, the production of services—if it is to be fully made use of—might entail that a substantial portion of the work force must be absent from their jobs. The possibilities for such pauses and interruptions varies between different jobs and types of environment, of course, and hence in itself becomes a source of inequality.

Conclusion

Space was hardly mentioned in the foregoing sections. One may get the impression that I think that space is irrelevant for the treatment of the kind of problems dealt with here. And most social scientists would look at it that way. They would not mind sampling biographies from anywhere and exposing them to the ordinary battery of statistical analysis.

But I am thinking of a frame that permits a good amount of deductive reasoning. And that frame is there, I think, only as far as we are able to integrate time with space.

Behind events projected onto the separate individuals in a population lie transactions with other individuals and objects around them. But transactions require for the most part nearness in space. Movement can be allowed to take only a limited amount of time. Transacting populations are predominantly populations that live fairly close together as in a city or village. This is a circumstance which adds a further dimension to the budgeting process. Demand and supply must be catered for rather locally all the time. This gives rise to a complicated mixture of cooperation and competition. And for the indivisible individual the mixture is a strong determinant on the content of his biography. Take a simple example.

Assume that a firm in a small town decides to expand its activities and for that purpose draws in some few hundred new employees. These will then cooperate at the work-place so from the point of view of the firm all is fine. But if the expansion is rapidly executed, the same persons are likely to have to compete on a congested housing market with the result that some—hardly the better paid ones—have to disperse and commute to work in longer journeys.

There is also a type of 'negative' competition which is most frequently disregarded. When people withdraw from interaction within a certain locality, it is inevitable that they correspondingly destroy activity programmes existing there before. This reduces the number of potential choices for the remaining population without them being able to influence the matter. There are localized examples of how this process of deterioration of social functions rages in areas of out-migration or in the city areas from which the more wealthy population strata move away. In a more general fashion the same effect arises when automobile usage reaches such proportions that the remaining population without cars is too small to provide a base for public transport at a feasible price.

As long as we take only time into account we can continue to live with the faith that everybody has a wide free choice and that this choice does not affect those people one is not dealing with directly. But the picture becomes quite different as soon as we start to consider the whole population living together within a bounded space of daily reach. Then we must admit that the local finitude of time and space makes everything hang together in a complex way. But this hanging together can be looked into rather rigorously if one tries to apply a space-time trajectory perspective. The insights that will come out are important and should have consequences both for individual awareness and for political ambitions.

Afterword: Towards a Time-Space Structured Approach to Society and Environment

Tommy Carlstein and Nigel Thrift

On substance and concept

The aim of this book is fourfold: first, to increase the awareness of time aspect of societal organization; secondly to bring time-oriented studies in the other social sciences to the attention of those already aware of space; thirdly, to bring together major raw materials and semi-finished products which can provide inputs for new models and theories; and finally to suggest new avenues of progress in this general field of study.

Some major attempts and approaches are presented in the three volumes of this book; this chapter is more by way of a retrospective assessment of still extant problems and the prospects for their solution. The discussion of limitations on existing work should not be seen as criticism because the objectives that we have formulated are often different from those of other contributors—scholars with their own specific aims, interests and points of departure in mind. However, in trying to enlarge the scope, we must point to obvious facts—that some studies have been more sectoral than others, some have been more comprehensive in their treatment of time and space, some have been confined to a particular time horizon, such as the day, some are limited to specific environments (e.g. urban or rural), and so on. Again it is apparent that some treat time perception without dealing with the time-space structure of society, and that some deal with the temporal organization of activity without including time allocation.

What we want to point out is that there are new and more effective combinations of approaches, that greater precision in the use of concepts is necessary when merging different models, and that better generalizations and more comprehensive models can be built. Neither should it be forgotten that there are new and exciting fields of substance that should be incorporated and which would probably be much better *understood* using a time and space allocation and organization approach—subjects like technology, politics and bureaucracy. There is much that could be said and done, but in the present context we shall confine ourselves to a minimum of essential points which need to be brought out into the open in order to stimulate further dialogue and development.

On the other hand, we would not want this book to be seen in isolation. It would obviously be pretentious not to emphasize at this stage that there are several established schools in the field, such as the Multinational Comparative Time-Budget group, the Chapin group at North Carolina in the USA, the Time-Geography Group in Sweden, or the Becker time-allocation school in economics. The book to hand represents only a select portion, which further has a strong bias towards the Anglo–American language area. Material available in French, German, Spanish, Swedish, Bulgarian, Polish, Russian or Japanese is for instance, grossly under-represented although it exists. Therefore, in this Afterword we try to at least touch upon some of the approaches not contained in this book, especially the Becker school in economics.

A time-space approach can herald the possibility of integration of diverse substance, but only if there is a greater and more precise delination of substance in the real world which is to be the object of study. There is an obvious need to establish a more nearly one to one correlation between substance and concept, if more complex and comprehensive time-space model-building is to pay dividends. This will be discussed further below, but at this stage it should be stressed that agreement must be reached on certain basic concepts if there is to be genuine additivity of knowledge and intellectual progress. There are a number of semi-private languages in circulation used in the analysis of socio-economic and human ecological systems in a time-space framework. Many of these languages are not consistent when viewed in a wider perspective, and it is of interest to discuss how they can be readapted and redefined.

The present book does *not* advocate the carving out of some separate niche in the social science field, which deals with time-space social science. To create another sub-discipline will not solve any problems in a social science already segmented and overspecialized. What the introduction of time and space as explicit dimensions in all their facets promises to achieve is instead to promote the *integration of diversified areas of knowledge*. It also increases the potential for bridging the gap between socio-economic science on the one side and bio-ecological and technological science on the other.

This is something which has not really been attained by, for instance, 'general systems theory', which is specific in form but quite arbitrary in content. It has been boldly claimed that general systems theory has been instrumental in integrating various branches of science. Perhaps it has had some contributory effects. The dominant imprint, however, seems to have been one of systematic labelling of diverse substances with the same names. Like the quantitative revolutions in the various social sciences including human geography, mathematical and other general languages of formalization are useful for certain deductive purposes,[1] but they have given no guidelines on how to join and couple a given set of concepts and given models to the elements in the real world. This is a completely missing link in general systems theory.

Because of the tendency of geographers to reify space and sometimes make substance out of form, or the tendency to reify time when studying time aspects of society, it becomes necessary to make a general statement with regard to substance. The real world substance analysed by a time-space structured social science does not depart in any way from that ordinarily studied in the various social sciences. It consists of human individuals and populations, animal and plant populations as they interact with man, activities, time, space, artefacts, constructions, institutions, groups, organizations, signals, information, money, norms, values, goals, decisions, control, power, domains, interests, resources, raw materials, production, consumption, distribution, transport, movement, mobility, communications, media, cognitions, perceptions, ideologies, cosmologies, and so on. Remember there are substantive aspects of time and space as well, hence their inclusion in this list. It is not in the choice of substance that the time-space approach differs. It is in the conceptualization of substance and the organization of substance into models with a greater use of the formal qualities of time and space that the difference will be found. It is because of the universally pervasive properties of time and space as locational, allocational and existential dimensions of most substance that the two dimensions are so useful in structuring our understanding of the elements and processes found in the real world. This is a main and irrevocable contention of this book.

It is useful at this stage to recollect any major sub-systems of real-world societies which have been left unstudied in time-space oriented social science and which have been given an ugly sister treatment in the present book. At least two areas present themselves, namely the technological and the political.

From a social science point of view technology has been maltreated for decades because, unlike all other sectors of human activity and thought, it has not become the focus of a social science discipline of its own. Technology and its role in society have been delegated to a horde of technical scientists and engineers, whose partial and myopic perspective has done much to pave the way for misapplications on a grand scale. Technological aspects are sometimes inputs in other social science disciplines, but never in a pervasive and dominant fashion. Technology is just an exogenous variable! There are several reasons why a science of technology in society has not developed spontaneously. One is that the lion's share of basic concepts, models or theories in social science have been geared to a substance that is psychological, institutional or pecuniary in kind rather than activity, material or biologically substance-oriented. When technology has been studied by social scientists, this heritage of mind, moral and money has made these studies so rudimentary that they have been of little use in monitoring technological development. Commonly both the human population-activity-machine-energy component or the bio-ecological one has been conspicuous by its absence and it is only in border disciplines like geography, architecture and ecology that technology has been given any serious basic consideration (Carlstein 1974c). If systematically and imaginatively exploited, the dimensions of time, space and energy could yield much to integrate our understanding of the functions, role and dynamics of technology in society. As Hägerstrand (1974b) has argued, it is technology as a cultural product which separates biological ecology from human ecology as a bio-social science:

> Man clearly forms a biological population among all others.... (But) between man and other populations lies a world of symbols and artefacts of his own creations.... Man is thus living and acting in the intersection of two separate but in many respects similar worlds, the biological and the technological.... To me it seems as if human technology fundamentally represents an effort to mimic the natural world of organisms.... More important is to note that fabricated entities have certain formal population characteristics. I think it is safe to say that all material things fabricated by humans have typical 'life-times'—at least in terms of useful 'life'. They have birth-rates controlled by socio-economic forces. They own different degrees of mobility and they have age-distributions—all traits which mean

a lot for human living conditions. The similarity between the man-made world and living communities goes further. Technology exhibits its own 'food-chains' in the sense that more complicated artefacts must be composed of less complicated parts in long chains. Specialization and complexity begin to make these chains as problematic to keep in balance as their living equivalents. . . .

Hägerstrand goes on to argue how both organisms and artefacts can be visualized as paths in time-space which form a web, how each path is subject to individual or environmental time-space constraints, how entities must be synchronized and synchorized, and how all these activities must take place in pockets of operations and domains in time-space which ensure the completion of projects (cf. also Hägerstrand 1974a). There is no doubt that if we are to grasp how the human population interacts with the population of artefacts created by humans, we must start to develop a conceptual model which inter-connects the activities of people, artefacts and cultigens into one system, in which artefacts are seen as a special kind of population with its own input–output relations and time-space requirements. Some of the basic concepts for such a model have been suggested by Hägerstrand already (Hägerstrand 1973b; 1974a; 1974b). It is also apparent that economizing with human time, settlement space and energy are interrelated, in that using less of one tends to increase the use of another. These kinds of substitution effects must be inves-tigated in a framework of allocation, budgeting and economizing in real terms rather than in the conventional and by now somewhat discredited pecuniary format.

The other neglected area is that of politics, although the various aspects of administration and communications between organizations have already been touched upon by Olander and Carlstein above. The fact that decisions are made in a situational context with time-space coordinates, the fact that political projects and communication between sub-groups in a population are time consuming or the fact that geographic space and time is segmented into a fabric of domains all must be borne in mind when studying how behaviour and systems are politically controlled. The struggle for time and space resources and the competition between projects introduces another aspect (cf. Hägers-trand 1973b). Much fruitful reinterpretation of politico-administrative pro-cesses can be carried out in a structural framework of time and space, and various *capacity* assessments of political communication and institutions (Carlstein 1975c) can also be very useful if one wishes to find means of ex-panding democratic participation in decision-making. Research into already existing literature on political systems would no doubt be very rewarding in developing a theory of how political activity is integrated with other forms of activity and interaction. Some time studies seem to hint at this. A public administration specialist, Lee, studied how administrators perceive time in rela-tion to their tasks and positions (Hahn Been Lee 1967; 1968). Another study called 'Waiting, exchange and power: The distribution of time in social systems' (Schwartz 1974, 1975) gives a further hint of a possible theme in this field. But it is important to integrate the spatial components of politico-administration systems (cf. Christaller's administrative principle) with that of time and time-consuming activities. This field is so rewarding in terms of being 'under-researched' that it could be a major field of time-space geography and time-space oriented social science at large. It is important, however, not to have a sectoral view of political and administrative process, but to see this as an activity just as subject to time allocation and economizing as others.

As was pointed out before, the various approaches presented in this book are often partial in that they cover some temporal and spatial aspects of society and human activity but not others. Those dealing with time use have not dealt with time allocation for various reasons, and those analysing perception and cognition have ignored the activity or social inter-actional component. Many time frameworks have totally neglected the spatial dimension and the structure of human settlement, for instance, most of the work done by economists or that by the students of 'time-budgets' (e.g. in Szalai, ed. 1972). Likewise the perhaps most inclusive and internally consistent approach, that based on the time-geographic model of the Lund School, has so far been deficient in considering the role of perception and cognition.

Uniting these approaches is not a matter of simple addition of concepts however, because the various frameworks are based on entirely different postulates. Concepts in one approach cannot be extended to another without modification and reduction of internal logical errors and inconsistencies. If they are Lakatos's degenerating problems shift sets in: Geography already has enough tacked-together models.

Perhaps the most interesting experiment is to confront schemes which are able to hold their own on the basics of their inherent criteria of achievement, with other schemes, paradigms and models. This is not simply because it is a requirement for further amalgamation and fusion, but rather because it tends to reveal the intrinsic logical weaknesses of the various approaches. Not only does it expose major inadequacies when confronted with reality but also how some frameworks suffer from strategic conceptual flaws.

From time-use survey to population-cum-activity systems in time-space

With the spread of the clock and the calendar as regulators of industrial work organization (see Parkes and Thrift, *TSST*, Volume 1), it is not surprising that time-use studies and activity accounting have come about as powerful analytical instruments as well as monitoring devices. The main disparity between *time-use studies* and other descriptions of human activities has been one of greater specification and quantitative precision. It *does* matter whether individuals perform certain activities one hour or six hours per day, or one day or seven days per week, and these quantitative differences can reach such a magnitude that they attain qualitative significance as well. Regardless of the setting—rural versus urban, agricultural versus industrial—or of the specific activity—work versus leisure or television versus cinema consumption—the quest for precision and accounting of time and other resources required numerical specification of the relative duration, frequency and temporal location of activities. This was the *raison d'être* behind 'time-budget' studies, as they have come to be applied to most sectors of activities.

Time Budgets

Rather than just revising the existing time-budget studies, some important observations will be made concerning the role of the more conventional time-budget studies and time-use surveys, with special regard to their role in the design of future general theories on population and activity in time-space.

A basic problem of time-use studies has been that of *activity classification*. If human action and behaviour is to be sorted into discrete entities or quanta called 'activities', there must be criteria defining the various activities so that they do not overlap. To this end a good many activity classifications have been devised and some have, rightly, been designed with a particular problem sector in view, such as the differences between male and female activities, the extent to which people are engaged in various forms of leisure activity, the time spent on television and its relation to optimum broadcasting hours for certain target populations, and so on. In the multinational comparative time-budget study (cf. Szalai 1972), the object was the comparison of activity patterns in urban industrial societies. It was thus a typical general time-budget study, which did not focus on certain specific sectors of activity, and in many respects it had a quite advanced activity classification. And yet there existed one broad miscellaneous activity category, namely 'work'. Its deceptively familiar sound reduced it to a catchall. Whether people were driving lorries, mining coal, serving at a restaurant, teaching children, acting as politicians, or building houses, their activity was homogenized and subsumed under the heading of 'work'. The only way in which 'work' was specific was when it occurred in homes and consisted of domestic work. It is perhaps not surprising that in this particular study there was at a general aggregate level surprisingly little variation in the activity patterns of about a dozen different nations. This is not intended to be a serious criticism of a study which did not set out to study 'work' and its variations in content, but it points out an important bias and limitation of this project. A further point can also be made. If we are to develop time-use studies and their concomitant activity classifications into something more comprehensive, and if we are to use them to understand the role of technology in society, such an omission will not do. Usually it is only in time-use studies in agriculture settings that due respect has been paid to the variety of non-domestic productive tasks (cf. *inter alia* Erixon 1938; Kay 1964; Tax 1963). Exceptions are perhaps those studies in which activities done at work have been the only activities studied, as in time-and-motion studies. But regardless of whether one wants to extend the theoretical perspective to technology, to psychological factors of stress or satisfaction, or even whether one wishes to catch the effects of shift-work, a new and adequate activity classification must be worked out which is tailored to these purposes. The same criticism can be applied to the undifferentiated way in which economists deal with time allocation and the concept of 'labour', which is another widely used umbrella category (see below).

Another important consideration is whether time-use studies want to describe a special activity such as movement or transport. It is, of course, an essential prerequisite to distinguish between *stationary* and *mobile* activities if one is to include the effect of space and relative spatial location. Time can be saved by reorganizing activities in space, or conversely, one can spend more time on travel. One way (there are others) in which the settlement system of a region impinges on time-use is through the relative spatial location of different activities. In combination with the travel mode this generally determines the amount of time spent on travel and movement. There are many activity classifications which are totally insensitive to this fact, and this means that the portion of other activities displaced by movement in a daily time-account cannot be established, let alone the effects of travelling at a different speed or reorganizing the settlement system to save time. In an effort to extend the 'time-budget' approach to explicit spatial settings, this item in any activity classification is a *sine qua non*.

Diaries

There are many other dilemmas in the conventional time-budget survey. The usual method of collecting time-budget information is a diary in which respondents fill in the times at which they carried out each activity during the day. This is not the place to refer to all the problems and pitfalls associated with diaries. Apart from the purely financial costs, which can be prohibitive even for a conventional sample large enough to avoid the problems of small samples when disaggregation takes place, another problem is whether there will then be information overload in relation to the limited time resources of the analyst. Catch 22! The latter problem can be particularly apparent if the interval at which respondents are asked to record activity is too small. If the mesh is too large, on the other hand, one runs the risk of losing many of the short-term activities of the day which from a timing and interaction viewpoint are very significant. Many critical activities in projects are not particularly time consuming in themselves but are necessary ingredients in daily or longer term projects, such as leaving a child at school. Many other problems exist with diaries, for instance whether or not to use a predetermined activity classification at the risk of losing information which does not fit neatly into the categories chosen. Alternatively, days of research time must be spent in reinterpreting the activities described individually by each respondent. Then again if both activity and place are to be recorded, numerous questions of spatial precision crop up.

Although the diary technique has many advantages over recall interviews and participant observation techniques (ideally it should be used in conjunction with them) a major drawback with diaries is that it is difficult for children and the aged to fill them out and these 'categories' are *people* too. It should be unnecessary to point this out, but many surveys carried out have an unhealthy interest in those who are not handicapped, those who are not too young to be literate nor old enough to be written off. Especially when sampling procedures are aimed at individuals rather than households, the focus is on the healthy and productive while other categories are often left out.

Statistical design and processing shows up another mountain range to be crossed, peaks such as sampling procedures in the selection of respondents, the processing of materials acquired, the methods of aggregating information, and not least the extent to which processed material can be used as a basis for wider generalizations on how the system under study works. The philosophy in this field is still underdeveloped and the introduction of space has not made things easier. Obviously, the *modus operandi* selected by various researchers is generally geared towards some defined end, descriptive or theoretical, although the editors of this book have all encountered research groups with time-'budget' data which they did not really know what to do with; and by the time they did know they were painfully aware of the limitations of their data set. This has particularly been the case with statistically-oriented social scientists and with statisticians at central bureaus working with 'social indicators' who have found time-use data to be the new tool in the indicative arsenal. While it would be unfair to deny the applicability of such data on an *a priori* basis, a sincere attitude should be encouraged in trying to understand what these data are supposed to be indicative of. To start using such data as input in the planning process without knowing what they imply is irresponsible towards the people the planners serve, and the state of the art is such that at present the majority of areas of application of aggregate time-use data are not justifiable.

Sampling

The way in which the real world is chopped up into entities for observation and into elements for sampling is intimately related to how the same pieces can be put together again in order to make generalizations about the workings of the system as a whole. Although there are many formal guidelines as to how sampling can be carried out in order to attain reliable and generalizable information and evidence, there are also substantive aspects to sampling which require previous theoretical and empirical understanding of the problem area, not just familiarity with statistical techniques. Sampling is even necessary in the time economy of the analyst, he or she cannot collect information for an entire period and population in a region![1] But in its essence, all sampling entails cutting the real-world cake into some kind of slices and there are many implications of slicing a compound total reality in different ways. These issues are inextricably interwoven with those of contextual analysis, aggregation problems and generalization of findings, as well as theory construction.

Starting with the purely formal problems of statistically treated time-use data as collected through diaries, it can be found that too often complex parametric statistics are used essentially to describe data that would be better presented in tabular form. Often simple accounting conveys all the information necessary. When these statistics are used for inference, numerous problems arise. If spatial coordinates are included for each activity there is obviously the problem of spatial dependency in the data leading to spurious results. This makes use of correlation techniques such as factor analysis very risky (Hepple 1976). But often the more serious problem is the very considerable theoretical objections to the use of parametric statistics in this area, which will definitely mean redefinition of many of the significance tests currently in use. The reason is that although in this case the analysis is of a number of activity episodes treated as a set of observations, they are not independent in the statistical sense because the sample is not one of episodes but more commonly of individuals. Once an individual has been sampled, the probability that an activity in his immediate history will occur in the sample goes to unity (e.g. breakfast, work). Similarly for any individual not sampled the probability must go to zero. In such circumstances none of the standard parametric significance tests can be used because they all assume the analysis being tested is an analysis of the sample of observations, each of which, if drawn randomly in the normal way, has a probability equal to that for any other event in the population. Thus if parametric statistics are to be used at all, it must be strictly as summary measures (Cullen and Phelps 1975; Thrift 1976).

Returning to the way in which sampling designs select among real world elements, it would perhaps be useful to indicate the range of a particular type of sample of a population's total time. This will be done with the aid of some time-geographic diagrams. In many of the time-use studies up to the present which have dealt with the daily cycle of activities, attempts have been made to select one 'representative' day in order to study the sample population selected among a total population in a given region. If one selects every fifth individual, this would be something like Figure 1. This day is taken as representative of all the days of the year. The problem with this kind of sampling over time is that the day chosen may not be 'representative' for obvious reasons—it may have been an exceptionally stormy day, a national holiday, the day when the bus drivers were on strike, and so on. Then there are seasonal variations as well as the more obvious variations between weekdays and weekends. The latter problem is often settled by taking one weekday and one weekend day, but even here we find that Saturday is not the same as Sunday, and even that Monday is different from Wednesday, and Wednesday from Friday. Extending the sample to cover a whole week and its variation can solve this problem, but then there is so much data that the sample has to be reduced to cover one person

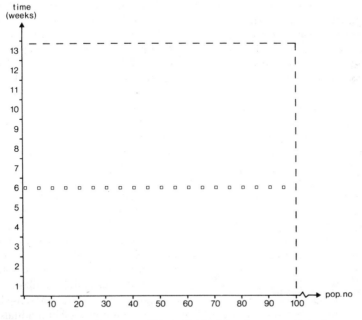

Figure 1 Sampling every fifth individual for the same single day.

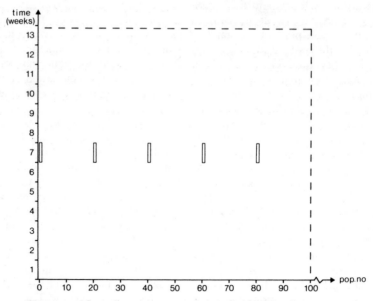

Figure 2 Sampling every twentieth individual for the same week.

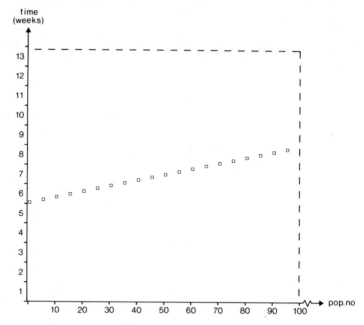

Figure 3 Spreading the sample of every fifth individual over several successive days, i.e. both over time and the population.

out of twenty, as in Figure 2. But both of these alternatives have the dis-
advantage of concentrating the fieldwork of data collection into one short spell,
which requires a far greater number of fieldworkers, interviewers and diary
instructors, etc. If instead one spreads the sample over both time and the
population, one can distribute the time for data collection a researcher has
available more evenly and at the same time avoid incidental factors which
affect the activities of people. These are averaged out, as in Figure 3. Another
possibility is to repeat the same procedure at several seasons, and collect the
data for the same individuals but on three or four occasions over the year
and even vary the weekday and include weekend days on some 25 per cent
of the occasions a person has to fill in his diary, as in Figure 4. So, there is
always a choice between studying more, different individuals for a short time
(e.g. one day) or studying fewer individuals each for a longer consecutive
time (e.g. one week), as in Figure 3. The latter makes it possible to study longer
activity sequences affecting one individual and how some activities in a project
can be postponed. It also allows a better basis for the study of activity
frequencies within a longer time span.

Each method has its special advantages and disadvantages, but the problem
encountered is that if one collects data for an 'average' day of some kind, the
generalization is only valid for a fictitious average day! It is not applicable to
any real day. Once the sampling is done and the data aggregated, they cannot
be disaggregated again. They cannot be applied to any kind of genuine micro-
analysis or be used as an input in micro-planning. In fact, it is very dubious
whether they can be used in macro-planning either, except as the crudest form
of indicators.

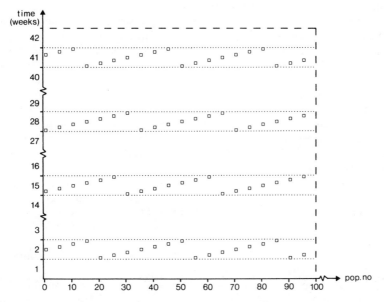

Figure 4 Spreading the sample of every fifth individual over several days and over
several different seasons of the year.

One of the difficulties with time-budget studies is that they have to take *individuals* as the basic units, and because it is intended to use inferential statistics from the start, individuals are sampled in some broader (and often spatially undefined) population. This kind of analysis is bound to ignore many of the *coordination* aspects of human activity, and it treats people in an atomistic and isolated way at which survey workers and statisticians have become experts. Of course, some observed activities are individual and so less coordinated, but others are collective and indeed *demand* coordination. This generally means that they require several individuals to be present in the *same place* at the *same time*. A quick reflection on our private experience makes this plain indeed. We have all had to attend school classes, places of work, and meetings of voluntary organizations which are synchronized collective activities. Many meetings cannot begin until a quorum or even all members are present. With the growth of the tertiary and quaternary sectors of industrialized societies such situations have become ever more common and time demanding in time and population size terms. Then in all kinds of agricultural and industrial work, there is a wide variety of tasks and projects which simply cannot be performed by single individuals. An extreme case is perhaps an assembly line in a car factory. All such *coupling constraints* (Häger-strand 1970a) have been severely neglected when sampling procedures cull out individuals in a population more or less at random, as has been the case in many time-budget surveys.

In the same fashion, household members coordinate (synchronize and synchorize) their activities, and if one intends to study the household sector, it should be the household or *domestic unit* which should be the sampling unit, not separate individuals! The way in which a household member allocates her or his time is a function of the division of 'labour' (or better the division of activities), the extent to which members delegate activities among themselves, the extent to which they share the use of room and equipment, such as the kitchen, bathroom, television, cars and so on. And the fact that they share the same financial resources determines the external activities they are able to engage in to a major degree. Finally, household members collectively care for one another and assist one another in (say) cooking (and, for instance, in the care of younger children, on a continuous basis). To snatch individuals out of this organizational context through ill-designed sampling techniques and later statistically aggregate them into some kind of 'activity pattern' is in many respects a rather futile endeavour. To go on from there and try to forecast changes in patterns or predict the effects of partial changes of activities on the population is extremely misleading. For example, if on this basis researchers recommend policy measures which may seem acceptable at the aggregate level, the effects of such a policy might be extremely disruptive at the household level. The sampling of individuals in isolation *does not permit* generalizations on house-hold units as functional entities.

Of course this is not to claim that the household is the only sampling unit. The problem at hand may be best solved and understood by using an organization, firm, institution, or place or work or service as the basic unit. This is because this takes into account the internal time (and space) organization of the unit and internal coordination, such as manning pro-grammes and shift-work schedules. There are several such studies of student populations (Cullen and Godson 1971; Bullock *et al.* 1971, or firms (Poor, ed., 1970) of children's day nurseries (Mårtensson 1977), and of the movement of government organizations to new locations (e.g. Mårtensson 1974).

Space can be another basis for sampling. One can systematically select spatial areas in which the whole population is observed and for which information is collected. If one studies a large urban area, such a sample design might be the best choice if one wishes to get an idea of the internal variations in a city. (Cf. chapter 9 and 10 above.)

As previously mentioned, a logical consequence of sampling individuals by pure statistical criteria is that individuals are snatched out of their organizational and spatial-environmental context. Time-budget surveys, with their focus on actually performed activities, have had remarkably little to tell about the temporal organization of society. As initially outlined by people like Moore (1963), each society has a temporal structure and organization, which is a result of *interaction* between individuals in various situations and settings. What may be one person's shopping hours may be another's working hours, for instance, and there is a great deal of interdependence between various individuals occupying different positions in the overall structure. Hence, when a randomly chosen set of individuals and their activity 'patterns' in a time period like a day, are detached and statistically aggregated, this does not give a true mapping of the temporal organization of society, except in the very trivial sense that most people sleep at night, go to work in the day, and watch television in the evenings. Similar aggregate patterns and profiles are in many respects a statistical abstraction which curiously enough has no real counterpart in society. To base policy upon such results is in many cases a kind of academic shadow-boxing.

This is exactly why the time-geographic model is so useful as a logical point of departure. When individuals and objects are looked upon as paths or trajectories which have come from one place and are heading forward in time to other places, and when they form webs of interaction, individuals are placed in a *context*. When such trajectories are more closely examined, the perspective chosen helps the analyst carefully to disentangle the strand from the total web in a meaningful way. Perhaps, then, the proper unit for observation is not the isolated individual but the various mechanisms by which couplings are made in the web, or the capacity of individuals to form couplings and select among potential couplings in a given portion of time-space.

Hägerstrand has commented upon the difference between what he calls the compositional and the contextual approach. One is anatomical in nature—a system is cut up into finer and finer components and organized into a set of hierarchical levels, sometimes in terms of statistical levels of aggregation. The other is contextual and treats a social event in its setting (Hägerstrand 1974c).

What is needed before a deeper causal analysis is possible is constructive work based on new concepts, rather than more conventional statistical analysis. Hägerstrand points out that when events are statistically aggregated for periods in time and regions in space and investigated amounts are allowed to covary with one another, no picture is received of how activities and events are embedded in prior and posterior stages. He gives an example of how one can analyse an event, a traffic accident. It is possible, for instance, to seek the cause of the accident in the behaviour and personal qualities of the colliding parties and provide background 'ecological' data that the car stock has been growing greatly in the last decade and that the accident occurred in a built-up area. But rather than looking at the behaviour of individuals and aggregate system we must ask why the accident was possible at the start—why the situation was generated. It may have been that it was actually programmed into the system by the time organization of activities of various larger organizations in the environment. If one traces the paths backwards in time, it may be discovered that the cyclist school child, who was one of the parties, had to leave one place (say a biology lab) and be at another specialized place such as a gymnasium, at the same time as a lorry driver made one of his routine trips with goods from a storehouse to a building site. Both were independently entangled in routines which had been imposed on them by superior organizations, which led to the sharing of the same place at the same time. The important problem thus becomes to see how the overall activity programmes of various social units program individuals to use time and space and with what effects.[2]

> It is obvious that the enormous number of situations which constitute the life of society are mutually regulated by its components: people and objects that leave one situation and enter new ones in the same or a different place. These situations are chained to one another in a complicated web which is not void of structure. (Hägerstrand 1974d.)

The various continuity constraints on individuals and objects and how they constrain or allow chains of activity and situations to arise, as well as how the web develops over time in space, all this cannot be grasped by reckless sampling and picking out of entities here and there without an understanding of what is extracted and what remains. Which is not to argue that all forms of statistical treatment of data are wrong or useless. Often a combination of intuition and familiarity with every day life brings some substance into the analysis. Statistical activity 'patterns' and profiles of time-budget surveys do convey certain rough outlines of things like sex-role structure or diversity versus monotony of activities with categories of individuals, but remarkably little theory is generated and without such theory, guidance on how society can be reorganized is dangerous.

If we then come to prediction of temporal and spatial patterns we find what we might call the time-budget paradox. Most people can look at a person's diary for a week and, due to the routine nature of our lives, say with reasonable certainty what that person will be doing in the next few weeks. However, when the data are aggregated with other diary data the problem of prediction becomes much harder. Thus we can predict individual patterns better than aggregate patterns—a situation uncommon in the social sciences! The reason is that in aggregating one loses information which in prediction one then tries to replace! Thus the emphasis in time-budget prediction would seem to be on taking some mystical 'average' individuals and predicting their behaviour as representative of a particular group. Even some variance between individuals when constraints are less active (i.e. in leisure time) is so great that it cannot be *effectively* predicted.

Conclusions on the time-budget survey as an analytical instrument

Without discrediting an approach which has done much to provide insights and further our picture of human activities in social systems, it is still fair and useful to sum up the shortcomings of the conventional time-budget survey. This is done with a more ambitious objective in mind, namely the design of a more integrated and comprehensive time-space structured theory of society and habitat.

1   The time-budget survey often uses debatable sampling techniques and aggregation methods, which divorces time use from interaction, group formation, and time allocation in a population and settlement system. It becomes nearly impossible to determine causal structural relationships.

2   The short time perspective and concern with 'average' days neglects the structural implications of various time spans which are sub-sets of one another, e.g. how days are parts of weeks, or years are part of life (cycles).

3   Time use is not seen as a component in longer term *projects*.

4   Time-use surveys deal with *actual* behaviour as exhibited in *ex post* analysis, while alternative choices and options are never registered since alternatives not chosen are a form of non-behaviour which is less susceptible to crude observation and which must be deduced from situational premises.

5   The lack of consideration of the physical or spatial-geographic environment has numerous implications in that actual behaviour studied is already *adapted* to a particular environmental setting.

6   Since so little of the environment which constrains and generates particular behaviour and activity programmes (and projects) is considered, time-use studies can provide little but crude guidance on how the environment should be changed to promote certain forms of time-using activities. Hence such studies are inherently more powerful in detecting symptoms than in rectifying problems.

This having been said about time-budget studies of the conventional format, and recognizing their contribution and usefulness, a main purpose of this book has been to indicate how some of these shortcomings may be compensated for and how the framework can be enlarged to include time allocation, time organization and interaction in geographic space.

Time-allocation approaches: some notes on their past and future design

Time-allocation studies enquire into the mechanisms by which time is allocated as well as the consequences and opportunity costs of different alternatives. This is not done only at the individual level but also at aggregated levels such as groups, firms, organizations and regions and nations. Time-allocation studies are usually approached through a demand and supply structure of schema. Many research workers dealing mainly with time 'use' and temporal 'accounting' of activities refer to their work as time 'allocation' analysis, without being fully aware of the difference between time-use and time-allocation models.[3]

In the time-use studies of how time has been allocated *ex post facto* by units such as individuals, households or firms, the various mechanisms for allocating time are not automatically registered, and the sets of alternatives which were open to the unit have not been observed or otherwise included in the analysis. Of course, some studies fall somewhere in between the two types. On the whole, however, there are good grounds for making a distinction between the inductively based and empiricist time-use surveys and time-allocation studies, which must, of course, be firmly based in the real world but which seek to deduce the consequences of various ways of allocating human time. Hypothetico-deductive time-allocation studies also aim to explain the circumstances under which demand for time is met by supply. Of course, a demand and supply formulation does not necessarily entail a static equilibrium approach such as we are used to in economics. It can be dynamic and 'holochronic', for instance, by dint of looking at supply-demand interaction in terms of packing (cf. Carlstein above, and 1975d).

In the time-geographic design of time-allocation analysis, the time *supply* side is quite obvious; it is the human population which supplies time and the volume supplied in a given period is a function of population size and population characteristics such as age, skill, sex and various other capability constraints on who can supply time to what kind of activity. But who then *demands* time? The population? Well, in an ultimate sense this is obviously the case. But to view the population as a direct source of demand is less fruitful perhaps than recognizing that there are various intermediary mechanisms of time demand. These are embodied in the multitude of *human projects* conducted within various groups and organizations and which are a part of the *institutionalized activity system* of society.[4]

This abstraction of the activity system of society as a separate sub-system from the population requires some further justification, because in the *ex post* analysis of actual activities into time-'budgets', the two are imperceptibly fused. Time-use accounts describe the unique outcome of time allocation, not its process and mechanisms, hence the traditional difficulty of sorting out how much of actual time use was a function of choice and how much was enforced by the environment. But time demand is something related to the future although some demands are routine and repetitive, and the activity system includes future activities, as yet unconstrained by limited population-time supply, which may well in many sectors exceed supply.

It is through the notion of *project*[5] that the goal dimension in human affairs (and hence the future) is brought into the model. All biological organisms can be said to have inherited objectives and to be geared to the attainment of certain results, output or products, in the simplest case mere survival and reproduction; but in the case of humans these are not just inherited but culturally acquired. In a sense, the past is always product while the future is project, and each human individual starts off as a product but from his subjective view his life is a project. During life he entertains a range of individual projects of varying scale and duration, but he also participates in various collective projects which require coordination with other individuals in time and space. Projects are thus sequences of future activities of individuals and groups designed to materialize in certain forms of output. In the daily perspective, certain projects are only discernible in very small fragments of component activities, and the *gestation period* of the project, i.e. the time it takes to perform the whole of it, may be much longer. Projects range from very simple and repetitive tasks such as cooking a meal, sleeping, weeding a field or telling a story through to the larger scale ones such as producing a machine, cultivating a crop, writing a book or building a house. Building up extensive medical care services or educational systems are even larger scale projects; the apex is perhaps sending humans into outer space. If any meaningful analysis of human time demand is to be possible, it is not sufficient to deal with short-term projects in the daily round. These must be placed in a wider context and much more effort must go into the study of human projects and not merely the component activities as manifested in a very short time span. Here one undoubtedly enters the traditional domain of economics, but it is important to study projects in *real terms* as opposed to financial, as there are many capacity constraints that are inadequately reflected in the monetary system. Besides, there are many kinds of projects and component activities internal to households, firms, societies and organizations as well as political, military, religious, recreational and artistic activities which are not made subject to monetary transactions. These activities still mix and interact and compete for time resources in the population system. It should also be remembered that the allocation of human time is paralleled and synchronized with the economizing of other resource inputs into projects, such as settlement time-space, energy, machine-time and building-time. Thus shortage of either of the ingredient resources tends to have stop-go effects on human time inputs (Carlstein 1975a; 1975d).

There are several time-allocation schools in the field of economics, economic anthropology and human geography, and it is important to point out their specific assumptions, aims and commonalities. Many of these assumptions are strategic to their viability and usefulness in a broader and more ambitious context, such as their application to urban and regional planning or to the analysis of development problems. Since time allocation in economics has not been discussed so far, this will be done now.

Is time money? Time allocation in economics from Marx to Becker

The reason why there is relatively little explicit work on time allocation in economics is that, generally speaking, economists have been much more concerned with problems of production and exchange than with those of consumption or physical distribution. Hence much of the work on time has been implicit and concealed under the guise of '*labour*' and '*work*' as a factor of production. In the sense that the general level of employment, the labour participation rate and the division of labour reflect the macro-aspects of time allocation to work, the way time is used has for long been a concern of economists. Adam Smith's work on the wealth of nations (Smith 1776), in which it was maintained that the only source of wealth was production resulting from labour and resources, laid the foundation. Later Karl Marx developed a major interest in the specific relation between human time and labour, to which much of *Capital* (Marx 1867) is devoted. Marx, following on from predecessors like Ricardo, attributed the economic value of commodities to the labour expended on them. This notion was strategic to Marx's definition of surplus value. The main difficulty with the labour concept, of course, was that it only accounted for that portion of total population time which was spent on the general activity of 'work', and hence human time enters mainly as an input in the production of 'goods and services'.

Those were the beginnings, but with the further formalization of economics time was also employed as a periodic interval of accounting and as a variable for calculating interest and depreciation on money, stocks, and capital, as well as an auxiliary dimension for sorting out 'stocks' and 'flows' in the economy, something which was a basic necessity if economic analysis was to cohere with socio-economic realities.

Since the Second World War, economics has exhibited a slow but steadily growing concern with various aspects of time. Time has entered as an even more necessary dimension of reference in the study of business-cycle fluctuations and corresponding changes in employment volume. It was imperative to see how the variables of macro-economics such as investment, savings, production and consumption were interrelated over time, and with the adoption of Keynesian economics the timing or temporal location of government measures had to be finely adjusted to the temporal behaviour of the variables mentioned.

With the increased control exercised over the more violent oscillations of the economy, as well as the increased focus on the long-term aspects of growth and investment, especially in the newly independent countries, time again became a supporting pillar in the study of dynamics. There was a growing appreciation of the fact that conventional equilibrium formulations were too static to grapple with economic growth issues. Keynesian and other macro-economic theories became 'dynamized', and time in economic dynamics became as important as it had become in demographic dynamics. It was treated implicitly as a category for catching economic events, as well as a way of incorporating the unyielding logic of time's arrow and what physicists have called the asymmetry of time. The important trait to notice, however, is that the procedure was one of 'dynamizing' the conventional equilibrium formulations, and the basic world view of economics—the way in which it delineated reality into observables—was one that had descended quite directly from Smith, Marshall and so on down the line of Western economists. But time was only incorporated as a kind of appendix to the existing body of theory. The time dimension did as little to revolutionize economics as space did when Isard tried to introduce space through 'regional science' (Isard 1960) or as Richardson's more recent attempts at regional economics have done (Richardson 1969; 1971; 1973a; 1973b). (Isard has recently taken up *time* in his regional analysis but with questionable success. Cf. further *TSST*, Vol. 3.)

But reality is sometimes a force which intrudes on grand conceptual schemes. There were those economists who had an interest both in consumption and physical distribution and transport. At the micro- and meso-theoretical levels, it was inadequate to look at time allocation as a mere balance between work and what has been wrongly termed 'leisure'. (Non-work time is certainly far from being all 'leisure', as de Grazia (1962) has convincingly shown in his very broad analysis *On Time, Work and Leisure*.) Much of the activity in the subsistence sector, e.g. in the households, was just another form of production, something which becomes particularly obvious when services such as cooking, caring for children and the aged, and caring for the sick is moved into the monetary sector of the economy. Hence a fair portion of the growth of the GNP in post-war Western society, is not really based on an increase in the capacity of the economy per capita but on a redefinition and reorganization of time use which accompanied the enlargement of the monetarized sector at the cost of the subsistence sector. Particularly when personal care and services are taken into account it becomes evident how costly they really are when conducted outside the domestic setting.

The relation between the monetarized sector and the 'subsistence' sector, as well as the balance of time use between production-cum-work and consumption-cum-leisure activities, posed some vexing problems which did not fit comfortably into the orthodox framework, and there was growing awareness that they were associated with the occupation of time. In the Western countries, problems of labour-saving and capital intensive techniques, automation, unemployment and enforced leisure caused concern about the volume and distribution of work time (and non-work time) in the population. Likewise the increased capacity to produce goods (as distinct from services), which was another part of the rosy picture of the affluent society, made some economists and sociologists worry about leisure time and its alternative uses (Larrabee and Meyersohn 1958; Wilensky 1961; Dumazedier 1962; de Grazia 1962). The 'problems' of increased leisure were also catching up with the Communist countries in which the increased productivity in industry had been partially directed towards the shortening of working hours. Here the main concern was associated with the increased spatial mobility and use of weekend residences as well as with the fact that people did not engage in free time activities that were socially constructive (i.e. for the State). Some studies were therefore undertaken to map various features of this leisure problem as well as finding ways of channelling the free time of people in less private directions (Patrushev 1975; Lippold 1975). Of course, one of the problems of increased leisure was simply that it required additional investments in buildings and facilities.

The problem of how to deal with activities in the so-called 'subsistence' sector was one particularly felt in the less developed countries. While the response was slow in economics, the main discipline to take up the challenge was economic anthropology. In this field there have been a number of studies and approaches based on time-use and allocation (cf. below pp. 253–4).

It was with the growth of consumption theory that the beginnings of a more encompassing perspective on time allocation emerged in economics. But one of the first economists to explore comprehensively the theme of time was neither Becker nor Linder (cf. below) but the American economist George Soule who wrote a whole book on the subject of time allocation from an economist's viewpoint as early as 1955, under the illuminating title *Time for Living*. His ideas seem to have been comfortably forgotten by later economists who have either not searched the literature or who found Soule too insignificant to mention since his formulation was not econometric (cf. also the problem of amnesia and the discoverer's complex in social science, Sorokin 1956, Ch. 1). Even sociologists such as Moore (1963) and de Grazia (1962) seem to have missed Soule (which is surprising). Soule seems to be the first Anglo-American economist, however, with a sincere interest and comprehensive perspective on basic time-allocation problems of modern industrialized nations. In Chapter Six of his book called 'The Economy of Time', he makes a number of very interesting points with broad theoretical implications. He says, for instance,

> Still, however, economic theorists have not absorbed the concept of time formally into their basic thinking, as physical theorists have done. Specifically, economists have not regarded time as a scarce resource, coordinate with land, labour, and capital, and have not developed their theory of resource allocation on this four-dimensional framework. Yet the technological revolution cannot be understood without reference to the time factor, which in practice has been involved from the very beginning. Still less could there be an economic theory appropriate to the present and future of technological civilization without recognizing the immense and growing importance of time as a scarce resource. (Soule 1955, p. 89.)

Soule then goes on to raise the very uncomfortable question of the workings of the market economy as an allocation mechanism of human time: 'Does the market system apportion time to the uses best fitted to satisfy human needs, as economists argued that it apportioned land, labour, and capital?' The answer to this question is still largely unexplored because such a radical rethinking of conventional economics (as opposed to Marxian economics) was too difficult for all but a few. In the final section of chapter 6, Soule turns to issues of consumption (as he does elsewhere in his book), and makes all the basic observations which were later elaborated by consumption theorists such as Becker and Linder. Soule tackles the topic of consumption under the assertive heading 'Time is the Scarcest Resource':

> If time were unlimited, there could be no end to the potential demand for goods. But suppose the extreme case—suppose that nobody had to spend any hours at all in production of products for sale; suppose 'work' were all done by automatic machines. Still there would be a limit, within any year, of the amount of time a given population would have in which to use what might be sold to them! ... As that limit is approached, it will appear even more clearly than now that technological civilization ... is gradually making goods more abundant than the time in which to consume or enjoy them. ... Technology has mastered the art of saving time, but not the art of spending it. The situation which man under technology is approaching emphasizes the problem of economizing not so much land, labour, and capital as the time which is not devoted to earning a living. ... How will man proceed to allocate his time in satisfying them without the aid of prices and markets? Is it not clear that any effort to do so must emphasize a different set of values than those dominant in the nineteenth and early twentieth centuries? (Soule 1955; pp. 100–1.)

Apart from Soule and some Eastern European economists, the American economist Becker, and the Swedish economist Linder were among the very first to give time allocation explicit consideration in economics. Both did so in an attempt to deal with consumption problems in a more meaningful way. Becker starts off from where Soule had paved the way by noting that the effect of economic development has been a reduction in the work week (which is perhaps debatable) and that 'the allocation and efficiency of non-working time may now be more important to economic welfare than that of working time; yet the attention paid by economists to the latter dwarfs any paid to the former' (Becker 1965). This was exactly one of Soule's main tenets and like him Becker tries systematically to bring into the orbit of economic theory many of the time-economic problems that were formerly outside. The difference is that Becker's approach is formal and econometric in style, and Becker is probably the first Western economist to build models of time-allocation processes. It is therefore of great importance to assess the way in which these models work, their under-lying assumptions and their fit to reality, since Becker is one of the very few who have explored this important field shunned by other economists.

Having been previously a pioneer in the field of time-use for education and investment in 'human capital', as formulated earlier by T. W. Schultz (1961), Becker, in his first article (1965) aims to develop 'a general treatment of the allocation of time in all other non-work activities'. The basic units studied are individuals and households (rather than, for instance, firms), and his models are essentially behaviouristic in that the level of explanation is at the level of the decision-making unit rather than the environment, to which Becker gives a rather summary treatment. Becker integrates time allocation with monetary income and expenditure, thus presenting a kind of synthesis between a human time theory and a monetary-financial theory, which is indeed focused on fusing the former with the latter, i.e. incorporating time use and allocation within an already structured theory of the flow of income and money in an economic system. In short, time is translated into money and vice versa, and moreover, all time is assumed to be translatable into money. Since human time is a source of monetary income, time spent on non-work (i.e. on not working for wages) is a source of forgone earnings, for instance when a student studies instead of works or when a housewife spends time at home rather than at gainful employment. (This should make everyone aware of the tremendous costs of dying in terms of forgone earnings!) 'For example, the costs of a service like the theatre or a good like meat are generally simply said to be equal to their market prices, yet everyone would agree that the theatre or even dining take time, just as schooling does, time that could have been used productively. If so, the full costs of these activities would equal the sum of market prices and the forgone value of time used up', (Becker 1965, p. 494). Becker's approach is therefore typically a 'value of time' approach, in which the value of time is measured in monetary terms, but incorporating the fact that some households have good reasons for not working twenty-four hours per day (can this be so?) since this will not necessarily maximize the utility of households, as Becker sets out to explain. The concept of *full cost* is thus one of a set of parallel concepts necessary to carry out the 'theoretical analysis of choice that includes the cost of time on the same footing as the cost of market goods.' The reason for making time thus commensurable with goods is one which is necessary in order to redefine the notion of consumption.

In the concept of consumption used in Keynesian macro-economics, produc-tion is carried out by firms and government organizations, while consumption is the responsibility of households who do nothing but consume. This is clearly somewhat out of step with every-day experience, particularly in the views of modern women. A much more realistic stand on household activity is that much of it is production, and Becker uses this in pointing out that households 'combine *time* and market *goods* to produce more basic commodites.' He gives one example of a commodity, such as a play, which requires an input of actors, script, theatre and the playgoer's time, or sleeping which is a commodity depending on 'the input of a bed, house (pills?) and time'. Human consumption activity is thus divided into the production of discrete quanta of commodities which use human time and market goods as input. This is done according to household *production* functions, which could just as well be called consumption functions, since the view taken concerning household consumption makes it into a kind of production process with its own particular inputs and outputs as shown in the diagram below:

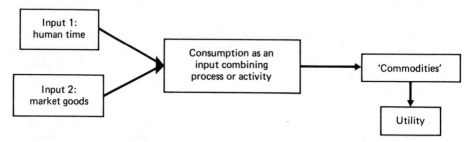

The concept of full cost is paralleled by the concept of *full income*, which is a hypothetical income accruing if a person were to work twenty-four hours per day, 365 days per year. The full price of an individual commodity produced is likewise the sum of direct market prices and indirect prices (i.e. income forgone by spending time on consuming or combining the commodity with time).

> The full-income approach provides a meaningful resource constraint and one firmly based on the fact that goods and time can be combined into a single overall constraint because time can be converted into goods through money income. It also incorporates a unified treatment of all substitutions of non-pecuniary for pecuniary income, regardless of the nature or whether they occur on the job or in the household. (Becker 1965, p. 498.)

Having thus arrived at convertibility and substitutability between money, goods and human time, some commodities produced in the household setting are more earnings intensive, goods intensive or time intensive in their use of the total resource of full income. Full income is defined as the total time available multiplied by the earnings per hour (the wage rate) plus other pecuniary sources of income.

What then is the *output* of the individual and household consumption process and how does one measure it? The output has the form of 'commodities' which upon consumption are a source of utility, which all individuals and households try to maximize (of course). Each commodity is a discrete quantum which adds to the next in providing utility. The commodities need not be specified in kind, since the important thing is not that they consist of eating a meal, sleeping, or playing tennis but rather that they are sources of 'psychic income' [*sic*] and utility. How then is utility output measured? It is well established (in economic theory) that the marginal utility of a rational consumer is equal to the marginal costs, which is identical with price in a perfectly competitive market, and hence utility output can be measured in terms of price input, and utility is maximized by maximizing income. Hence, the marginal forgone earnings are indicative of the price of time, and using more time or goods respectively depends on the marginal costs of using more goods in producing a given 'commodity' or the marginal cost of using more time on the 'commodity'. There are a good many substitution effects which make households more goods-intensive or time-intensive in their consumption behaviour. Should time become more valuable in terms of money, we want to consume less time and more goods, i.e. make our forms of consumption more goods-intensive. If poor and uneducated, we want to consume more time and less costly goods (apparently) and indeed have little choice.

The essential foundations laid in the Becker article of 1965 are used in the more elaborate treatise, *The Allocation of Time and Goods over the Life Cycle* (Ghez and Becker 1975). This extends the framework to allocation problems in a life-cycle perspective. By adding the investment function in 'human capital', the three primary kinds of activities of households become work, consumption, and education. Since the time perspective is extended to several decades it introduces a new time factor into the model, things like interest rates on capital, time preferences with regard to consumption, a savings function and a function of depreciation of goods used must be introduced. It is, for instance, a fact that the marginal cost of producing human capital is higher when a person is older than when he is young, or is less skilled and earning less because of this.

There are several criticisms which can be launched against Becker's approach with regard to the realism of the assumptions made, the way an individual and household-based model is tested on indirect aggregate data for a non-household population, or the way that a supposedly dynamic theory is tested on atemporal cross-section data. In comparison with other time-allocation studies in sociology, it is apparent that his activity classification is extremely rough, dealing mainly with three kinds of activity, and that there is no spatial dimension at all—for instance travel time is not included to reflect the fact that households interact in time and space. Another major deficiency is that it is a purely behaviouristic theory, which is about a set of Robinson Crusoe families each stuck on an island, in which educational resources avail themselves *automatically* when demand arises over the life cycle. Neither the availability of educational institutions nor the wage rate are determined exogenously to the family but are endogenous variables(!). Households are utility maximizers and they produce unspecifiable 'commodities'. These household consumption functions are not independently derived either, and the whole model seems in too many respects to be derived from the material on which it is tested. It is thus hardly a genuine *theory* of time allocation, but a basically untested model, which relates certain crude and aggregate measures of time use to certain aggregate measures of pecuniary flows affecting an aggregate of households.

At the behaviouristic level of the household, there are some predictions which can be made on a very general level, but these deal more with the allocation of goods and time for age groups or cohorts of the population in a cross-section perspective. It can hardly be applied as a prediction of consumption patterns within a decade or two to come, because by then a good many system interdependencies may have cropped up which the model cannot handle. It cannot be generalized beyond the household level to deal with any other kind of larger scale unit.

The use of utility theory is another kind of apparent sophistication which is extremely debatable from an empirical viewpoint. The way in which this framework is used is more realistic perhaps than the conventional way in which goods are seen as objects of choice in utility functions. Becker and Ghez turn the problem around and see how utility is *derived* from the output side of a household production function into which time and goods enter as an input. But on the other hand, the 'commodities' produced by households are not measurable and the approach still assumes Economic Man maximizing behaviour, revealed preferences and the rest of the debatable assumptions of neoclassical economics.

Another fundamental and very important objection can also be raised in terms of (literally) human values. Becker and Ghez assume that a price tag can be put on every human activity. Everything can be converted into cold cash, to put it severely. This makes the approach very culture-specific in that it cannot be applied to the developing countries, nor to all sectors in developed countries. Likewise, it cannot be applied to children and, typically enough, there are no children in the Becker and Ghez model. Life starts at fifteen or twenty years of age in most of the diagrams, and children only enter as a kind of service and time demanding good before that time.

The *monetary-value-of-time* approach is also beset with certain problems if it is applied to a sector like transport planning. It has been seen before in similar applications how it becomes more economical to cover the landscape with tarmac only if the people driving on it have high enough salaries. Other bizarre conclusions arising from this value-of-time approach are that when estimating the costs of traffic accidents, it is much cheaper to run over a woman, child or unemployed worker than a well paid company director. Similarly rich men should go to jail for less time than poor men—the value of their time is higher. Of course, this does not imply that either Becker or Ghez actually maintain similar beliefs at a personal level. But the point is that once one starts translating everything into money, certain logical consequences follow, and it is very easy to start applying certain optimization criteria postulated for one purpose to whole new fields in which they certainly should not be used. It thus seems likely that money-equals-time approaches are much more power-ful in amplifying inequalities between different social strata than when being used in planning to promote equality and socio-economic justice. The latter point remains to be seen, but a sceptical approach should be taken.

We should also take note of Linder's study of time use and consumption (Linder 1970) which was published in Sweden under the title 'The restless Welfare Man: An economic study of time shortage in the affluent society' but had the rather insipid title *The Harried Leisure Class* in its English version. This book is full of interesting observations on the temporal organization of modern post-industrial societies, especially on time for consumption. But it goes far beyond that by dealing with working hours, time spent on consumption decisions, time for cultural activities, saving and redistributing human time, ceilings to work and consumption, and even cross-cultural comparisons on time perception and the rate at which activities are performed. In a short mathe-matical appendix a few of these varied observations are summarized, and even here there is a minor but unimportant element of utility theory applied. In terms of substance, Linder's analysis is much broader than Becker's. Concomitantly Linder has had great difficulties in formalizing this diverse material into econometric equation systems. In the substitution between model and reality, Linder can be said to sacrifice the former, while Becker and Ghez forfeit the latter (thereby gaining more prestige in certain economic circles).

In an historical perspective it is interesting to note that arguments over time and utility theory date back to the previous century. The German demographer and statistician Becker who together with another German statistician and economist, Wilhelm Lexis (1837–1914), developed the concepts of life-lines and life-tables so basic to demography, was very aware of time problems. As mentioned earlier, Hägerstrand generalized the notion of life-lines to life paths in time-space, which form the demographic and population-dynamic basis for the time-geographic model. Lexis (whose work in probability theory was a greater inspiration to Keynes), is reported to have been very critical of utility theory and questioned at a very early stage the convexity and continuity assumptions of preference orderings. Moreover, he did not accept the theorem of equalization of marginal utilities, since the time element in demand and consumption introduces numerous complications.

> Want and satisfaction are both felt and exercised over time. At one and the same time only a limited set of wants can be satisfied. One can eat, drink, sleep, and work, but these activities are to some extent mutually exclusive. Thus, the individual has to decide what sequence to follow in satisfying his set of wants. This sequence will be determined, according to Lexis, by the intensity of wants and by their periodicity, the most fundamental rhythms being the day, the year, and one life-time. The demand of an individual will be classified and exercised accordingly. Intensive wants will be satisfied first, on a daily basis, depending on the periodicity of recurrence of wants. Other, less intensive wants will be satisfied after full satisfaction of the intensive wants has been achieved.

> [This] in turn requires a reformulation of the theory of demand and implies the necessity of defining the demand for (consumption of) each good at different times and quantitatively different. (International Encyclopedia of the Social Sciences, Vol. 9, pp. 761–6).

One can conclude that time-allocation theory, whether based on a utility formulation or not, can hardly be abstracted from time and space as existential dimensions. In economics time allocation is not seen in a spatial perspective at all, and it employs a utility format which is in itself static and full of temporal contradictions which have not yet been sorted out. A fundamental rethink of the existential temporal and spatial premises of utility theory is necessary.

Another economist with a long and profound interest in time, especially in relation to decision-making and the future, is G. L. S. Shackle (cf. also *TSST*, Vol. 1), Building on Keynes's idea of a kaleidoscopic equilibrium among other things, Shackle (1958; 1969; 1972) became interested in what he termed 'expectation time'. This has often been called existential economics, but essentially it is an approach to decision theory within the framework of economics. Much of economic theory tends mysteriously to assume, explicitly or implicitly, that humans have complete knowledge of what their circumstances are. Choice and decision making apply only to actions to be taken in the future, whose consequences will work themselves out in the further future. The future is unobservable and knowledge of it can only be by inference. But novelty, new knowledge, decisions themselves (if deserving of the name by being a cut between past and future) are by their nature beyond the reach of inference. Thus decisions can be rational only in a special sense—that of exploiting to the best present effect, on the decision-maker's state of mind—the scope afforded to imagination by what is known and by the gaps in that knowledge. Thus Shackle's theory tries to answer the question how far, and how, can humans know what their circumstances are. 'Expectation' therefore confines itself as a concept to what is deemed possible framed as 'potential surprise'— a measure of disbelief about events.

Of course, there are several components in a decision theory. A distinction useful in this context is that between decisions on the allocation of human time and decisions about the allocation of other resources that take place in existential time. Likewise in political life and elsewhere, decisions take time to make; there are decision-making projects which involve time-consuming processes, for instance, gaining background information. Decision making is an *activity* which must be seen in the broader context of temporal and spatial organization of society, a structure which must be systematically incorporated, as should the communication between all kinds of specialized decision-makers and those who 'consume' the effects of decisions taken.

Time allocation in real terms

Human time is a real resource, while money as a pecuniary means of transaction is a derived resource with quite different properties. Even if financial transactions were to apply to all human actions (and those of machines and other 'capital'), money would still merely reflect these underlying processes and only limited integration and causality in society and environment would be mediated by monetary flows. Part of the crisis in economics and the failure of this discipline to cope with many problems of socio-economic structure, development and ecology is founded on the fact that economics refuses to make substantive distinctions that are crucial to real economizing and long-term policy. Monetary price tags make virtually everything sold and bought commensurable, as if a chemist would evaluate all kinds of atoms in terms of one kind, e.g. hydrogen atoms. (This is what Becker does by his use of shadow prices in his time-allocation models.) As stressed by a recent critic of the economic disciplines (Schumacher 1974), *basic incommensurabilities* of various resources and goods have made it necessary to look at economy, ecology and technology in new ways, and qualitative distinctions cannot be obliterated in the analysis of resource utilization because of certain homogenizing features in their financial control and accounting.

As a response to this growing awareness and recognition, special theories of resource use, turnover, conversion and depletion have emerged for resources such as energy (cf. Odum 1971), water, land, soil, vegetation, fauna, etc. To this field can also be said to belong the field of time allocation in a genuine sense (but also including time-use studies). However, just as human time is allocated, economized and applied to different goals and projects, so is the time of animals and even plants and artefacts if one cares to extend the perspective beyond the human species and see things in a broader ecological system. Thus with the aid of 'telemetric' methods, many studies are now being made of the 'time budgets' of various species of animals by marking them with a transmitter and following their diurnal and seasonal activities over time (in fact, their day-, week-, year- or life-paths are being recorded).

Time thus becomes a dimension allowing *formal* commensurability between substantively different things, as does space. It is thus possible to analyse the temporal allocation of many different resources, organisms and artefacts, and this is the direction in which it would seem most useful to develop time-space structured studies. Hence, the translation of human time into money is in many respects likely to prove itself a scientific cul-de-sac, one which should be left to the most orthodox economists. One interesting research area to improve is the labour theory of value which would seem to have a rewarding prospect. But the real and lasting uses of time-space social science are to be found in the view of time allocation in real terms (in substantive terms). Only this allows (at our current stage) time allocation to be treated in conjunction with the temporal and spatial organization of society and habitat.

Towards a broader time and space structured science of society and environment

The final section of this afterword will take up some additional fields of study which have been given only perfunctory attention in the preceding chapters, but which serve as examples of how wide the scope of time-space conceptualizations of society and habitat can be. The areas discussed below are also intended to serve as a stimulus to further research efforts, since they are both important and interesting. However, there are many others, so the fields mentioned are no more than *examples* and many more could be added, for instance time-allocation problems of political participation in democratic states, the time-space organization imposed by the choice of certain technologies, the relation between allocation of human time and settlement space and the monetary mechanisms of allocation in modern economies, subtle topics such as the meaning of time for individuals at various stages of their life cycle, and all-embracing topics such as the role of temporal and spatial organization in the national development of Third World countries.

Historical reinterpretation

It is perhaps not unfair to make the assertion that the study of history has most often been conducted on an empiricist basis in the sense of being a study of what has actually occurred and with what consequences. Of course, the trend is now towards development of social history which is less focused on historical reconstruction of events and more oriented towards the analysis of various social formations. But the descriptive bias of many historians has further militated against the theoretical approach of seeing actual history as a sub-set of possible histories, and in the search for watersheds in these time lines which switch history from the abstract 'what could have been' to the concrete 'what is'.

Be that as it may, there is a wealth of descriptive studies of historical processes which need to be transformed into a more theoretical format, thus allowing comparative and generalized kinds of historical and social scientific understanding. This can only be done through the reinterpretation of existing materials.

It is here that time-space types of models can be of use, for instance, in studying how a given society was structured and what kinds of lives, life-cycles or biographies it generated for its population. This kind of history would not need to be elitist and concentrate on those who rule and decide in society. It would rather be focused on analysing representative individuals in a given social formation and studying their daily, annual and total life cycles. A typical study amenable to such reinterpretation is that by Soustelle (1964) on the daily life of the Aztecs (*la vie quotidienne*). One could focus on the elementary structures of this kind of society by looking at sub-systems such as the daily round, the division of the labour, time and cosmology, the life-cycle, the family, the city, the state and so on. Many of these sub-systems have already been studied in the more formalized approaches to time-use and time-allocation, the life-cycle, the developmental cycle of the domestic groups (cf. Goody 1958), and the various time-geographic models of settlement, population and activity. What can be done in time-space structured studies is first to 'decompose' the given historical record and then reinterpret this in terms of temporal and spatial organization. This data base can then be synthesized and used as input in more comprehensive model building and theory formulation, whereby different social formations can be explained and compared.

The fact that time and space relations are measurable means that a strict reinterpretation on the basis of more developed sub-models can possibly work as a way of making a dominantly qualitative material more quantitative, since even qualitative information on where and when actions and events occur in relation to one another gives the quantitative constraints within which a given sub-system can possibly operate. Of course, such reinterpretation of qualitative data assumes a close interplay between data and model building, but using the temporal and spatial dimensions more fully as structuring dimensions (which has been less common up till now), will allow this. As the time-space models on which data can be projected, as it were, become more developed, the scope for more fruitful and fuller systematization of historical materials will increase. The fitting of reinterpreted facts into time-space models would in due time pave the way for more deductive forms of reasoning in sorting out the possible worlds from the impossible ones. This would be especially helpful in prehistory and archaeology where one needs to maximize the inference from those facts which can be established with reasonable certainty. The range of possible solutions may often seem great until the constraints are systematically aggregated, which can only be done with the aid of models and theories.

In the case of Great Britain, work on the reconstruction of time budgets has already been shown to be possible, such as in the discussion on sources for English local history by Stephens (1973). There are a number of works containing information on daily activities and living conditions, from the early studies by Marx (1867) and Engels (1892) on the condition of the working class to a good many later studies such as those by Laslett (1965; 1972), Thompson (1968), Stedman-Jones (1971), Malcolmson (1974), Samuel (1975) and Stearns (1975). It is also possible of course to use diaries and biographies of notables such as Evelyn, Blundell, Heywood, Peps or Josselin to construct past time-space environments and then attempt to analyse them in terms of supply and demand for time, and other aspects (e.g. MacFarlane 1976). A recent contribution is the study of the country clergyman of the seventeenth century, Ralph Josselin (MacFarlane 1976).

Of course, most countries have writers of diaries and it would indeed be interesting to be able to make comparisons between the lines revealed therein on a broader scale between areas, epochs or social formations. In the Swedish case, where ethnologists have worked a great deal with historical materials on folk culture, Erixon (1938) constructed a complete time-budget for a farmer during the year 1860 for eight different times of the year. This was on the basis of diary materials and the memories of informants. Erixson outlines which time-allocation and time-organization factors ought to be included in anthropological, ethnographic or historical time studies of society. These included the conventional variables such as the daily round, the annual and the life cycles, the division of activities by sex, changes occurring over time and so on. Methodologically he also draws on the time and motion studies made by engineers in factories as well as the studies made in the United States on farmers' and homemakers' use of time. Erixson was one of the first anthropologists to take a more formalized approach to the temporal organization of society and its activities. The use of the time-geographic model for reinterpreting historical and ethnographic materials has also been discussed by Hägerstrand (1974a) with special emphasis on innovation problems.

Ethnographic reinterpretation and anthropology

Much of what has been said on historical materials applies equally to the use of ethnographic or social anthropological materials. This is not the place to review the various approaches to time use and time-space organization of society and environment as envisaged by anthropologists. However, a few points must be made beyond those mentioned elsewhere in the book.

There has been a traditional interest in time allocation and time use in anthropology, and there is also a fair amount of time-use data available, both in direct quantitative form and by way of precise qualitative description supported by examples of time use during a day or several days. More full-fledged descriptive studies of time use are those by Tax (1953) and Kay (1964) while studies with a strong time-use component would be those by Richards (1939) and Foster (1948). Then there are a good many other studies in Anglo-American anthropology where there are descriptions of daily time use or sample days for households and individuals, such as the studies by Lewis (1951), Jantzen (1963), Little (1967), Epstein (1968) and Reining (1970). But much more material than this is available, as is evident from the extensive review by the village studies group at the Institute of Development Studies at Sussex (cf. Connell and Lipton 1973, 1977).

At the other end of the scale are studies dealing with the mechanisms of time *allocation*. Here the leading scholars have been Firth (1967), Herskovits (1952), Barth (1967a; 1967b), Leach (1967) in a much neglected study on time allocation in rural Ceylon (Sri Lanka), and Sahlins (1972). Mary Douglas has been another anthropologist with a general interest in the temporal organization of society (1962; 1963) and she has more recently been looking into time-allocation processes related to consumption.

The above studies have rarely been structuralist in orientation, in the way Gregory (*TSST*, Vol. 1) defines structuralist analysis, although some are in the general Radcliffe-Brown sense. Some approaches focus on the individual and his or her time allocation, choice and opportunity costs without really grasping the way time allocation is an interactional phenomenon (an approach criticized by Carlstein (1975d)). There is therefore a strong behaviouristic bias in these studies. Salisbury (1962) has contributed a very interesting study on time allocation and innovation in New Guinea, which is hard to pin a label upon. He has already been described as a 'formalist' in the rather sterile debate which has raged in economic anthropology, but regardless of this 'default', his study incorporates the use and allocation of human time in a very thorough and wide sense which sets it apart from much of the earlier work involving time in anthropology. Much of Godelier's structuralist critique of Salisbury's study is valid in its own right, on the other hand a great deal of it has been based on the search for the identity within the discipline of *economic* anthropology rather than *general* anthropology. Time allocation is far too useful a field to be confined to economic anthropology as such although this is where it has been most thoroughly applied in anthropology, for instance in the study by Sahlins (1972) which has received great attention. (However, Sahlins seems to be rather out of touch with other studies on time use, temporal organization and time allocation that are available in the social science literature.) What is also evident in the present status of time-use, allocation and organization studies in anthropology is the apparently widening gap between economic and ecological anthropology. Much of the reason for this is the lack of models of time-space relationships which permit a rigorous incorporation of the settlement system, land use, spatially located inputs and outputs in production and other processes. (Here the time-geographic model could be a useful synthetic device.) Likewise, anthropology would benefit from making time use and temporal organization of society subject to more explicit modelling in all sectors of society, not just the economy. Even structuralist-Marxist anthropology in its various models suffers from 'atemporality' in spite of the greater emphasis on history and diachronic study, because time is still only treated as an aid in the study of process and not so much as a resource or locational framework. Space is generally conspicuous by its total absence as a structuring dimension, in spite of the materialist bias that ought to have rendered it analytically useful. Accepting the labour theory of value does not negate the regard that use and exchange must have for location critieria, or the way that production is a function of time allocation.

Time, space and structuralism

Structuralist models have many advantages in explaining and understanding societies as social formations (as pointed out by Gregory in *TSST*, Vol. 1) although the usefulness of its underlying philosophy is not always borne out in its different manifestations. The strong points of structuralist approaches include their rejection of empiricism and the view of the actually observable as a sub-set of the possible alternatives contained within a broader structure. This is the classic distinction in linguistics between grammar and syntax on the one hand, and its spoken and written manifestations on the other. In social science, human behaviour as actually observed corresponds to these expressions of society, which in the structuralist's opinion cannot be understood without our having grasped the structures which generate such behaviour. In the field of time-space oriented social science, the study of time-use patterns and 'time budgets' in the classical sociological sense essentially belong to the realm of behaviouristic studies. The econometric time-allocation models of Ghez and Becker (1975) belong to a sophisticated variant of behaviourism, where the behaviour of individuals in market situations is generalized inductively and built into a formal deductive model of behaviour. What sets Ghez and Becker firmly apart from the structuralist approaches is their atomistic view of the socio-economic system as a mere reflection of individual behaviour. In economic anthropology, Barth (1967) tries to get at the basis on which allocations are made (and not merely overt time-use behaviour), but he is an anthropological counterpart of Ghez and Becker in that his view of the *system* is still too atomistic. Time allocation as an interaction phenomenon within a population and the environment is not genuinely tackled. It is incorrect to assume that the empirically established variants of behaviour of individuals and households constitute the total choice space at the socio-economic system level.

Labels such as 'structuralist' and 'behaviourist' can only serve as crude indicators however, and many other more subtle distinctions are necessary to pinpoint the merits of particular approaches or the directions of fruitful scholarly developments. Accepting many of the basic virtues of structuralist approaches, formats and models, the case can also be made that this school would benefit greatly from an infusion of time-space structured studies. This has not really been the case on a broad enough basis in spite of the interest expressed by leading structuralist exponents such as Lévi-Strauss (1966) or Godelier (1969; 1975). In the Marxist-structuralist approaches, space plays an insignificant role both as a natural resource, a room resource and a locational framework, i.e. both in terms of substance and form, as is evident from Gregory's discussion. Most anthropological studies in the structuralist vein are still remarkably weak in their handling of human settlement and the use of space, due to a lack of spatially structured concepts and models. But they are generally much stronger than geographic studies in explaining the processes by which land is owned and reallocated.

Time has entered structuralist-Marxist models in several ways. Their historical focus often places them in a *diachronic* framework, they look into the processes of production and reproduction of elements, structures and even total social formations. The stress on labour and utilization coupled with a more substantive approach to economic processes introduces a fairly strong focus on time use, at least in the context of labour. Structuralism has thereby taken a fair step forward in relation to more static and synchronic functionalist studies, such as the action approach of Talcott Parsons (1951). However, the structuralist frameworks are far from *holochronic*, as this concept has been defined in the present book. The holochronic framework of time-geography, which totally incorporates space, and the settlement system as well, could do much to improve the analysis of how processes of production and reproduction operate within particular social formations. The reason for this is that it allows for a capacity assessment of maintenance of systems as well as capacity for social transformation. Structuralism, as for instance espoused by Godelier in his analysis, 'Modes of production, kinship and demographic structures', is still methodologically weak in grappling with the broad interrelationships of ecology, superstructure and infrastructure. His population-base arguments (Godelier 1975) in relation to the viability of certain kinship systems, constitute, roughly speaking, an anthropological counterpart to the very elaborate theory of population scale, thresholds, etc. and occurrence of certain institutions which Christaller demonstrated in his central-place theory as early as 1933.

As a final remark on structuralism, it is perhaps natural for geographers to lament the micro role that spatial (geometic) structure of social and eco-logical processes takes in the present structuralist approach. One reason is the way that geographers tend to confuse observable spatial *pattern* with structure. Another is that the role of the 'artificial' world of man as a semiological study in itself has been obscured. A third is that in ignoring the temporal domain or domains, geography has given little inspiration to structuralists. Here time-geography can help since it deals well with the artificial environment and, of course, with time. But structuralism also needs to incorporate time more fully into itself, it needs to 'motivate its models by reintroducing dynamics, time and evolution of structures', (Thom 1972, p. 72). It is only in this way that the transformation problem can be realistically solved. Thus in the time-space structured approach is one way to more cooperation between geography and structuralist (and in particular structuralist-Marxist) studies in neighbour-ing disciplines.

Scale in relation to structure and process

That time and space are dimensions for measuring size and scale has been dealt with by Holly in volume 3 of *TSST*. For substance which is more obviously tangible such as material objects, organisms or land, space provides a simple general yardstick, while for objects or organisms as well as events and activities, time serves a corresponding purpose. Of course, a good many phenomena have size properties that are not directly measured in time or space terms, for instance various measures of capacity, performance, weight, strength, and so on. There are a number of *substantive* ways in which to measure size and scale which do not directly involve space and time.

Quantification as expressed both in everyday reckoning and accounting as well as in science and technology is a cultural means of handling the fact that most phenomena in the human environment appear in *quanta* or packages of certain sizes, quanta which are spatially distinct and often also temporally discrete. Many *size* properties are thus stated in terms of *aggregates of quanta* (individuals, corpuscles, units or specified entities) such as population size. But this way of using the size concept is tantamount to an individualization of an aggregate, since what is actually meant in the above case is population *number*. However, the *quantization* of nature and society itself is something which is taken for granted. Quantification often takes the quanta in which phenomena appear as given in the analysis of *relations between aggregates*, and hence it is not surprising that the 'quantitative revolutions' in the various social sciences have still not produced much explicit theory on why different natural and cultural phenomena appear in given sizes and quanta, the general relationships between sizes of quanta, or the relations between size (scale), structure and process. For instance, what is the size or scale a certain component must have to function in a wider system or what are the threshold relations between different components in an integrated socio-environmental system? Existing theories relating size and structure seem to be essentially sectoral in scope, since they deal mostly with relations internal to a sector, an economic domain, an urban system, a population system, a technical system and so on. Few theories relate the scale and size of elements belonging to different spheres to one another. Zipf's treatise (1949) which covers substances as diverse as language and cities seems to be one of the few available so far, but it is generally inadequate to grapple with broad human ecological issues such as those raised by Schumacher (see below). So are the intrinsically interesting studies of the size relations between different species in biological ecology, although they could serve as a model for the kind of studies needed in human ecology.

Since change is often more readily observed than structure, processes of scale transformation have probably received most attention in the field of size-structure analysis. Demography has tackled the issue for decades, taking human population as its focal point, and economics, economic history, historical geography, etc. have looked into the structural effects of rise and decline in certain industries. Since this impinges heavily on everyday living conditions, besides being politically controversial, it has not escaped analysis by all social scientists. The same holds true for world population growth and urbanization processes. While Christaller's theory of central places is one relating size to structure and function (Christaller 1933; 1966) and is thus one of the few genuine quantum theories of social structure, it is inherently static and deals little with transformation and process. There are also an increasing number of studies on the effects of urban size and the merits and demerits thereof (e.g. Neutze 1965; Richardson 1973b). Richardson's survey and analysis is based on comprehensive materials but illustrates the great need for further studies in the field as well as some of the limitations of the current way in which economics deals with these issues.

A recent more general socio-ecological discussion with an anti-economics flavour is that of Schumacher (1974) which deals with scale in technology in relation to the ecological predicament of modern societies. It takes a strong stand against the prevailing trends towards increase in scale in many forms of industrial production, as is borne out in the title *Small is Beautiful*. The analysis is persuasive and intuitively appealing as well as having a base in the findings of others. Due to its interweaving of moral issues with scientific, its ambitious scope and its popularity, this study might be rejected by hard-line scientists. Its great value, however, lies in the many crucial issues it raises about the scale at which many human activites are being conducted, the inherent dangers of this and the structural changes which are necessary to remedy the situation. The book illustrates the great urgency of looking into the scale factor in society and habitat.

Although there are many substantive ways of measuring size and scale, such as the number of people serviced by a given industry, the units of output per time period and so on, most issues of scale have a combined substantive and time-space aspect to them. One can take the aspect of *group size* as an example. This has been of traditional concern in many branches of social science. Lévi-Strauss (1963) has pointed out that 'there is an obvious relation between the functioning and even durability of the social structure and the actual size of the population. It is thus becoming increasingly evident that form properties exist which are immediately and directly related to the absolute size of the population, whatever the group under consideration. These should be the first to be taken into account in an interpretation of other properties.' However, there is also a relation between the group size and the kinds of activities that a group can carry out, as well as between group volume (size x duration) and the volume of collective activity. Likewise there is a relationship between the size of words (minimal symbol quanta) and the rate at which verbal communication can proceed (Carlstein 1975c). Zipf (1949) also wanted to show that a principle of effort minimization made the most frequently used the shortest ones, which can also be interpreted as a means of reducing the size of the minimal information quanta in order to allow a greater transfer of information per time unit.

Perhaps the key with which time-space approaches will unlock the door to quantum relations among socio-environmental phenomena is the analysis of time-space properties of *activities*. Activities are units of process and discrete quanta which have duration and which must also occupy space. There are size or volume relations between activities, on the one hand, and individuals, equipment, buildings, or action spaces on the other. Likewise, human groups of different kinds have varying carrying capacity for activities just as land does. The various time-allocation mechanisms involved also give certain size relationships between group size, volume of communication, size of territories, durations of meetings, specialization of roles and so on. Capability constraints of size are transferred between segments of the same system, so that one element *sizes* or gives maximum or minimum size to another. The archaic English verb *to size*, i.e. to shape the size of something, has the same generative implication as when a structuralist says that an existing social formation can only be understood through the mechanisms which produce and pattern it.

Problems of size and structure are thus facets of the same diamond and just as hard to scratch. But scale problems in time-space oriented social analysis are not merely a problem of choosing the appropriate *scale of observation* in time and space. They go far beyond that to cover the quantum aspects of socio-environmental systems, size and carrying capacity, scale transformation and its broader effects, and the sizing of processes and elements as a function of the size of generating mechanisms. Finally, they entail an analysis of *finitude*, or limited size, that which necessitates both allocation and conservation of resources.

Social justice, welfare and healthy societies

Another field where time-space structured studies have already been applied is in the analysis of various dimensions of social justice, welfare and health. This is, of course, a large field so only a few instances will be taken up to give support to the general contention that space-time approaches can be useful, both at the stage of problem identification and at the practical level of planning and implementing social reforms. Like all other kinds of applicable social science, it can of course be misapplied but there is nothing new in that. Likewise, a method which is excellent for identifying a certain problem (as empirical time-budget studies often are) may be very poor in delivering sound prescriptions as to how it should be eliminated.

Citizen *participation* in various cultural activities, for example, has been the object of a Canadian study (Department of the Secretary of State 1974) in which non-work time activities of various population categories were analysed with the objective of supporting those branches of cultural expressions which have perhaps become suppressed by overall socio-economic development. Time-allocation studies of citizen participation in various organized activities and the role conflicts of participating in different ones have also been subject to analysis (e.g. in Sweden by the Hägerstrand research team). An obvious field of study is the relationship between work and non-work activities, amply documented in the studies of the Multinational Comparative Time-Budget group (cf. Szalai, ed., 1972). While there are many studies available on the effects of shift-work or non-work activities, it is curious how little interest has been focused on assessing whether the long-term reduction of working hours in most industrial nations has been partly offset by longer commuting times as a function of urban sprawl and longer travel distances. At a corresponding micro-level, it would be interesting to conduct comparative analyses of the extent to which spatial specialization of premises for different activities have led to the expansion of 'mono-culture' types of sterile environments and to an imposition of passive leisure activities. Comparisons between Vancouver, Halifax and Port Albertini seem to indicate that the more passive leisure activities such as television viewing attract the highest percentage of participants for the greatest length of time in the large cities (Jim Hayes, personal communication). The list of studies focusing on various aspects of social structure and welfare can be endless, and several concrete examples have been given throughout this book already. The social indicator school has taken up time-use studies to derive real-term indices of various socio-economic conditions, with a varying degree of success because of the nature of aggregate indices, and time use can be used as a basis for such social accounts (as opposed to financial, cf. Meier 1959; Patruschev 1975).

One special field of time-use analysis is the study of *sex roles* and time expenditure on various activities. This is generally a dimension of most time-use studies, and can be both descriptive and prescriptive, for instance in rectifying the balance between men and women through various social reforms. Or time-space structured approaches can be used for an analysis of sex roles and the structure of the environment (e.g. Palm and Pred 1974). The use of the individual path model as a means of understanding how roles are temporarily and spatially interwoven or separated in an environment seems to be important. For, should there exist the political will for a greater equality between men and women, a good many reforms will have to be carried out in the physical environment and station structure if men and women are to operate on a more equal opportunity basis, for instance with regard to public transport, relative locations of jobs, the dovetailing of work hours and the like.

What is perhaps characteristic of the state of the art at present is that there have been a good many sectoral applications of time-use studies. Similarly, in society, there are different organizations and agencies designing and deciding over sectoral activity systems, e.g. regulating working hours, opening and manning hours of service facilities, time schedules of schools, meeting times of political or voluntary organizations, and the timetables of public transport systems. But just as there was once a need for *cross-sectoral* spatial planning, there is a corresponding need in many cities (and even nations) for a corresponding *temporal planning*. At least some voluntary coordination between different organizations and interest groups who affect the same population is a minimum requirement to prevent sectoral sub-optimization from becoming a major burden. A long-term *time organizational policy* may also become necessary at the national level, as there are many contradictory trends both in industrialized and less technologically developed societies. Capital intensification, for instance, often leads to a rise in productivity of capital and labour, at the same time as it assumes a more continuous use of capital over the diurnal cycle and throughout the year. Thus there are those who argue that a shorter working week is impossible unless more is invested in plant and machinery to raise the productivity of labour. At the same time, this entails more shift work and continuous operation, which makes free time more difficult to use for social contacts, contacts in the family, and so on, each family member being caught in his or her own timetables and activity schedules. Hence the 'free' time gained through a shorter working week cannot be used to normal ends if it is located out of phase with the activities of others upon whom a person depends. For instance the more institutionalized, specialized and differentiated household members become in their respective roles the fewer degrees of freedom they can get in their daily activity programme, the more difficult certain kinds of programme become (cf. Blakelock 1960; Hägerstrand 1972c; de Grazia 1962). But the scope for temporal coordination of activities between different groups and individuals is to a considerable extent dependent upon the spatial layout and structure of society. This is an important research area.

Assessing future technology and societal organization

Time-space structure studies have much potential power in dealing with the future, not merely the past and the present. The possibilities of assessing innovations and their impact have already been discussed, for instance, in chapter 8. However, several studies made elsewhere take up future technology and socio-environmental organization from a time-allocation and spatial structural viewpoint. Obviously, time's arrow or the asymmetry of time does not make the future a part of human experience, so the very method of dealing with the future must rely on an analysis of possible future states, given certain trends or possibilities rooted in the present. A strong element of deductive reasoning is likewise necessary in interrelating single component trends into a composite whole.

As Hägerstrand (1972b) has pointed out in a population-cum-activity centred futurological study, there are several formal characteristics of time-space analytical approaches which render them suitable to this kind of problem area. One is the cross-sectoral nature of time-allocation processes in that diverse activities from different sectors interfere with one another in a fashion which does not follow sectoral logic alone. Budgeting constraints and the competition for finite time and space resources provide the outer limits within which possible organizational forms must fit. Treating resources in real terms is also a way of circumventing the analytical obstacles induced by the fluid qualities of pecuniary flows. In a monetary regulatory system, all kinds of adjustments in the form of changing prices and elasticities, inflation, devaluation of currencies or introduced credit restrictions crop up over time to bring the monetary system in line with real conditions. It is notoriously difficult to use monetary entities and measures over longer time periods. The major stabilizing basis for futurological studies of this kind is found in demographic conditions, the human population as a source of time supply. The population system, especially as conceived in the time-geographic model, forms the core of society and within a given time period, a life time is taken as an unbroken flow (cf. chapter 12 above). Given the distribution of tasks and capabilities of this population, the carrying capacity for different time-demanding activities and organizational forms can be assessed in various ways. At a macro-level, sectoral expansion or contraction of certain forms of activity will generate temporal and spatial conflict zones which are specific to certain areas or times of the day, year or life cycle. Major changes in work organization, the service sector, in rate of political participation or recreational time and space demands are thus reflected in a systematic way, and a time-space study of population and activities elucidates many structural consequences of trends and innovations as well as the potential capacity for accommodation and adjustment, at both the macro and micro levels.

It seems to be a very useful step in this kind of perspective to deal with *model populations* before grappling with large real populations in specific regions. This is the approach of Ellegård, Hägerstrand and Lenntorp 1975, 1977) in their analysis 'Activity organization and the generation of daily travel', where two future alternatives were investigated, one a low energy and the other a high energy consuming society. Many variables were exogenously given, such as the development of the population, certain basic values of the people, economic development and matters of distribution of output and benefits, apart from the energy component. Likewise the settlement system was assumed to be more dispersed in the high-energy level alternative, while the low energy case showed spatial concentration to reduce energy spent on transport and the heating of houses. The next step consisted of an evaluation of what kind of *temporal organization* of society this would entail, especially with regard to the heavy time-demanding activities of non-domestic production, services and education, for instance the extent to which capital intensification in the energy-rich alternative would lead to more continuous production and more shift work. The introduction of a more general six-hour work day was also assumed. All these ingredients were then weighed and projected onto the(sample) model population of a convenient size (1,000 persons) in terms of the time demands for a typical work day (Figure 5). This distribution of major activities outside the home was then used to derive an aggregate profile for *travel segments* (or travel bits), i.e. the temporal distribution of journeys (Figure 6).

The latter was further broken down into a matrix of relative frequencies of journeys between different kinds of stations and the travel for other purposes than work and education. Another disaggregation was that of the total population into sample household of different composition, e.g. people in

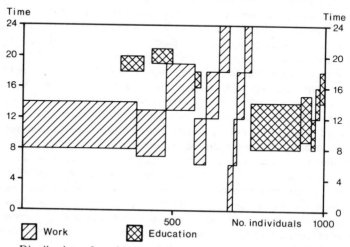

Figure 5 Distribution of working and education time for the model population. (Source: Ellegård–Hägerstrand–Lenntorp 1975)

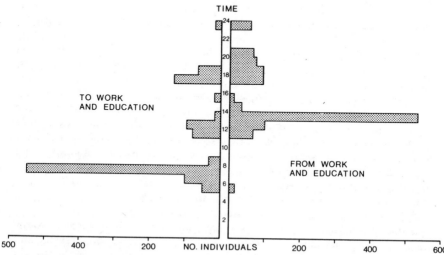

Figure 6 Distribution of journeys over a twenty-four hour period. Only journeys immediately before and after work and education are included. (Source: Ellegård–Hägerstrand–Lenntorp 1975)

gainful employment, in part-time education, in ordinary school, and pre-school children or people working in the home. This was done in order to evaluate the effects of certain dominant macro-structural features at the household and individual level. The classification of the population is thus based on their kind of time use for dominant activities. Within the same research project, a more recent study of breaking down a model population into component households has been carried out by Gustavsson (1976), where the model population has been systematically sampled from a slightly larger population in a southern Swedish community. It should be noted that in the specific case of future assessments of the transport sector, *spatial* organization can partly be taken as given, due to the many infrastructural investments on which society has become dependent. Partly it can be regarded as a policy variable in case a nation wants to economize on human time or (perhaps versus) various forms of energy. The actual expenditure of both energy and time on travel must thus be calculated for different kinds of human settlement, at the same time as there may be other factors shaping the settlement structure.

Parallel to these efforts, there have also been time-organization studies made on how the legal system operates in booking and reserving both human time and other resources for future use (through contracts, institutional boundaries, etc.), thus making resources more available to certain projects and organizations than others (Wallin 1974a). Similar studies have been made on the relation between careers in the life cycle and stability of settlement and residence (Wallin 1974b). The project and domain concepts as incorporated in time-geography (Hägerstrand 1973b) seem very useful in dealing with both the *reservation* and *preservation* of resources for the future, which is again another vast realm open for further systematic enquiry based on temporal-cum-spatial conceptualization.

Conclusion

In substantive terms, it would be less than profitable to sum up the materials presented in this volume in some nutshell statements. A major objective of the book was to illustrate the whole spectrum of studies departing from the general recognition that society and environment have an important spatial and temporal structure which science and policy cannot afford to neglect. The volume further aimed to stimulate more study and research on the topic so that a more coherent body of theory in socio-environmental science can emerge, hoping that this will be put to a just and constructive application. This Afterword was designed to round off the book by indicating certain gaps in our knowledge, pointing out the existence of materials that were not covered by the chapters for which the editors have been able to provide room. This would not have been possible without the many interesting contributions to the book covering a diversity of subjects. Finally, the editors wanted to show that the temporal and spatial structuring of studies can become a means of multidisciplinary integration rather than a new hobby-horse within some discipline. It is hoped that the general field presented here will evoke enthusiasm among many different specialists, give them additional perspectives and generate new discoveries, and that these discoveries are additive and can be fused with those of others. Here time is again a vital factor.

Bibliography

Abler, R., Adams, J. and Gould, P. (1971) *Spatial Organization: The Geographer's View of the World*. Englewood Cliffs: Prentice Hall Inc.

Alexander, S. (1920) *Space, Time and Deity*. New York: Macmillan

Allan, W. (1949) 'Studies in African Land Usage in Northern Rhodesia,' *Rhodes–Livingstone Institute Paper* 15, Manchester.

Anderson, J. (1971) 'Space-time budgets and activity studies in urban geography and planning,' *Environment and Planning* 3, 353–68.

Armstrong, B. J. L. and Pushkarev, B. (1973) *The Office Industry: Patterns of Growth and Location*. Cambridge, Mass.: MIT Press.

Barth, F. (1959) 'The land use patterns of migratory tribes in South Persia,' *Norsk Geografisk Tidskrift* 17, 1–11.

—— (1961) *Nomads of South Persia: The Basseri Tribe of the Khamseh Confederacy*. Boston: Little Brown and Co.

—— (1967a) 'Economic Spheres in Darfur,' in Firth, R. (ed.), *Themes in Economic Anthropology*. London: Tavistock.

—— (1967b) 'On the study of social change,' *American Anthropologist* 69, pp. 661–9.

Baumol, W. J. and Oates, W. E. (1972) Kostnadssjukan inom tjänstesektorn och levnadsstandarden. *Skandinaviska Enskilda Bankens Kvarfalsskrift* 2.

BBC Audience Research Department (1965) *The People's Activities*. London: BBC Publications.

Becker, G. S. (1965) 'A theory of the allocation of time,' *Economic Journal* 75, pp. 493–517.

Bellan, R. (1971) *The Evolving City*. New York: Pitman.

Bjerke, K. (1970) 'An integrated social and demographic statistical system,' *Statistisk Tidskrift*.

Blakelock, E. (1960) 'A new look at the new leisure,' *Administrative Science Quarterly*, 4, pp. 446–67.

Blaut, J. (1961) 'Space and Process,' *The Professional Geographer* 13, pp. 1–7.

Bliss, C. (1958) 'Periodic regression in biology and climatology,' *Connecticut Agricultural Experiment Station, Bulletin* 615, New Haven.

Bohannan, P. (1953) 'Concepts of time among the Tiv of Nigeria,' *Southwestern Journal of Anthropology* 9, pp. 251–62.

Bohannan, P. and Bohannan, L. (1968) *Tiv Economy*. London: Longmans.

Bohannan, P. and Dalton, G. (eds) (1962) *Markets in Africa*. Northwestern University Press.

Boserup, E. (1965) *The Conditions of Agricultural Growth: The Economics of Agrarian Change under Population Pressure.* London: George Allen and Unwin.

Boston Globe (1972) 'Druggists to meet to ask protection,' *Boston Glove*, 19 August, p. 4.

Brail, R. K. (1969) *Activity System Investigations: Strategy for Model Design.* University of North Carolina Ph.D. Thesis. (Also: Ann Arbor, Mich.: University Microfilms.)

Bromley, R. J. (1974) 'Periodic markets, daily markets and fairs: A bibliography,' *Monash Publications in Geography* 10. Melbourne.

Brookfield, H. C. (1969a) 'On the environment as perceived', in Board, C., Chorley, R. J., Haggett, P. and Stoddart, D. R. (eds), *Progress in Geography* Vol. 1. London: Edward Arnold.

—— (ed.) (1969b) *Pacific Market Places: A Collection of Essays.* Canberra: Australian National University Press.

—— (1973) 'Full circle in Chimbu: A study of trends and cycles', in Brookfield, H. C. (ed.), *The Pacific in Transition.* London: Edward Arnold.

Brown, L. A. (1968) *Diffusion Dynamics: A Review and Revision of the Quantitative Theory of the Spatial Diffusion of Innovation.* Lund Studies in Geography, Series B, 29.

—— (1968) *Diffusion processes and location*, Bibliography Series Number 4. Philadelphia: Regional Science Research Institute.

—— (1975) 'The market and infrastructure context of adoption: A spatial perspective on the diffusion of innovation,' *Economic Geography* 51, pp. 185–216.

Brown, L. and Cox, K. R. (1971) 'Empirical regularities in the diffusion of innovation,' *Annals of the Association of American Geographers* 61, 551–9.

Brown, L. A. and Golledge, R. G. (1971), 'Some Approaches to Spatial Search Behavior,' paper read to Association of American Geographers Meeting, Boston, 1971.

Brown, R. (1958) *Words and Things*, New York: Free Press of Glencoe.

Buck, J. L. (1937) *Land Utilization in China.*

Buckley, W. (1967) *Sociology and modern systems theory*, Englewood Cliffs, NJ: Prentice-Hall.

Bullock, N. (1970) 'An approach to the simulation of activities: a university example,' *Land Use and Built Form Studies, Working Paper* 21, Cambridge.

Bullock, N., Dickens, P., Steadman, P., Taylor, E. and Willoughby, T. (1970) 'Surveys of space and activities: Reading University,' *Land Use and Built Form Studies, Working Paper* 40, Cambridge University.

Bullock, N., Dickens, P., Steadman, P., Taylor, E. and Tomlinson, J. (1971) 'Development of an activities model,' *Land Use and Built Form Studies, Working Paper* 41, Cambridge University.

Bullock, N., Dickens, P., Shapcott, M. and Steadman, P. (1974) 'Time budgets and models of urban activity patterns', *Social Trends* 5, pp. 1–19.

Buttimer, A. (1976) 'Grasping the dynamism of the life world,' *Annals of the Association of American Geographers* 66, pp. 277–92.

Buttimer, A. and Hägerstrand, T. (forthcoming) *Dwelling.* (tentative title).

Carlsson, S. (1951) *Executive Behaviour: A Study of the Work Load and the Working Methods of Managing Directors.* Stockholm.

Carlstein, T. (1970) *Införandet av skolgång i ett agrart bysamhälle.* Mimeo. Department of Geography, University of Lund.

266 Bibliography

—— (1972) *Regional or Spatial Sociology?* Mimeo. Department of Geography, University of Lund.

—— (1973) *Population, Activities and Settlement as a System: The Case of Shifting Cultivation.* Mimeo. Department of Geography, University of Lund.

—— (1974a) *Time Allocation, Innovation and Agrarian Change: Outline of a Research Project.* Mimeo. Department of Geography, University of Lund.

—— (1974b) *Time Allocation.* Mimeo. Department of Geography, University of Lund.

—— (1972b) *Development as a Packing Process in Space and Time.* Mimeo. Department of Geography, University of Lund.

—— (1974c) 'Technology, time use and regional development,' *Rapporter och Notiser* 11, Lund.

—— (1975a) 'A time-geographic approach to time allocation and socio-ecological systems,' *Rapporter och Notiser* 20. Lund.

—— (1975b) *Shifting Cultivation: A preliminary model of packing and interaction.* Mimeo. Department of Geography, University of Lund.

—— (1975c) 'Time allocation, group size and communication,' *Rapporter och Notiser* 21. Lund.

—— (1975d) *Time Allocation: On the Capacity for Human Interaction in Space and Time.* Mimeo. Department of Geography, University of Lund.

—— (1975e) *A Village School as a Time-Demanding Innovation.* Mimeo. Department of Geography, University of Lund.

Carlstein, T., Lenntorp, B. and Mårtensson, S. (1968) 'Individers dygnsbanor i några hushållstyper,' *Urbaniserings-processen* 17. Lund: Department of Social and Economic Geography.

Central Statistical office (1974) *Social Trends* 5. London: Her Majesty's Stationery Office.

Chapin, F. S. Jr. (1965) *Urban Land Use Planning.* Urbana: University of Illinois Press.

—— (1966) 'Time budget studies and city planning,' Paper presented at the Time-Budget Round-Table at the Sixth World Congress of Sociology, Evian.

—— (1966b) 'The use of time budgets in the study of urban living patterns,' *Research Previews* 13, 1–6.

—— (1968a) 'Activity systems and urban structure: A working schema,' Journal of the American Institute of Planners 34, pp. 11–18.

—— (1968b) 'Activity systems as a source of inputs for land use models,' in Hemmens, G. C. (ed.), *Urban Development Models.* Washington, DC: Highway Research Board.

—— (1970) 'Activity analysis or the human use of urban space,' *Town and Country Planning.*

—— (1971) 'Free time activities and the quality of urban life,' *Journal of the American Institute of Planners* 37, 411–17.

—— (1974) *Human Activity Patterns in the City: Things People Do in Time and in Space.* New York: John Wiley and Sons.

Chapin, F. Stuart Jr. and Hightower, H. C. (1965) 'Household activity patterns and land use'. *Journal of American Institute of Planners* 31, pp. 222–31.

—— (1966) *Household Activity Systems: a pilot investigation,* Chapel Hill: Centre for Urban and Regional Studies, Institute for Research in Social Science, University of North Carolina.

—— (1966) 'Household Activity Systems,' *Urban Research Monograph, Center for Urban and Regional Studies, University of North Carolina.*

Chapin, F. S. Jr. and Weiss, S. F. (1968) 'A probabilistic model for residential growth', *Transportation Research* 2, pp. 375–90.

Chapin, F. S. Jr. and Logan, T. H. (1968) 'Patterns of time and space use.' in Perloff, H. S. (ed.), *The Quality of the Urban Environment*. Baltimore: The Johns Hopkins Press for Resources for the Future, Inc.

Chapin, F. S. Jr. and Brail, R. K. (1969) 'Human Activity Systems in the Metropolitan United States,' *Environment and Behaviour* 1, 107–30.

Chapin, F. S. Jr., Butler, E. W. and Patten, F. C. (forthcoming) *Blackways in the Inner City*. Urbana: University of Illinois Press.

Chapman, M. (1970) *Population Movement in Tribal Society: The Case of Duidui and Pichahila, British Solomon Islands*. Doctoral Dissertation, University of Washington.

Chisholm, M. (1962) *Rural Settlement and Land Use*. London: Hutchinson University Library.

Christaller, W. (1933) *Die zentralen Orte in Süddeutschland*. Jena. Transl. by Baskin, C. W. 1966 as *Central Places in Southern Germany*. Englewood Cliffs, NJ: Prentice Hall, Inc.

Chow, Y. S., Robbins, H. and Siegmund, D. (1971) *Great Expectations: The Theory of Optimal Stopping*. Boston: Houghton Mifflin.

Cleave, J. H. (1974) *African Farmers: Labour Use in the Development of Smallholder Agriculture*. New York: Praeger Publishers.

Colby, C. E. (1933) 'Centrifugal and centripetal forces in urban geography,' reprinted in Mayer, H. M. and Kohl, C. F. (eds), *Readings in Urban Geography*. Chicago: University of Chicago Press. pp. 287–98.

Conklin, H. C. (1957) *Hanunóo Agriculture: A Report on an Integral System of Shifting Cultivation in the Philippines*. FAO Forestry Development Papers 12. Rome.

—— (1961) 'The study of shifting cultivation,' *Current Anthropology* 2, 27–61.

Contini, B. (1968) 'The value of time in bargaining negotiations: Some experimental evidence,' *American Economic Review* 58, 374–93.

Connell, J. and Lipton, M. (1973) 'Assessing village labour situations in developing countries,' *Institute of Development Studies Discussion Paper* 35. Brighton. Also publ. 1977 by Oxford University Press, Delhi. 180 pp.

Cullen, I. G. (1972) 'Space, time and the disruption of behavior in cities', *Environment and Planning* 4, pp. 459–70.

—— (1976) 'Human Geography, Regional Science and Individual Spatial Behaviour', *Environment and Planning* 8, pp. 397–409.

Cullen, I. and Godson, V. (1972) *The structure of activity patterns*, Joint Unit for Planning Research, University College London and The London School of Economics.

—— (1975) 'Urban networks: the structure of activity patterns'. *Progress in Planning*, 4, pp. 5–96.

Cullen, I. and Phelps, E. (1975) *Diary Techniques and the Problems of Urban Life*. London: Joint Unit for Planning Research, Social Science Research Council Report HR 2336.

Deo, N. (1974) *Graph Theory with Applications to Engineering and Computer Science*. Englewood Cliffs: Prentice-Hall.

Department of Employment (1974) 'Women and work: A statistical survey,' *Manpower Paper* 9. London: Her Majesty's Stationery Office.

Department of the Secretary of State (1974) *Citizen's Participation in Non-work Time Activities*, vol. I. Ottawa.

Doherty, W. (1973) 'Courthouses seen as family classrooms,' *Boston Globe*, 30 January, p. 1.

Doob, L. W. (1961) *Communication in Africa*. New Haven: Yale University Press.

—— (1971) *Patterning of Time*. New Haven: Yale University Press.

Douglas, M. (1962) 'Lele Economy compared to the Bushong,' in Bohannan, P. and Dalton, G. (eds), *Markets in Africa*. Northwestern University Press.

—— (1963) *The Lele of the Kasai*. London: Oxford University Press.

Downs, R. (1970) 'The Cognitive Structure of an Urban Shopping Centre,' *Environment and Behaviour* 2, 13–39.

Duckham, A. N. (1963) *Agriculture Synthesis: The Farming Year*. London: Chatto and Windus.

Dumazedier, J. (1962) *Vers un civilization du loisir?* Paris.

Ehrlich, P. R., Ehrlich, A. H. and Holdren, J. P. (1973) *Human Ecology*. San Francisco: W. H. Freeman.

Eighmy, Thomas H. (1972) 'Rural periodic markets and the extension of an urban system,' *Economic Geography* 48, 299–315.

Einstein, A. (1922) *The Meaning of Relativity*. Princeton, Princeton University Press.

Ellegård, K., Hägerstrand, T. and Lenntorp, B. (1975): 'Activity organization and the generation of daily travel: Two future alternatives,' *Rapporter och Notiser* 23, Lund. Also in *Economic Geography* 1977, forthcoming.

Engels, F. (1892, 1968) *The Condition of the Working Class in England in 1944*. London.

Engström, M. (1970) 'Regional arbetsfördelning: Nya drag i förvärvsarbetets regionala organisation i Sverige,' *Meddelanden från Lunds Universitets Geografiska Institution, Avhandlingar* 65.

Engström, M. G., Sahlberg, B. (1973) 'Travel demand, transport systems and regional development: Models in coordinated planning,' *Lund Studies in Geography*, Series B, 39.

Epstein, T. S. (1962) *Economic Development and Social Change in South India*. Manchester: Manchester University Press.

Epstein, S. (1968) *Capitalism, Primitive and Modern: Some Aspects of Tolai Economic Growth*. Canberra: Australian National University Press.

Erixon, S. (1938) 'Regional European Ethnology II, functional analysis–time studies,' *Folkliv* 3, 263–94.

Erlandsson, U. (1976) *Företagsutveckling och utrymmesbehov*. Lund: Gleerup.

Erlandsson, U. and Johansson, B. (1976) *Utrymmeskonsumtion i produktionen*. Mimeo. Department of Geography, University of Lund.

Firth, R. (ed.) (1967) *Themes in Economic Anthropology*. London: Tavistock.

Flowerdew, R. (1974) 'Extensions to a model of residential choice', paper presented to the Annual Conference, Institute of British Geographers, Norwich.

—— (1976) 'Search strategies and stopping rules in residential mobility,' *Transactions, Institute of British Geographers*. N.S. 1, pp. 47–57.

Foster, G. M. (1948) 'Empire's children: The people of Tzintzuntzan,' *Smithsonian Institution, Institute of Social Anthropology*, Publication 6.

Frankenhaeuser, M. (1972) Synpunkter på forskning om människan i framtidens samhälle. Ds Ju 1972: 24. Stockholm: Justitiedepartementet.

Freeman, J. D. (1955) 'Iban Agriculture,' *Colonial Research Studies* 18. London: HMSO.

Friedman, Jonathan (1972) *System, Structure and Contradiction in the Evolution of*

'*Asiatic*' *Social Formations*. Ph.D. thesis, Columbia University, New York. 400 p.

Fuchs, V. R. (1968) 'The service economy,' *National Bureau of Economic Research. General Series* 87. New York.

Galbraith, J. K. (1958) *The Affluent Society*. New York: New American Library.

Geertz, C. (1963) *Agricultural Involution: The Processes of Ecological Change in Indonesia.*

Ghez, G. R. and Becker, G. S. (1975) *The Allocation of Time and Goods over the Life-Cycle*. National Bureau of Economic Research. New York: Columbia University Press.

Glass, D. and Singer, J. (1972) *Urban Stress*. New York: Academic Press.

Goddard, J. B. (1973) *Office Linkages and Location*. Oxford: Pergamon Press.

Goddard, J. and Morris, D. M. (1975) *The Communications Factor in Office Decentralization*. Mimeograph. London School of Economics.

Godelier, M. (1969) 'La monnaie de sel des Baruya de Nouvelle-Guinée,' *L'Homme* 9, 5–37.

—— (1972) *Rationality and Irrationality in Economics*. London: NLB.

—— (1973) *Horizon, trajets marxistes en anthropologie*. Paris: Maspero.

—— (1975) 'Modes of Production, Kinship, and Demographic Structures,' in Bloch, M. (ed.), *Marxist Analyses and Social Anthropology*. London: Malaby Press.

Good, C. M. (1970) 'Rural Markets and Trade in East Africa,' *University of Chicago, Department of Geography Research Paper* 128.

Goody, J. (ed.) (1958) *The Developmental Cycle in Domestic Groups*. Cambridge: Cambridge University Press.

Gottman, J. (1970) 'Urban centrality and the inter-weaving of quaternary functions,' *Ekistics* 29, 322–31.

—— (1972) 'Urban centrality and the inter-weaving of quaternary activities', in Bell, G. and Tyrwhitt, J. (eds), *Human Identity and the Urban Environment*. Baltimore: Penguin Books, pp. 499–515.

Gould, P. (1969) *Spatial Diffusion*. Association of American Geographers, Commission on College Geography Resource Paper 4.

De Grazia, S. (1962) *Of Time, Work and Leisure*. New York: Twentieth Century Fund.

Gustavsson, G. (1976) *Konsistensprövning inom en modellbefolkning*. Mimeo. Department of Geography, University of Lund.

Gustavsson, G., Hägerstrand, T. and Lenntorp, B. (1975) 'Tidsgeografiska bilder av dagens och fråmtidens resbehov,' *Rapporter och Notiser* 16. Lund: Geografiska institutionen.

Hägerstrand, T. (1947) 'En landsbygdsbefolknings förflyttningsröelser. Studier över migrationen på grund av Asby sockens flyttningslängder 1840–1944, *Svensk Geografisk Årsbok* 23, 114–42.

—— (1953) *Innovationsförloppet ur korologisk synpunkt*. Meddelanden från Lunds Universitets Geografiska Institution, Avhandlingar, 25. Lund. 304 pp. Transl. by Pred, A. 1967, *Innovation Diffusion as a Spatial Process*. Chicago: Chicago University Press.

—— (1963) 'Geographic Measurements of Migration: Swedish Data,' in Sutter, J. (ed.), *Human Displacements: Measurement Methodological Aspects*. Monaco, pp. 61–83.

—— (1967). *Innovation Diffusion as a Spatial Process*, transl. by Pred, A. Chicago: Chicago University Press.

—— (1969a) 'On the Definition of Migration,' *Scandinavian Population Studies* 1, pp. 63–72. Reprinted 1975 in: Jones, E. (ed.), *Readings in Social Geography*. Oxford: Oxford University Press.

—— (1969b) 'A socio-environmental web-model,' in Eriksson, G. A. (ed.), 'Studier i planeringsmetodik,' *Memorandum från Ekonomisk-Geografiska Institutionen* 9, 19–28. Abo.

—— (1970a) 'What about people in Regional Science?' *Papers of the Regional Science Association* 24, 7–21.

—— (1970b) 'Tidsanvändning och omgivningsstruktur,' in *Statens Offentliga Utredningar* 14 (4): 1–146.

—— (1970c) 'Frihet och tvång i Stockholm och Rusksele. Några observationer av individ och familj i skilda svenska omgivningar,' In *Forskning och samhällsutveckling*, pp. 66–77, Stockholm: Allmänna Förlaget.

—— (1972a) 'Tätortsgrupper som regionsamhällen. Tillgången till förvärvsarbete och tjänster utanför de större städerna,' in *Regioner att leva i. En rapport från ERU*. Stockholm: Allmänna Förlaget.

—— (1972b) *Om en konsistent individorienterad samhällsbeskrivning för framtidsstudiebruk*. Stockholm: Justitiedepartementet Ds Ju 1972: 25

—— (1972c) 'The impact of social organization and environment upon the time use of individuals and households,' *Plan (International)*, pp. 24–30. Stockholm.

—— (1973a) *The Impact of Transport on the Quality of Life*. Fifth International Symposium on Theory and Practice in Transport Economics. European Council of Ministers of Transport. Athens.

—— (1973b) 'The domain of Human Geography,' in Chorley, R. J. (ed.), *Directions in Geography*. London: Methuen.

—— (1974a) 'On socio-technical ecology and the study of innovations,' *Ethnologica Europaea* 7, pp. 17–34.

—— (1974b) 'Ecology under one perspective,' in Bylund, E., Linderholm, H. and Rune, O. (eds.), *Ecological Problems of the Circumpolar Area*. Luleå: Norrbottens Museum.

—— (1974c) 'Tidsgeografisk beskrivning—syfte och postulat,' *Svensk Geografisk Årsbok* 50, pp. 86–94.

—— (1975a) 'Survival and arena: On the life-history of individuals in relation to their geographical environment,' *The Monadnock* 49, pp. 9–29.

—— (1975b) 'Space, Time and Human Conditions,' in Karlqvist, A., Lundqvist, L. and Snickars, F. (eds), *Dynamic Allocation of Urban Space*. pp. 3–12. Farnborough: Saxon House.

Hägerstrand, T. and Lenntorp, B. (1974) 'Samhällsorganisation i tidsgeografiskt perspektiv,' *Statens Offentliga Utredningar 1974: 2, Bilaga 2, Ortssystem och Levnadsvillkor*. Stockholm.

Hammer, P. G., Jr. (1973) *Critique of Role of Time Allocation in River Basin Model*. EPA–600/5–73–007. Washington: US Government Printing Office.

Hammer, P. G., Jr. and Chapin, F. S., Jr. (1972) *Human Time Allocations, A Case Study of Washington DC*. Center for Urban and Regional Studies, University of North Carolina, Chapel Hill.

Harary, F. (1969) *Graph Theory*. Reading, Mass.: Addison–Wesley.

Harris, A. I. (1966) *Labour Mobility Survey: Labour Mobility in Great Britain 1953– 63*. London: Her Majesty's Stationery Office.

Hartshorne, R. (1946) *The Nature of Geography*. Association of American Geographers.

Harvey, D. (1969) 'Conceptual and Measurement Problems in the Cognitive

Behavioural Approach to Location Theory,' in Cox and Golledge (eds), *Behavioural Problems in Geography*. Northwestern University Studies in Geography 17, pp. 35–68.

Hastrup, F. (1970) Danish 'Vangelag' *Kulturgeografi* 114, pp. 96–100.

Hawley, A. (1950) *Human Ecology*. New York: Ronald Press.

Hedberg, B. (1970) 'Kontaktsystem inom svenskt näringsliv: En studie av organisationers externa personkontakter,' *Meddelanden från Lunds Universitets Geografiska Institution, Avhandlingar* 64.

Hepple, L. W. (1976) 'A maximum likelihood model for econometric estimation with spatial series,' In Masser, I. (ed.): *Theory and Practice in Regional Science*. London: Pion.

Herskovits, M. J. (1952) *Economic Anthropology: The Economic Life of Primitive Peoples*. New York: Norton.

Hightower, H. C. (1965) *Recreation Activity Analysis: Towards a Spatial and Aspatial Methodology for Urban Planning*. Ph.D. thesis, University of North Carolina. (Also in University Microfilms, Ann Arbor, Mich.)

Hill, P. and Smith, R. T. H. (1972) 'The spatial and temporal synchronization of periodic markets: Evidence from four emirates in Northern Nigeria,' *Economic Geography* 48, pp. 345–55.

Hiller, W. and Leaman, A. (1973) 'Paradoxes of the Man–Environment Paradigm,' *Architectural Design*, pp. 507–511.

Hitchcock, J. R. (1968) *Urbanness and Daily Activity Patterns*. Ph.D. thesis, University of North Carolina. (Also in University Microfilms, Ann Arbor, Mich.)

Hodder, B. W. and Ukwu, U. I. (1969) *Markets in West Africa: Studies of Markets and Trade among the Yoruba and Ibo*. Ibadan: Ibadan University Press.

Hole, W. V. and Attenburrow, J. J. (1966) *Houses and People*. London: Her Majesty's Stationery Office.

Howard, R. A. (1960) *Dynamic Programming and Markov Processes*. Cambridge, Mass.: MIT Press.

Howell, J. T. (1973) *Hard Living on Clay Street*. Garden City, NY: Anchor Press/Doubleday.

Hultblad, F. (1968) 'Övergång från nomadism till agrar bosättning i Jokkmokks socken,' *Meddelanden från Uppsala Universitets Geografiska Institutioner* Ser A 230. Stockholm: Almqvist och Wiksell.

Isard, W. (1960) *Methods of Regional Analysis*. Cambridge, Mass: MIT Press.

Isard, W. and Liossatos, P. (1972) 'On optimal development over space and time,' *Regional Science Perspectives* 3.

—— (1973a) 'Transport rate and pollution as basic variables in space-time developments,' *London Studies in Regional Science* 4.

—— (1973b) 'Space-time development and a general transfer principle,' *The Regional Science Association Papers* 30, pp. 17–38.

—— (1973c) 'Transport investment and optimal space-time development,' *Regional Science Association Papers* 31, pp. 31–48.

—— (1975a) 'Parallels from physics for space-time development models, part I, *Regional and Urban Economics*, 5, pp. 1–34.

—— (1973d) 'Social injustice and optimal space-time development,' *Journal of Peace Science* 1, pp. 69–93.

—— (1975b) 'Parallels from physics for space-time development models, part II. Interpretation and extensions of the basic model,' *Regional Science Association Papers* 34, pp. 43–66.

—— (1975c) 'Optimal space-time development: A summary presentation,' in Karlqvist, A., Lundqvist, L. and Snickars, F. (eds), *Dynamic Allocation in Urban Space*. London: Saxon House.

Isard, W. and Kanemoto, Y. (1976) 'Stages in space-time development,' *Regional Science Association Papers* 37, pp. 99–131.

Izikowitz, K. G. (1951) 'Lamet: Hill peasants in French Indochina,' *Etnologiska Studier* 17, Göteborg. 375 pp.

Janelle, D. G. (1966) *Spatial Reorganization and Time-Space Convergence*. Ph.D. thesis, Michigan State University.

—— (1968a) 'Spatial reorganization: A model and a concept,' *Annals of the Association of American Geographers* 58, pp. 348–64. Also in: Bell, G. and Tyrwhitt, J. (eds), 1972. *Human Identity in the Urban Environment*. Baltimore: Penguin Books.

—— (1968b) 'Central place development in a time-space framework,' *The Professional Geographer* 20.

Jantzen, C. R. (1963) *A Study in the Theory and Methodology of Community Time Allocation*. Ph.D. thesis, Michigan State University. (Also in University Microfilms, Ann Arbor, Mich.)

Javeau, C. (1975) 'Methodological problems in time-budget studies: A preliminary inventory,' in Michelson, W. (ed.), *Time Budgets and Social Activity*. Centre for Urban and Community Studies, Major Report 4. Toronto.

Jensch, G. (1957) 'Das ländlische Jahr in Deutschen Agrarlandschaften,' *Abhandlungen des Geographischen Instituts der Freien Universität Berlin* 3.

Johnson, D. L. (1969) 'The Nature of Nomadism,' *University of Chicago, Department of Geography Research Paper* 118.

Johnson, J. H., Salt, J. and Wood, P. A. (1974) *Housing and the Migration of Labour in England and Wales*. Farnborough: Saxon House.

Jones, P. M. (1975) 'The analysis and modelling of multi-trip journeys,' *Oxford University Transport Studies Unit, Working Paper* 6.

Kay, G. (1964) 'Chief Kalaba's Village,' *The Rhodes–Livingstone Papers* 35, Manchester: Manchester University Press. 95 pp.

Knight, C. G. (1974) *Ecology and Change: Rural Modernization in an African Community*. New York: Academic Press.

Koopmans, T. J. (1957) *Three Essays on the State of Economic Science*. New York: McGraw Hill.

Korsch, B. M. and Negrete, W. F. (1972) 'Doctor–patient communication,' *Scientific American* 227, no 2.

Kotuk, R. (1971) 'A scary village,' *Village Voice*, 10 June, 1, p. 54. New York City.

Kranz, P. (1970) 'What do people do all day?' *Behavioural Science* 15, pp. 286–91.

Lamberton, D. M. (ed.) (1971) *Economics of Information and Knowledge: Selected Readings*. Harmondsworth: Penguin Books.

Larrabee, E. and Meyersohn, R. (1958) *Mass Leisure*. Glencoe: Free Press.

Laslett, P. (1965) *The World We Have Lost*. London: Methuen.

—— (ed.) (1972) *Household and Family in Past Time*. Cambridge: Cambridge University Press.

Leach, E. R. (1966) 'Two essays concerning the symbolic representation of time,' in Leach, E. R. *Rethinking Anthropology*. London: The Athlone Press.

—— (1967) *The Economy of Time in Dry Zone Rural Ceylon*. Paper presented at the Seminar for International Studies, Lund University, Sweden. 12 p.

Lee, Hahn-Been (1968) 'From ecology to time: A time orientation approach to the study of public administration,' *Ekistics* 25, pp. 432–8.

Lenntorp, B. (1970) 'PESASP—en modell för beräkning av alternativa banor,' *Urbaniseringsprocessen* 38. Lund: The Department of Geography.

—— (1973) *Tidsgeografiska synpunkter på transportanalyser.* Mimeo. Department of Geography, University of Lund.

—— (1974a) 'Transporter i dygnsprogrammet,' *Statens Offentliga Utredningar 1974:2, Bilaga 2, Ortssystem och levnadsvillkor.* Stockholm.

—— (1974b) 'Grupperingar och arrangemang av odelbara enheter,' *Svensk Geografisk Årsbok* 50, 95–113. Lund.

——(1976a) 'A time-space structured study of the travel possibilities of the public transport passenger,' *Rapporter och Notiser* 24. Lund: Department of Social and Economic Geography.

—— (1976b) 'Paths in space-time environments: A time-geographic study of movement possibilities of individuals,' *Lund Studies in Geography, Series B*, 44. 150 pp.

—— (1977) 'A time-geographic approach to individuals' daily movements,' *Rapporter och Notiser* 33. Lund: Department of Social and Economic Geography.

Lévi-Strauss, C. (1963) *Structural Anthropology.* New York: Anchor Books.

Lewis, O. (1951) *Life in a Mexican Village: Tepoztlán Restudied.* Urbana: University of Illinois Press.

Lexis, W. (1875) *Einleitung in die Theorie der Bevölkerungsstatistik.* Strasbourg: Trubner.

Linder, S. B. (1970) *The Harried Leisure Class.* New York: Columbia University Press.

Linton, R. (1933) 'The Tanala: A Hill Tribe of Madagascar,' *Field Museum of Natural History, Anthropological Series* 22. Chicago.

Lippold, G. (1975) *The Modelling of the Relationship of Use of Time and Consumption.* IIASA, Schloss Laxenburg, Vienna.

Little, K. L. (1951, 1967) *The Mende of Sierra Leone.* London: Routledge and Kegan Paul.

Locke, J. (1690) *An Essay Concerning Human Understanding.*

Long, N. (1968) *Social Change and the Individual: A Study of the Social and Religious Responses to Innovation in a Zambian Rural Community.* Manchester: Manchester University Press.

Lowry, W. P. (1967) 'The climate of cities,' *Scientific American* 217 (2) 15–23.

Lucas, J. R. (1973) *A Treatise on Time and Space.* London: Methuen.

Lynch, K. (1972) *What Time Is This Place?* Cambridge, Mass.: MIT Press.

McCall, J. J. (1965) 'The economics of information and optimal stopping rules,' *Journal of Business* 38, 300–17.

—— (1970) 'Economics of information and job search,' *Quarterly Journal of Economics* 84, 113–26.

MacFairlane, A. (1970) *The Family Life of Ralph Josselin, A Seventeenth Century Clergyman: An Essay in Historical Anthropology.* Cambridge: Cambridge University Press.

—— (1976) *The Diary of Ralph Josselin.* Oxford: Oxford University Press.

Malcolmson, X. (1974) *Popular Recreations in English Society, 1700–1850.* Cambridge: Cambridge University Press.

Martins, H. (1974) 'Time and theory in sociology,' In Rex, J. (ed.), *Approaches to Sociology.* London: Routledge and Kegan Paul.

Mårtensson, S. (1974a) 'Drag i hushållens levnadsvillkor', *Statens Offentliga Utredningar 1974:2, Bilaga 2, Ortssystem och levnadsvillkor.* Stockholm. Pp–233–264.

—— (1974b) 'Tidsbudgetstudier vid skogshögskolan', *ERU:s underlagsmaterial* U8. Stockholm: Arbetsmarknadsdepartementet. Pp 1–53.

—— (1977) 'Childhood interaction and temporal organization,' *Economic Geography* 53, pp. 99–125.

Marx, K. (1867) *Capital.* New York: Modern Library, 1906, III.

—— (1970) *Capital,* volume 1. London: Lawrence and Wishart (first published 1887).

—— (1971) *A contribution to the critique of political economy.* London: Lawrence and Wishart.

Maslow, A. H. (1970) *Motivation and Personality.* New York: Harper & Row.

Mayfield, R. C. (1972) 'The spatial structure of a selected interpersonal contact: A regional comparison of marriage distances in India,' in English, P. W. and Mayfield, R. C. *Man, Space, and Environment.* New York/London: Oxford University Press.

Mayfield, R. C. and Yapa, L. S. (1974) 'Information fields in rural Mysore,' *Economic Geography* 50, 313–23.

Mead, W. R. (1958a) *An Economic Geography of the Scandinavian States and Finland.* London: University of London Press.

—— (1958b) 'The seasonal round: A study of adjustment on Finland's pioneer fringe,' *Tijdschrift voor Economische en Sociale Geografie* 49, 157–62.

Meier, R. L. (1959) 'Human time allocation: A basis for social accounts,' *Journal of the American Institute of Planners* 15, 27–33.

—— (1962) *A Communications Theory of Urban Growth.* Cambridge, Mass.: The MIT Press.

—— (c. 1967) 'Notes on the creation of an efficient metropolis: Tokyo,' in Bell, G. and Tyrwitt, J. (eds), *Human Identity and the Urban Environment.* Baltimore: Penguin Books, 557–80.

Michelson, W. (1965a) 'A conceptual introduction to the use of the time budget for the purposes of physical planning,' In Michelson, W., ed. *Time Budgets and Social Activity* Centre for Urban and Community Studies, University of Toronto, Major Report No 4, pp. 66–75.

—— (1965a) *Retrospective observations on the use of time-budgets in the analysis of housing implications,* Paper presented at the symposium on 'Applications of time-budget research to policy questions in urban and regional settings', International Institute for Applied Systems Analysis, Schloss Laxenburg, Austria.

—— (forthcoming) *Environmental Choice, Human Behaviour and Residential Satisfaction.* New York, London: Oxford University Press.

Mintzberg, M. (1973) *The Nature of Managerial Work.* New York.

Moore, W. E. (1963) *Man, Time and Society.* New York: Wiley.

Morrill, R. L. and Pitts, F. R. (1967) 'Marriage, migration and the mean information field,' *Annals of the Association of American Geographers* 57.

Moses, L. N. and Williamson, H. F. (1963) 'Value of time, choice of mode, and the subsidy issue in urban transportation,' *Journal of Political Economy* 71, pp. 247–264.

National Industrial Conference Board (1927) *Night Work in Industry.* New York.

Neutze, G. M. (1965) *Economic Policy and the Size of Cities.* Canberra: Australia National University.

New York Times (1973a) 'The cost of living goes up every day, but the cost of leaving goes down every night', Eastern Airlines advertisement in *New York Times*, 14 August.

—— (1973b) 'British TV shuts down at 10:30 to save energy,' 18 December p. 20.

—— (1975) 'Madrid shuts down its nightlife earlier to save on energy,' 26 January, p. 11.

Newsweek (1973a) 'CBS radio all night news network, 4 a.m., Teaneck, New Jersey' advertisement in *Newsweek*, 2 April, p. 28–9.

—— (1973b) 'Down go the thermostats,' *Newsweek*, 19 November p. 110–12.

—— (1973c) 26 November, p. 84.

Norborg, K. (1968) *Jordbruksbefolkningen i Sverige*. Lund: Gleerup.

Odum, H. T. (1971) *Environment, Power, and Society*. New York: Wiley.

Olander, L. O. (1974) 'Företagens kontaktsituation,' *Svensk Geografist Årsbok* 50, 58–63.

Orme, J. E. (1969) *Time, Experience and Behaviour*. London: Iliffe Press.

Ottensman, J. R. (1972) *Systems of Urban Activities and Time: An Interpretative Review of the Literature*. Center for Urban and Regional Studies, University of North Carolina, Chapel Hill.

Palm, R. and Pred, A. (1974) 'A time-geographic perspective on problems of inequality for women,' *Institute of Urban and Regional Development, Working Paper* 236, University of California, Berkeley. Also in: Burnett, K. P. (ed.) 1976, *A Social Geography of Women*. Chicago: Maarouta Press.

Palmer, J. D. (1970) 'The many clocks of man,' *Natural History* 79, 53–9.

Parkes, D. (1973) 'Timing the city: A theme for urban environment planning', *Royal Australian Planning Institute Journal* 11, pp. 130–135.

—— (1974) 'Themes on time in urban social space', *University of Newcastle upon Tyne, Department of Geography Seminar Paper* 26, 1–59.

—— (1975) 'T-P graphs and the space-time factorial ecology of the city: An experiment,' *University of Newcastle N.S.W., Research Papers in Geography* 2.

Parkes, D. N. and Thrift, N. J. (1975) 'Timing space and spacing time', *Environment and Planning* 7, pp. 651–70.

Parkes, D. and Wallis, W. D. (forthcoming) *Locational Maps and Experiential Maps*.

Parks, R. H. (1967) Efficient estimation of a system of regression equations, when disturbances are both serially and contemporaneously correlated. *Journal of the American Statistical Association* 62, 500 9.

Parsons, T. (1951) The Social System. New York: The Free Press.

Patrushev, V. D. (1975) 'The Problem of Organizing Spare Time in Society under Conditions of the Scientific and Technological Revolution,' In Michelson, W. (ed), *Time Budgets and Social Activity*. Centre for Urban and Community Studies, University of Toronto.

Pelzer, K. J. (1945) 'Pioneer settlement in the Asiatic tropics,' *American Geographical Society Special Publications* 29. New York.

Persson, C. (1974) 'Kontaktarbete och framtida lokaliseringsförändringar: Modellstudier med tillämpning på statlig förvaltning,' *Meddelanden från Lunds Universitets Geografiska Institution, Avhandlingar* 71.

Poor, R. (ed.) (1970) *4 Days, 40 Hours: Reporting a Revolution in Work and Leisure*. London: Pan Books.

Popper, K. R. (1972) *Objective Knowledge: An Evolutionary Approach*. Oxford: Clarendon.

Pred, A. (1967, 1969) 'Behavior and location: foundation for a geographic and dynamic location theory'. Parts I and II. *Lund Studies in Geography, Series B, Human Geography* 27 and 28.

—— (1973a) 'The growth and development of systems of cities in advanced economies,' in Pred, A. R. and Törnqvist, G. (eds), 'Systems of Cities and Information Flows: Two Essays,' *Lund Studies in Geography, Series B* 38, 1–82.

—— (1973b) *Urban Growth and the Circulation of Information: The United States System of Cities, 1790–1840.* Cambridge: Harvard University Press.

—— (1973c) 'Urbanization, domestic planning problems and Swedish geographic research', in C. Board, *et al.* (eds), *Progress in Geography* Volume 5, New York: St Martin's Press, 1–76. London: Edward Arnold.

—— (1975) 'On the spatial structure of organizations and the complexity of metropolitan interdependence,' *The Regional Science Association, Papers* 35, 115–42.

Prial, F. J. (1972) 'Taxi industry, beset by problems, looks for ways to stay on duty', *New York Times,* 17 October.

Pyle, G. F. (1969) 'The diffusion of cholera in the United States,' *Geographical Analysis* 1, 59–75.

Rappaport, R. A. (1968) *Pigs for the Ancestors: Ritual in the Ecology of a New Guinea People.* New Haven and London: Yale University Press.

Reining, P. (1970) 'Social factors and food production in an East African peasant society: The Haya,' in McLoughlin, P. F. M. (ed.) *African Food Production Systems: Cases and Theory.* Baltimore and London: The Johns Hopkins Press.

Reszöházy, R. (1972) 'The methodological aspects of a study about the social notion of time in relation to economic development,' in Szalai, A. (ed.), *The Use of Time: Daily Activities of Urban and Sub-urban Populations in Twelve Countries.* The Hague: Mouton, 449–60.

—— (1970) *Temps social et developpement.* Brussells: La Renaissance.

Richards, A. I. (1939) *Land, Labour and Diet in Northern Rhodesia.* London: Oxford University Press.

Richardson, H. W. (1969) *Regional Economics: Location theory, urban structure and regional change.* London: Weidenfeld and Nicolson.

—— (1971) *Urban Economics.* Harmondsworth: Penguin Books.

—— (1973a) *Regional Growth Theory.* London: Macmillan.

—— (1973b) *The Economics of Urban Size.* Farnborough: Saxon House.

Riddell, J. B. (1970) *The Spatial Dynamics of Modernization in Sierra Leone: Structure; Diffusion, Response.* Evanston: Northwestern University Press.

Rogers, E. M. (1962) *Diffusion of Innovations.* New York: The Free Press of Glencoe.

—— (1969) *Modernization among Peasants: The Impact of Communication.* New York: Holt, Rinehart and Winston.

Rossi, P. H. (1955) *Why Families Move: A Study in the Social Psychology of Urban Residential Mobility.* Glencoe: The Free Press.

Rushton, G. (1969) 'Analysis of spatial behaviour by revealed space preference,' *Annals of the American Association of Geographers* 59, 391–400.

Sahlberg, B. (1970) 'Interregionala kontaktmönster: Personkontakter inom svenskt näringsliv,' *Meddelanden från Lunds Universitets Geografiska Institution, Avhandlinger* 63.

Sahlins, M. (1972) *Stone Age Economics.* London: Tavistock.

Salisbury, R. F. (1962) *From Stone to Steel: Economic Consequences of a Techno-*

logical Change in New Guinea. London and Melbourne: Cambridge University Press.

Samuel, R. (ed.) (1975) *Village Life and Labour.* London: Routledge and Kegan Paul.

De Schlippe, P. (1956) *Shifting Cultivation in Africa: The Zande System of Agriculture.* London: Routledge and Kegan Paul.

Scholz, F. (1974) 'Belutschistan: Eine sozialgeographische Studie des Wandels in einem Namadenland seit Beginn der Kolonialzeit,' *Göttinger Geographische Abhandlungen* 63. Göttingen: Verlag Erich Goltze.

Schultz, T. W. (1961) 'Investment in human capital,' *American Economic Review* 51.

Schumacher, E. F. (1974) *Small is Beautiful: A Study of Economics as if People Mattered.* London: Abacus.

Schwartz, B. (1974) 'Waiting, exchange and power: The distribution of time in social systems,' *American Journal of Sociology* 79, 841–70.

—— (1975) *Queuing and Waiting: Studies in the Social Organization of Access and Delay.* Chicago: University of Chicago Press.

Scudder, T. (1962) *The Ecology of the Gwembe Tonga.* Manchester: Manchester University Press.

Shackle, G. L. S. (1949, 1952) *Expectation in Economics,* Cambridge: Cambridge University Press.

—— (1958) *On Time in Economics.* Amsterdam: North Holland.

—— (1969) *Decision, Order and Time in Human Affairs.* Cambridge: Cambridge University Press.

—— (1970) *Expectation, Enterprise and Profit.* London: George Allen and Unwin.

—— (1972) *Epistemics and Economics: A Critique of Economic Doctrines.* Cambridge: Cambridge University Press.

Skinner, G. W. (1964–5) 'Marketing and social structure in rural China,' *Journal of Asian Studies* 24, 3–43, 195–228, 363–99.

Slater, D. (1973) 'Geography and Underdevelopment—1,' *Antipode* 5, 21–32.

Smith, Adam (1776) *An Inquiry into the Nature and Causes of the Wealth of Nations.*

Smith, M. W. (1952) 'Different cultural concepts of past, present, and future', *Psychiatry* 15, 395–400.

Soja, E. W. (1968) *The Geography of Modernization in Kenya.* Syracuse: Syracuse University Press.

Sorokin, P. (1956) *Fads and Foibles in Modern Sociology.* Chicago: Henry Regnery.

Sorokin, P. A. and Merton, R. K. (1937) 'Social time: A methodological and functional analysis,' *American Journal of Sociology* 42, 615–29.

Soule, G. (1955) *Time for Living.* New York: Viking Press.

Soustelle, J. (1964) *Daily Life of the Aztecs.* Harmondsworth: Penguin.

Spencer, J. E. (1966) *Shifting Cultivation in Southeastern Asia.* Berkeley and Los Angeles: University of California Press.

Stauder, J. (1971) *The Majangir: Ecology and Society of a Southwest Ethiopian People.* Cambridge: Cambridge University Press.

Stearns, X. (1975) *Lives of Labour.* London: Croom Helms.

Stedman-Jones, G. (1971) *Outcast London: A Study of the Relationships between Classes in Victorian Society.* Oxford: Oxford University Press.

Stephens, W. B. (1973) *Sources for English Local History.* Manchester: Manchester University Press.

Stewart, R. (1957) *Managers and their Jobs.* London.

Stigler, G. J. (1961) 'The economics of information,' *Journal of Political Economy* 69, 213–25.

Stine, J. H. (1962) 'Temporal aspects of tertiary production elements in Korea,' in Pitts, F. R., ed., *Urban Systems and Economic Development*. Eugene: University of Oregon, School of Business Administration.

Stone, P. J. (1970) 'Technical issues and solutions suggested by the international time budget study'. Mimeo, Harvard.

—— (1972) 'The analysis of time-budget data' in Szalai, A., *et al.* (eds), *The Use of Time*. The Hague: Mouton.

Szalai, A., Converse, P. E., Feldheim, P., Scheuch, E. K. and Stone, P. J. (eds) (1972) *The Use of Time: Daily Activities of Urban and Suburban Populations in Twelve Countries*. The Hague: Mouton.

Tax, S. (1963) *Penny Capitalism: A Guatemalan Indian Economy*. Chicago: The University of Chicago Press.

Taylor, P. J. and Parkes, D. (1975) 'A Kantian view of the city: a factorial–ecology experiment in space and time,' *Environment and Planning* A7, pp. 671–688.

Thom, R. (1972) 'Structuralism and biology,' in Waddington, C. H. (ed.), *Towards a theoretical biology 4: essays*. Edinburgh: Edinburgh University Press, 68–82.

Thomas, M. D. (1975) 'Growth pole theory, technological change, and regional economic growth,' *Papers of the Regional Science Association* 34, 3–25.

Thomas, M. D. and Le Heron, R. B. (1975) 'Perspectives on technological change and the process of diffusion in the manufacturing sector,' *Economic Geography* 51, 231–51.

Thomlinson, R. (1969) *Urban Structure*. New York: Random House.

Thompson, E. P. (1967) 'Time, work discipline and industrial capitalism,' *Past and Present* 38, 56–97. Reprinted in Flinn, M. W. and Smouth, T. C. (1974) *Essays in Social History*, Oxford: Clarendon Press, 39–77.

—— (1968) *The Making of the English Working Class*. Harmondsworth: Penguin.

Thorngren, B. (1967) 'Regional economic interaction and flows of information,' in *Proceedings of the Second Poland-Norden Regional Science Seminar*, Committee for Space Economy and Regional Planning in the Polish Academy of Sciences. Warsaw: PAN.

—— (1970) 'How do contact systems affect regional development,' *Environment and Planning* 2, 409–27.

—— (1973) 'Swedish office dispersal,' in Bannon, M. (ed), *Office Location and Regional Development*. Dublin: An Foras Forbartha.

Thrift, N. J. (1974) 'On time in geography: An explanation of temporal awareness and perception'. University of Bristol, Department of Geography. Seminar Paper, Series A, 25.

—— (1976a) 'Some more problems in time-space research and a Utopian prospectus', in Holly, B. P. (ed.), *Time-Space Budgets and Urban Research: A Symposium*. Discussion Paper 1, Department of Geography, Kent State University.

—— (1977) 'Time and Theory in Geography'. *Progress in Human Geography* 1, pp. 65–101.

Tomlinson, J., Bullock, N., Dickens, P., Steadman, P. and Taylor, E. (1973) 'A model of students' daily activity patterns,' *Environment and Planning* 5, 231–66.

Törnqvist, G. (1970) 'Contact systems and regional development,' *Lund Studies in Geography, Series B* 35.

—— (1973) 'Contact requirements and travel facilities: Contact models of Sweden and regional development alternatives in the future,' in Pred, A. and Törnqvist, G. (eds), 'Systems of Cities and Information Flows: Two Essays,' *Lund Studies in Geography, Series B* 38.

Wald, A. (1947) *Sequential Analysis*. New York: John Wiley and Sons.

Wall Street Journal (1967) 'More night people, more night life,' *Wall Street Journal*, 4 January.

Wallin, E. (1974a) *Rätten till framtida tillgångar*. Mimeo. Department of Geography, University of Lund. 23 p.

—— (1974b) 'Yrkesvalsprocessen och den regionala strukturen,' *Urbaniseringsprocessen* 51. Lund, 119 p.

Wärneryd, O. (1968) *Interdependence in Urban Systems*. Göteborg: Regionkonsult AB.

Westaway, E. J. (1974) 'Contact potentials and the occupational structure of the British urban system 1961–6: An empirical study,' *regional Studies* 8, 57–73.

Wilenski, H. L. (1961) 'The uneven distribution of leisure: The impact of economic growth on "free time",' *Social Problems* 9, 33–56.

Wilkinson, R. (1971) 'Hours of work and the twenty-four hour cycle of rest and activity,' in Warr. P. B. (ed), *Psychology at Work*. Harmondsworth: Penguin, P. 31–59. Also in Potten, D. and Sarre, P. (1974) *Dimensions of Society*. London: University of London Press, 249–72.

Wilkinson, R. G. (1973) *Poverty and Progress: An Ecological Model of Economic Development*. London: Methuen.

Wilson, M. (1951) *Good Company: A Study of Nyakyusa Age-Villages*. Oxford: Oxford University Press.

Young, M. and Wilmott, P. (1973) *The Symmetrical Family: A Study of Work and Leisure in the London Region*. Harmondsworth: Penguin Books.

Zipf, G. K. (1949) *Human Behaviour and the Principle of the Least Effort*. Cambridge: Addison-Wesley Press.

Index

HEANCE